D1132897

ROBERT H. LOWIE, ETHNOLOGIST
A Personal Record

ROBERT H. LOWIE
ETHNOLOGIST

A Personal Record

1959
Berkeley and Los Angeles
UNIVERSITY OF CALIFORNIA PRESS

UNIVERSITY OF CALIFORNIA PRESS
Berkeley and Los Angeles
CAMBRIDGE UNIVERSITY PRESS
London, England
© 1959, by The Regents of The University of California
Library of Congress Catalog Card Number: 59:8762
Manufactured in the United States of America

To My Beloved Wife

FOREWORD

This book is truly my husband's last will and testament. He began it in the fall of 1956, finished about half of it before his first operation in April, 1957, wrote all but one of the remaining chapters before his second operation in July, and struggled through the final one as best he could in the six weeks of life that remained to him. Some days he wrote five or six pages; some days, only five or six lines. But almost every day he sat at his desk for a while after breakfast and wrote until fatigue overtook him, often pathetically soon. On September 19 he wrote about two pages, told me happily that the book was finished, and asked me to arrange for the typing of the last chapter. Then he quoted a favorite Viennese song—subsequently played at his funeral—"Gern i leg d'Feder nieder." Thirty-six hours later he was dead.

My husband had three objectives in writing this book. He wanted, first, to tell young people what ethnographical study was like in the early decades of the twentieth century. Second, he wanted to put his own professional life on record. And, third, he wanted to stress methods of field work and their application under widely varying circumstances. Essentially this is a book about field work and what lessons it taught him, with his own experiences used as illustrative material. Now he has gone, but he has left behind him an expression of his personality, his work, his professional triumphs and disappointments, his industry, courage, versatility, and intelligence. In an appendix I have listed his publications. There will be a few more, since he had on hand several written but unpublished manuscripts, some of which will eventually appear.

His was a life of devotion and dedication to his work, to his principles, to his friends, and to his students. From the letters that have poured in since his death, I can only assume that to many young men and women he was a hero. It is my hope that through this last product from his ever-busy pen, future generations of young ethnologists may catch at least a glimpse of the combination of brilliance, charm, and humanity that was Robert H. Lowie.

Luella Cole Lowie

PREFACE

As one grows older and retires from the main stream of life's activities, one begins in thought to draw together the strands of his life and to assess his work—in short, to write his memoirs. To this general trend of age I am no exception. I venture to set forth the following chronicle, not merely because my life has been interesting to me; such grounds would be wholly inadequate. As I look back, I can see many useful lessons that a young ethnologist of today might derive from the story of my experiences, to the end that he might start at a more advanced point than I did and, consequently, travel further. I would certainly never presume to set up my life as a model; rather, I present it as a case study, with as much objectivity as possible, and without glossing over either my ineptitudes or my errors.

Wholly aside from any personal interest is the matter of history. A. L. Kroeber, Paul Radin, and I have seen anthropology develop from a struggling young field of specialization to the present moment of its expansion. We all remember attending meetings of the American Anthropological Association, at which we knew at least by sight every person present, so small was the total number of ethnologists in the country. The story of my life is also the story of anthropology during the first half of the twentieth century— of its problems, its methods, and its philosophy. Kroeber, Radin, and I belong to the same generation of men trained under Boas. Each of us has transmitted in his own fashion what he learned to succeeding generations, and each has added in his own way to the ever-growing fund of knowledge and methodology in our chosen field. Perhaps the chronicle of one of these lives may make the period clearer to those who come after us.

R. H. L.

CONTENTS

ILLUSTRATIONS

CHAPTER I

AN
ETHNOLOGIST
IS BORN

When I was a boy of eight or nine in Vienna, I got hold of an abridged version of the Leatherstocking saga. An older cousin and I also steeped ourselves in a series of *Indianerbüchel*, as the vernacular called them—paperbound booklets about adventures among the Redskins. As a consequence, we were fired with admiration for the Comanche tribe and firmly resolved to emigrate to the Far West in order to aid that valiant people against the villainous Apache. As a matter of fact, my parents brought me to New York a year or two later, though not for the exclusive purpose of furthering that particular project. Indeed, my childhood interest in Indians lay dormant for a good many years to come.

It was a foregone conclusion that I was to qualify for some profession. After leaving the public school system, I entered the College of the City of New York, choosing the classical in preference to the scientific curriculum. At first, I zealously devoted myself to Latin and a little later to Greek; but by the beginning of my junior year my thoughts were headed in another direction. Most of my friends happened to be nascent chemists, engineers, or biologists; and being somewhat older than I, they exerted a powerful influence on me. The only worthwhile aim in life, they preached, was "to add one's mite to the sum-total of human knowledge"—and that meant scientific research, preferably in the laboratory. In that period, facilities for such work at the College were meager, but I showed my good intentions by neglecting the classics in favor of a random extracurricular reading course in general science, plunging into Huxley, Spencer, and Haeckel, and poring over the old *Popular Science Monthly*. I hopefully bought a lobster and tried to dissect it with the aid of Huxley's book on *The Crayfish*. I haunted Central Park, learning to identify what trees were labeled, completely baffled for a while by the external resemblances of *Paulownia imperialis* and *Catalpa bignonioides*. I gathered leaves for a herbarium. A classmate, Louis R. Wolheim (later known to fame as the creator of the title role in Eugene O'Neill's *The Hairy Ape*), lent me a copy of Coulter's text on botany. With Frederick E. Breithut, subsequently head of the Department of Chemistry at Brooklyn College, I tackled *The Origin of Species*.

After getting my A. B., I never doubted that I was to go on toward some kind of research; the question was, in what field? Biology tempted me most, partly because my haphazard studies were largely in that direction, partly because the distinguished Columbia zoölogists, E. B. Wilson and Thomas H. Morgan, were then in their prime. However, the requirements were so rigorous that no one could hope to finish his studies in less than four years, whereas my funds—yet to be created by teaching in elementary school— would hardly be sufficient for that long a period. Chemistry, too, lured me; and I went so far as to take two courses at Columbia one summer, to give it a trial. I managed to pass, although what roused my interest were the philosophical questions bound up with the nature of matter and the logic of qualitative analysis, the elimination of one possibility after another until, by exclusion, an experimenter revealed the element in question. But it soon became clear that I lacked the manual skills required of a professional chemist.

What then? As an undergraduate I had taken a course in psychology. The text by John Dewey, written in his pre-Deweyish period, had attracted and impressed serious students. Though we had no laboratory work, I saw that the subject obviously admitted both of scientific research and of philosophical reasoning. It seemed the very thing for my taste. What was more, James McKeen Cattell, head of the department at Columbia, had become editor of the

Popular Science Monthly, a journal known to my circle of inti-
mates as *the* American champion of evolution. My friends approved the choice in principle, and one summer day in the Catskills in 1904 Fred Breithut and I sat down to scrutinize the
relevant Columbia catalogues and to outline a suitable curriculum
for me. The pamphlets contained biographical sketches of the
academic staff. We were particularly impressed with the professional career of Franz Boas, who was to be sure not a professor of
psychology, but of anthropology; but at least, he lectured in the
same major administrative division. So we decided that I should
major in anthropology, while taking psychology as my minor; and
I enrolled, accordingly, in the fall of the year.

Professor Boas was doubtless the leader among American anthropologists, and inspired his students with a sense of the dignity of his
science as a branch of knowledge that demanded as rigorous standards of research as any of the older disciplines. But his pedagogy
was odd. Though he was then lecturing on the cultures of American aborigines—a course from which a tyro would have profited—
he ignored this work in mapping out my first year's schedule.
Instead, he corralled me into his two highly specialized courses,
one on North American Indian languages, and one on the theory
of statistics. In addition, he urged me to register for the erudite
Swiss-American Adolphe Bandelier's lectures on Spanish sources
of Latin-American ethnography and archaeology. Since I knew
nothing whatsoever about Latin-American ethnography and archaeology, the best conceivable initiation into their bibliography
could hardly prove meaningful.

As for Boas's own offerings, the work on languages was good
fun, but rather too advanced for me at that stage, while the discussion of statistics left me in a state of utter befuddlement. It was
only by taking it all over again in my second year that I gained
some glimmerings of understanding. The seminar, too, was on
altogether too high a level for a newcomer. In it Boas broached
the ideas he had been crystallizing during years of delving into the
facts of primitive mentality; but much of the argument was lost
on an apprentice very imperfectly prepared by the Viennese *Indianerbüchel*. In those days of my novitiate it was the adjunct
professor, Livingston Farrand, an able teacher and executive, and

later president of Cornell, who encouraged me to feel that I was not an utter failure. It was also Farrand who urged me to volunteer my services to Clark Wissler, soon after the latter's appointment as head of the Department of Anthropology at the American Museum of Natural History. My volunteer work led to an institutional connection that lasted about fifteen years.

Accordingly, in my second and third graduate years, between the Museum and Columbia, I came to engage in a great variety of tasks. For Wissler I installed a synoptic exhibit of fire-making apparatus and measured a series of human palates, incidentally making observations on the transverse palatine suture. Under Boas I had another fling at aboriginal languages and pored over his raw data on Toronto school children, hoping to utilize his measurements for a statistical dissertation. I attended lectures on Chinese and Japanese civilization by Berthold Laufer (already eminent among Sinologues); and to satisfy my minor I took courses with Cattell and Robert S. Woodworth. It was, however, ethnography or rather ethnology, the interpretative approach to ethnographic facts, that attracted me most.

From references by the professors at Columbia, from the accounts of more experienced fellow students, from talks with William Jones (the quarter-breed Fox Indian who had graduated from Harvard and taken his doctorate under Boas), I gathered that ethnologists practiced a mysterious something called "field work." It was evidently the surest, most direct way of contributing to ethnographic knowledge; it corresponded to the chemist's laboratory, and an ethnologist who had never met aborigines in the flesh seemed like a scientist who wrote learnedly about the constitution of matter, but had never seen a precipitate in a test tube. But how an impecunious student could get to a native tribe remained a problem. The solution came unexpectedly one day when Wissler asked me whether I should care to go to the Lemhi Shoshone in central Idaho. I knew nothing about them, not even that they were closely related in speech to those heroic Comanche who had thrilled me as a boy. However, I jumped at the chance offered and prepared, as well as I could, for my maiden effort as a practicing ethnographer.

Today, or even twenty years ago, such preparation would be

relatively easy, for virtually all major areas of the globe have become sufficiently known for an experienced old hand to provide
an apprentice with specific clues. Unbelievable as it may seem, in
1906 most of aboriginal North America was, if not *terra incognita*,
yet only slightly known from a scientific point of view. This certainly held for nearly all members of the Shoshonean family. A
century before my prospective investigation Lewis and Clark had
been in Lemhi territory, and Wissler referred me to their *Original
Journals*. The great explorers were doubtless excellent observers,
but their stay with the Shoshone was brief; and although their
notes on externals were good, they recorded little indeed on religious and social life. What other early travelers had to say about
kindred or neighboring groups was rather less satisfactory. A
graduate student at Columbia, H. H. St. Clair, had collected specimens and tales among the Shoshone of Wyoming, but that branch
had conformed far more closely to the Plains Indian pattern of
life than to that of their kinsmen in Idaho. Though Boas and
Wissler gave me excellent advice of a general nature about field
research, the contemporary state of Americanist knowledge pre-
cluded their suggesting much in the way of fruitful specific clues.

If nowadays it is hard to picture the state of ethnographic
ignorance as late as 1906, it is no less difficult for a young anthropologist of today to visualize the earlier conditions of transportation in the Far West. Some Indian reservations were indeed tra-
versed by a main railroad line, but many were to be reached only
by changing to a branch line, possibly with narrow-gauge tracks;
and after getting to his station, the traveler might still have a
journey of fifty or a hundred miles by horse-stage ahead of him.
The even more remote parts of Canada naturally involved still
greater difficulties, as I shall have occasion to explain. Railroad
trains, too, were hardly up to present standards. Traveling on a
pass en route to Lemhi, I was not allowed to board the better
trains, so that it took me thirty-eight hours to reach Chicago. Indeed, for years to come, extra fare was charged for any train that
covered the distance between the two metropolises in less than
twenty-four hours.

Sometimes even one's goal remained in doubt when setting out.
This held true for my maiden trip, for rumors had reached Wissler

that the Lemhi Indians were to be moved from their old haunts to the Fort Hall Reservation near Pocatello, about two hundred miles south, there to be merged with related groups of Shoshone and Bannock. For some reason it proved impossible to learn from Washington officialdom whether the displacement was even then an accomplished fact. Accordingly, I had to go first to Fort Hall and find out what the situation was.

At Fort Hall, then, occurred my first contact with American Indians. It was far from encouraging, for I committed a typical beginner's *faux pas*. Arriving at a time when most of the resident Indians were gathered outside the Agency to receive their periodical rations, I thought I would seize the opportunity of pumping them. I soon discovered that that was *not* the right approach. The Shoshone either curtly refused to answer or made fun of me or began asking *me* questions. In despair I promised a pound of tobacco for a story of the ancient times. At last my bribe tempted a youngish bystander to tell me a very fragmentary myth about the legendary Weasel; beyond that nothing could be extracted from anyone, even though I publicly rewarded the raconteur in accordance with my promise, far beyond his merits.

Fortunately the lad who interpreted for me knew what was wrong. He took me aside and asked whether I could meet him on the following day at an aged aunt's, who was living at Inkom, about ten miles away. He felt that in the bosom of her family the aunt was sure to "open up." There turned out to be no morning train to Inkom, so I walked all the way. The old lady proved agreeable, and so at last I was able to take down my first text in an aboriginal tongue. My phonetics were terrible, but I did get a fairly complete version of an animal tale widely known among the Indians of the Great Basin and California. I was further rewarded by a firsthand observation of ancient mortuary custom. My interpreter had just deserted a comfortable log cabin because of his uncle's death in it.

The officials at Fort Hall informed me that the Lemhi had been granted a year of grace, hence were still to be found on their own reservation. After a very brief stay I proceeded northward. The trip illustrates what I have said about conditions of travel. At Pocatello I boarded a train of the Oregon Short Line, which took me as far as Red Rock, Montana, where I had to spend the night in a tiny hotel. There was no way of locking my room; and in the middle of the night my slumbers were interrupted by a belated wayfarer, who burst in but withdrew apologetically enough. Early the next day an antediluvian stagecoach, such as one sees in western films of the good old days, took me to the Great Divide, where I stopped for the night at a halfway house. Late the following afternoon I finally landed at Lemhi Agency. The trip from Pocatello, Idaho, to Lemhi, Idaho, took as long as that from New York to Pocatello and was certainly far more strenuous.

In those days it was hardly politic for a stranger to appear on a reservation without credentials, since he was likely to be ordered off by the superintendent in charge as a potential source of danger to the government's wards, conceivably as a card sharp or liquor dealer. Accordingly, Wissler had given me a letter from Washington, explaining my business, and introducing me to whatever federal officials I might have to deal with. Armed with this document, I was courteously received and allowed to join the employees' mess. The agent also assigned me a room to sleep in.

At this point it may be well to anticipate and explain that I have also camped with Indians, but not frequently. The obvious advantages are balanced by equal drawbacks. Of course by living among one's subjects one has them potentially under constant observation. But privacy is impossible. Moreover, you often have to beat off your host's dogs in the middle of the night and remain unperturbed when his children wander casually in and spit all over your floor. So I have availed myself of a great variety of accommodations, choosing the most comfortable when that was consistent with my work. I have roomed in the houses of halfbreeds, in a railroad station, in the attic over a general store, in the homes of government officials, in an abandoned house, in boxcars, outdoors on the ground, and probably in other places that I have since forgotten.

One of my first worries was how to get about the reservation, because the Indians lived widely scattered instead of being settled in a village near the Agency. A few of them could be reached afoot, but they were not the most promising informants. I therefore learned to straddle a horse and after a while managed to ride several miles at a time, though not with ease, let alone elegance.

More vital still was the matter of informants and interpreters. None of the old people spoke more than a few words of English. Before leaving New York I had called on the painter, De Cost Smith, who had spent a summer at Lemhi, camped near the chief, Tendoy. Here was a likely depository of ancient lore. I found Tendoy pleasant enough, especially when I presented him with a silver dollar, which I mendaciously represented as a gift from the artist. "Me heap savvy Smith," was his response, and that was rather better than his average age-mates' English. It was hardly possible to probe the depths of the Lemhi soul without the aid of a go-between. But there was the rub. Exactly one man on the reservation spoke fluent English, which he had picked up during a long stay in California. He was living on a farm with his aged mother, whom I pumped, with his aid, for one day. After that he saw no reason to work for me at the rate of a dollar and a half or two dollars a day, the maximum pay I could afford. A quarter for an hour's interpreting was regarded as standard wages at the time; for transportation furnished by the interpreter I naturally paid extra.

After this ephemeral collaboration I was reduced to a, ethnographically speaking, hand-to-mouth existence. I was advised to try out the half-grown Indian boys who had been to the "day school," that is, had attended classes for several hours a day and then returned to their homes. There, however, they heard and used nothing but Shoshone, so that even several years of "day school" produced lamentable results. A pupil might acquire enough English to help his mother buy a kettle at the trader's, but never much more than that. His pronunciation was often literally unintelligible, his vocabulary as a rule too meager for a simple interview with one of the old sages of the tribe or for the accurate rendering of folk tales. I dismissed one schoolboy after another and tried to learn what I could of the language, but with the choice of teachers at my disposal I did not get far.

To be sure, there were things to be directly observed, but not many. The natives of the present states of Idaho, Nevada, and Oregon had always been very simple folk in dress, dwellings, arts, and ceremonies, had always lacked the colorful aspects of Plains or Pueblo Indian life. By the time of my visit they had substituted trader's goods for many aboriginal utensils and they wore trader's clothes. Although some canvas-covered tipis were still in use, the majority of the Indians lived in cabins. The externals of living were on the level of poor, rural, white people. The Lemhi Shoshone are a small-statured people and appeared to me to be an unimpressive, ill-clad lot, shockingly disappointing for anyone cherishing romantic ideas of the noble savage. Here and there I saw baskets of native weave, occasionally I watched a woman sewing a moccasin with awl and sinew instead of with needle and thread, and once I noted the successive steps in smoking a deer hide.

Perhaps the most frequent and most stimulating aboriginal manifestation to be witnessed was gambling. Wherever a sizable group of men was gathered together, the favorite pastime was either the equivalent of our "button, button, who's got the button" or the throwing of native "dice." These latter were really lots, for the objects cast were about nine-inch willow sticks, generally plain on one side and marked on the other with burned-in designs. The lots were thrown on a flat stone in sets of four, the several combinations being scored according to an elaborate system.

The "button" game, widespread among the Indians west of the Rockies and usually known as the "hand-game," was even livelier. Two players or two couples, always of the same sex, were pitted against each other. The "buttons" were small bones or sticks, one plain, the other wrapped with string. Opponents faced each other kneeling at a distance of several feet. In singles, a player, first maneuvering his set under a blanket, hid one bone in each hand, then began singing, beating his breast and rhythmically moving his hands. His opponent carefully watched the movements, then tried to guess the position of the plain "button." If he pointed correctly, he took over the play; otherwise he had to give up a tally stick. The side that lost all its counters also lost the game and the stakes, which were fairly heavy considering the poverty of the betters. When I needed change for a five dollar bill, I merely had to cast about for a crowd of dice or hand-game players and pick up the appropriate number of silver coins from those spread out between the contenders.

Interest in these games was intense. Spectators watched eagerly, and sympathizers with one side would kneel alongside the team, carrying the tune and swinging their arms in unison. The Lemhi were untiring at this diversion. Once a party of Cree Indians who had come down from Canada for a visit were entertained all night playing the hand-game. Incidentally, they completely "cleaned out" their hosts.

Actually, I was not having a bad time at all, for my experiences, if not spectacular, were novel and at times amusing enough. Outstanding was my participation in a social dance at a time when I was blessed with a tolerably intelligible interpreter. The affair was scheduled to take place in a roofless barn. Arriving early, we found virtually the whole population there, men on one side, women on the other, the musicians in the center round a fire and plying a big drum to the accompaniment of their chant. For the longest time nothing happened. At last a woman got up, approached one of the drummers, and began pulling at his blanket. He played coy, remaining in his position, but she kept on pulling away until he yielded. He put his arm around her shoulders, and standing next to each other they glided clockwise about the fire. With the ice broken, the women took heart, and soon many couples were circling about, with unattached boys closing the ring. To my delight the squaw who did my laundering invited me and the two of us shuffled along with the rest. When the drummers stopped, the couples broke up and to my surprise my washerwoman opened a beaded purse and handed me a dime; my interpreter, I discovered, was getting only a nickel from *his* partner. However, my lady's generosity was not motivated by my personal charms. As my interpreter explained, it was my duty to invite her at the next dance and to pay her twice the amount received from her. In other words, she had contrived a safe one-hundred per cent investment. However, not content, she returned to the charge at the third dance, bringing a chum with her, so that I had to circle about with both women, an arm around each one's shoulders. I got two fees for my efforts and was duty bound to double them in my final performance of the night.

This was an experience to write home about; and there were minor incidents that tickled my risibilities. Little escaped the attention of the Lemhi. First they named me Four-eyes because of my spectacles. A little later my hirsute forearms and chest earned me the sobriquet of Bear-white-man; and on appearing one day with a visored cap, I was promptly dubbed Night-hawk-lies-down, because the projecting part of my headgear was supposed to suggest the posture of that bird at rest. Once the chief's son enigmatically pointed at me and began gesticulating vigorously, lowering and raising both hands. Finally, he translated: "You, how much snow?" I was as bewildered as before, though it turned out to be standard sign language for asking my age—how many winters had I seen. The movements of the hands indicated the falling of rain or snow.

This sort of thing was good fun and I enjoyed it. But it did not add up to much material for my notebooks. By the end of six weeks or so the situation got on my nerves. After all, I was a probationer trying to vindicate his worthiness. It was not by any means clear whether my mission was a success or a failure. The most maddening thing about it all was that whatever trappings or tatters of civilization these people had adopted, their mental set was that of the Stone Age. Everybody was afraid of being photographed. Even middle-aged men had no understanding of clocks and watches; when Tendoy's eldest son wanted to make an appointment he indicated the time of day by pointing at the position of the sun. Women regularly observed a restricted diet during several days' stay in a menstrual hut. A relatively sophisticated man assured me that his wife would keep on bleeding unless she abstained from meat during her period. I was also told that only a crazy man would talk to his mother-in-law. The trouble was not that the aboriginal mentality had disappeared, but simply that for lack of communication, I was unable to get at it except in driblets.

A layman may ask why I had not learned the language before setting out for Idaho. Alas! for Shoshone, as for the overwhelming majority of America's aboriginal tongues, there were no grammar or conversation books from which an ethnographer could acquire a practical speaking knowledge. Even today such preparation is possible only in a very few cases.

Why not settle down among a people for as long as it took to learn their speech before we attempted to study their ways of life?

Doubtless this would have been the ideal procedure, but no institution in the country would have financed it. Many of these native languages are extremely difficult, both phonetically and grammatically; to master one of them would take as long as to gain familiarity with Greek. Moreover, there are dozens of them, totally different from one another. After painfully acquiring facility in one place an investigator sent to another would have to start all over again. In the meantime, however, many native cultures were bound to vanish under the influence of white civilization; if the data were to be put on record, the mere handful of ethnographers would have to go hither and yon without time for intensive linguistic study. A missionary bent on converting the natives and translating the Bible into the vernacular might take the requisite time and even get financial support for his efforts, but never an ethnologist.

In short, an American field worker often faced serious practical problems. Either he had to rely on informants probably alienated from their own people while they had learned English in such eastern schools as Carlisle or Hampton, or he had to employ interpreters. Where good interpreters were unavailable, as at Lemhi, he was simply out of luck. So, while enjoying myself I muddled along, not without misgivings about the outcome of it all.

I would have gathered even less information than I did had it not been for the help of a middle-aged Shoshone neighbor of mine known to the whites as Jack Grouse. In his earlier days he had been baptized by Mormons and had picked up some English which, although atrocious in pronunciation, was on the whole more readily intelligible than that of the schoolboys. From time to time I could persuade him to dictate a story to me, generally at the rate of twenty-five or fifty cents a tale. However, he was unwilling to get the reputation of one who divulged valuable tribal knowledge. If a visitor happened to peep in during our labors, Jack would at once clear his skirts of me, moving away from me and pretending that I, too, was merely there on a neighborly call. Jack's *obiter dicta* were full of revelatory glimpses of Lemhi psychology, as represented by one who had had some contacts with the outside world. I only wish I had jotted them all down. One example must suffice.

Most Shoshonean tribes have a solar myth in which the Sun figures as at one time so close to the earth that he burned people to death. The Indians gathered in a council, which appointed the Cottontail Rabbit to hide in a hole from which he was to shoot the Sun the following morning. At sunrise the next day Cottontail let fly his arrows at the enemy as he became visible above the horizon, but they were all burned up. At last he used his firedrill as a dart. Now the Sun came tumbling down, scorching the Rabbit's neck and legs where the markings can still be seen. The Indians then raised the Sun to his present position. After finishing this story, Jack adorned it with an epilogue all his own: "Once," he said, "I was hunting a cottontail. He was sitting down and was going to run away when I was trying to shoot him. So I said to him, 'What! You shot the Sun and are afraid of *me?*' He believed me, and so I killed him." This was the mentality of a Lemhi sophisticate in 1906.

I was collecting data but not very rapidly. Then suddenly business picked up. A young man of eighteen or twenty returned from a boarding school after several years' absence. He spoke fine English and was willing to work for me; moreover one of his grandfathers, Red-shirt, a renowned medicine man, was willing to serve as informant, since his own flesh and blood profited thereby. Versions of myths were far more satisfactory when put into English by a competent translator than when retailed in Jack Grouse's halting jargon. I even obtained a very intimate, if brief, account of Red-shirt's communion with the supernatural. Some twenty years before, having disobeyed his guardian spirit's commands, he sickened and died. His soul, about ten inches tall, came out of his thigh, stepped forward, and glanced back at its corpse. Suddenly it was transplanted to a lower world, where the Father (God) greeted it and sent it back to live again. The old man would not believe what the missionaries or the other medicine men had to say about the hereafter; he *knew* because he had been there.

My last fortnight at Lemhi thus proved more profitable than the preceding two months. The results were not spectacular, but they did fill in gaps in knowledge and satisfied Wissler. Apart from random data, I had collected a sizable body of myths and tales, incidentally hitting on a suitable topic for my doctoral dissertation, instead of the statistical one I had been tending toward for want of a better. I had gained some insight into one of the simplest of American cultures and was able to sketch its relations with its neighbors. Moreover, I had won my spurs: I had done field work.

CHAPTER 2

IN ALBERTA
AND
MONTANA

I should have preferred to go back to the Lemhi to stay long enough or return often enough to master Shoshone, and, thenceforward to conduct my ethnographic research by interviewing natives without an intermediary. But I have already explained why in the circumstances such intensive work on any one "tribelet" was out of the question. Specifically, Wissler himself was a specialist on the Blackfoot Indians and the Plains as a whole; he was eager to fill in the innumerable lacunae in knowledge of that area, so often written about, yet scientifically in large measure unexplored. Oddly enough, even today there is no comprehensive account of the Sioux (technically, "Dakota"), who figure so largely in history texts, travel books, and popular writings; and the first scientific, though still untechnical work on the Comanche, who had so deeply stirred me as a boy, did not appear until 1952!

Given his special interests, Wissler naturally sent me on a reconnoitering tour of the High Plains. I was to spend a few days with the Northern Blackfoot of southern Alberta in order to take down in the original the myth of a singing rock that revealed itself at a time of famine and enabled the tribe to drive buffalo into a pound. After briefly looking in on a Cree camp not far away, with an eye to future research possibilities, I was then to betake myself to a third tribe in the same province for a more thorough study. These were the Canadian or "Stoney" branch of the Assiniboine, greatly influenced by their Cree neighbors, but like all the tribe a fairly recent offshoot of the Dakota, whose dialects they could understand. On the Stoney reservation I was to await further orders, for Wissler had not yet decided on my final stopping place for the summer.

Accordingly, in the spring of 1907 I set out for Montreal, whence I proceeded via the Canadian Pacific to Gleichen, Alberta, the stop nearest to the Blackfoot reservation. The last census had credited Gleichen with ninety-nine residents, most of whom were to be found at any time in various stages of inebriation in one or the other of the two local saloons. I was fortunate enough to arrive at an opportune time. Apropos of King Edward's birthday the authorities had granted the Indians a holiday week, and accordingly all the Blackfoot had assembled in an old-fashioned camp circle, with the nearest tipis only a few yards across the railroad tracks from the station. The problem was again one of communication; how was I to get a suitable interpreter? The keeper of the general store recommended a young Blackfoot named Rex, but at the same time imparted some disturbing news. It seemed that the Indians were at the moment in a state of passive rebellion against the white authorities—for what reason I never discovered —and the storekeeper warned me that as soon as I asked for Rex, the Indians would promptly hide him. The problem was, then, to get them to bring him to me. For this purpose I hit upon the following stratagem.

Not many years before the start of my expedition, A. C. Haddon, the well-known British anthropologist, had realized that many primitive folk amused themselves with the equivalent of the European cat's cradle. That is to say, they made string figures, not necessarily transferring the string from one player to another, but sometimes with refinements of their own, such as using the toes and even the teeth to produce a design or associating the figures with a serious magical purpose. An English writer had published a book on cat's cradle as played in the four quarters of the globe. A method had been devised for accurately describing every move of the digits, so that the reader of an account could reproduce every stage from beginning to end. A fellow student who also planned to go into the field that year urged me to join him in learning some of the figures as part of our preparation, and we actually mastered a number of them. Utilizing this newly acquired accomplishment at Gleichen, I began strolling through the camp, developing different figures with a piece of string while apparently looking neither right nor left. The Blackfoot came out of their tipis, staring at me in rapt attention, and finally themselves summoned Rex to discover the meaning of my strange antics. Thus I obtained an interpreter for my week's stay.

I wish it had been possible to remain for months. The myth Wissler needed was soon written down, but there was much to be seen during that week's celebrations. All the display of colorful aboriginal living which I had so sorely missed among the Lemhi was now spread out before my eyes. Never again have I seen so close an approximation to what life within an old Plains camp circle must have been like; nowhere again have I seen so many painted lodges. I recall particularly one with the figure of a snake coiled around the tent cover. Sauntering about, I saw a middle-aged Indian preening himself in public with the help of a looking-glass, while his wife combed his hair. Gifts were being passed back and forth lavishly, reminding me of what I had read about the potlatches of Northwest Coast Indians. I witnessed a round dance like the one I had joined in at Lemhi, except that the men did not clasp their partners' shoulders. Men alone performed the "Grass" dance, some of them naked except for breechclouts, moccasins, and ornaments, others in buckskin shirts and fringed leggings. Without understanding it, I even stumbled upon part of a sacred ceremony, in which the twenty members of a woman's society constructed a lodge for their ritual. Two days later I saw four of them crawling on their knees (not hands) and ceremonially touching the central pole of the structure.

Venturing to go beyond my stipulated task, I asked some general questions about tribal bands and military associations. I also jotted down a few folk tales. One story I heard is worth mentioning. It did not take me long, even at that stage of callowness, to detect that the narrator was calmly blending Biblical episodes with native ideas of cosmogony, ascribing most of creation to Jesus. Only one thing (I forget what) proved beyond his powers, so he had to appeal to the Thunderbird, the giant eagle whose flapping wings, according to many Indian mythologies, cause thunder. This mythical being helped Jesus and "that is why the Americans put his picture on their silver dollars."

With profound regret I tore myself away from the Blackfoot and set out to investigate the chances for effective future work with a Cree group at Hobbema. The prospects did not seem favorable, though much later David G. Mandelbaum succeeded in obtaining much valuable information from other divisions of this far-flung people. At Hobbema the old ways seemed to have been largely abandoned, and I accomplished nothing beyond writing down a few folk tales. The place is ineradicable in memory only because it was the only one in which I deliberately bilked a creditor —oddly enough, from sheer delicacy. On the strength of my credentials the widowed agent received me cordially, entertained me most hospitably for several days, and regaled me with accounts of the half-breed rebellion in those parts. I honestly felt that it would be an affront if I asked for a bill, so after much soul searching I went off without paying for my board and lodging.

There followed the season's major enterprise, a seven-weeks' stay among the Stoney Assiniboine at Morley, Alberta, in the foothills of the Rockies. At first I took a room at the principal trading post of the reservation and remained there while practically all the Stoneys went off to the fair at Calgary. When they returned, they scattered so far from the post that it would have been impossible to work with them had I remained there. Accordingly, I outfitted at the store and camped with my interpreter, his family's tent on one side of mine, his mother's on the other side. He did offer me the use of the frame house he occupied during the winter, but one peep into its squalid interior decided me in favor of outdoor life. The old woman provided me with firewood and water, but I had little confidence in Stoney cuisine and did my own cooking. As for the water, an inspection of its source convinced me that, for me at least, it would be unsafe to drink. Therefore at every meal I prepared large quantities of tea for my only beverage, using the surplus to wash my dishes, instead of heating water for the purpose. In later years I grew skeptical of my own recollections about this prolonged abstention from water, so on a trip to Europe I tried for several weeks to do without it. I found it wholly possible, though in my test case the substitute was not tea. As for my cookery, it was not particularly varied or choice; often, on returning to camp from a long day's journey on horseback, I would merely open a can or two for my evening meal.

My horsemanship greatly improved on the rocky trails of the Stoney reserve, for the Indians lived at considerable distances from one another. They were willing enough informants, and I collected a respectable body of myths and folk tales from them, but the people seemed a sad come-down after the picturesque Blackfoot. They had been strongly missionized and exposed to other white influences, not only in their outward life, like the Lemhi, but in their general attitude as well.

My interpreter was a sturdy, solid, good-natured full-blood, very fond of his children, and willing to assist me; but he lacked any pretense to sparkling intelligence and his English, though passable, shone only in comparison with the Lemhi schoolboys'. He did, however, contribute a classical epitome of Caucasian civilization. I had been discussing the prohibition of speech already noted among the Shoshone, between a man and his wife's mother. I explained that white men had no such taboo; we not only talked freely to our mothers-in-law, but even quarreled with them. The reply was: "White people will do anything!" Obviously, though the social structure of the Stoneys had broken down, they were tenacious of ancient rules of etiquette.

After a long period of waiting among the Assiniboine, I got my orders for the season's last stop. I was to make a preliminary visit to the Crow Indians in southern Montana, whose reservation I reached via Great Falls, Helena, and Billings—a devious but at that time the best route from my starting point in Alberta. Though my funds allowed only a month's investigation, this month laid the foundation for far and away the most important part of my field research in later years.

From the very start of my stay with the Crow I was delighted. For one thing, there was no interpreter problem. Contrary to my previous experiences in Idaho and Alberta, there were plenty of men in their thirties and forties who had been to eastern schools, spoke excellent English, yet retained contact with their own people and with ancient customs. Some of them took pride in wearing their hair long and braided, while adorning their persons with native decorations. They were, moreover, a good-looking, impressive lot, with a fair number of six-footers among them. As for the older generation, from which I naturally recruited my chief informants, all of them had lived the old life of buffalo hunters and warriors. They proudly showed me the scars of arrowpoints on their bodies, and few retained an unmutilated left hand, having sacrificed a finger joint either in trying to gain a spirit's compassion when seeking a vision or in mourning a deceased relative. Altogether the Crow had enjoyed a much richer life than the Lemhi and had retained proportionately more of its external signs; and the older people were clinging to ancient beliefs as tenaciously as the Shoshone. Of the tribes I had met, they bore the closest resemblance to the Northern Blackfoot, whom I had been so loath to leave.

Ignorant as I still was of ethnography, I could not help making discoveries and corroborating or expanding older information. About forty years previously Lewis H. Morgan had found a clan organization among the Crow and reported that children took their mother's clan name. In a general wave of skepticism, doubt had been thrown on his findings by reputable ethnologists; but without any prejudice in the matter I soon discovered that Morgan had been right. I learned about the Tobacco organization that annually planted a sacred weed and that was split up into many coördinate chapters. Famous braves vividly described to me their exploits on the warpath; and the tragic story of a young warrior, personally known to many of my interlocutors, was told with a Homeric grandeur that has haunted me ever since. How the bits I garnered here and there hung together, I naturally did not yet understand during this first visit, but it was clear that on the Crow reservation I had struck a gold mine.

CHAPTER 3

TO
LAKE
ATHABASKA

To my sorrow I did not for some time get a chance to exploit the treasure trove I had discovered among the Crow. Once more Wissler had plans of his own. In 1908 I was to make a reconnaissance trip to the Chipewyan Indians on and about Lake Athabaska, in the northernmost part of Alberta and Saskatchewan, not far from ten degrees north of the international boundary. As a result, I experienced the scientifically least productive, but humanly most exciting of my expeditions. I came to see parts of the Dominion very few Canadians have ever visited, traveling by conveyances quite different from those most ethnographers have been accustomed to.

At that time Vilhjalmur Stefansson, who had already been to the Arctic and was subsequently to gain fame as an explorer and author, was commissioned by the Museum to investigate certain Eskimo groups. For a comparatively short distance his and my projected route coincided, so it was natural that we should travel together as far as my destination. However, it was imperative for me to read proof of my doctoral dissertation before I left New York. Stefansson decided that he could not wait for me, so I went by myself after all.

Though in many ways entirely different, this third trip of mine in some ways paralleled my first, at least from a subjective point of view. Like the Lemhi, the Chipewyan had always had an extremely simple mode of life; and neither had been the subject of investigation by a modern ethnologist. Yet, as Lewis' and Clark's journals had left us a valuable account of the northern Shoshone in 1805, so Samuel Hearne, dispatched by the Hudson's Bay Company to explore northern territories, had produced a priceless account of the Chipewyan and their Cree neighbors as seen by him in the years 1769 to 1772. His book, *A Journey from Prince of Wales's Fort in Hudson's Bay to the Northern Ocean*, not only describes aboriginal customs in admirable detail, but also fascinates the reader by the author's naïveté and unconscious humor. I studied the volume by way of preparation and thereafter periodically reread it for the sheer pleasure of it.

There was still another parallel between my two journeys. In 1906 no one could or would tell Wissler whether the Lemhi were still in their hereditary territory in central Idaho or already on their new reservation farther south. Two years later he was equally unsuccessful in extracting corresponding information from the headquarters of the Hudson's Bay Company in Winnipeg. That is to say, no one could tell him how soon I should have to be on the Athabaska River in order to embark in one of the Company's northbound scows. As I later discovered, there was a legitimate reason for official reticence, to wit, pure ignorance. There simply was no calendrically fixed schedule for the Company's fleet; it left as early as the local officials deemed it wise to make a start. The date could not be foretold in Winnipeg, nor even in Edmonton.

To forestall the risk of my being left behind for an indefinite period, Wissler had me set out earlier than usual. I left New York on May 5, and put in a day in Winnipeg to consult officials of the Hudson's Bay Company there. Though they could not advise me about the nonexistent schedule, I got from them in exchange for cash a three-hundred dollar letter of credit, commending me to all the employees of the Company of Gentlemen Adventurers Trading into Hudson's Bay. My next stop was Edmonton, the provincial capital and great fur emporium, on the North Saskatchewan River. In 1908 it was also the northernmost railroad point in Canada, though still in the southern half of Alberta. Here, too, I paid my respects to the local representatives of the Company, and left my trunk in its storeroom after transferring to duffel bags what was needed for the trip.

Though still in the dark about the exact time of departure of the fleet bound for the Company's northern posts, I learned that the date was probably not far ahead. The point of embarkation, Athabaska Landing, a hundred and five miles to the north, could be reached only by horse stage, the journey taking two days. For the night we put up at a halfway stopping place, where I shared the floor of a barn with possibly ten fellow travelers.

I arrived at the Landing on the second evening of the journey and put up at the only available hotel. Accommodations were scant, so I shared a room and bed with a pleasant middle-aged Scotsman. Though not late, I had not much time to spare: the advance guard of eight scows had already gone down, that is, north, and the remaining seven boats were scheduled to leave in the morning under the command of a Mr. Kelly, officially ranking as "purser." The crew was composed of *métis*, representing various degrees of White-Indian mixture; their foreman, technically "guide," was a breed of partly Orkney Island ancestry, for at one time the Company had a special predilection for recruits from that region.

We did not leave the following morning. It turned out that Athabaska Landing was the last outpost of unrestricted indulgence in alcohol. Residents farther north had to obtain special permits and to pay a tax on every gallon of liquor they imported. Accordingly, our crew made the best of this last golden opportunity and the men were not lightly pried loose from the bar of the saloon. Late in the afternoon I overheard Kelly urging the guide to get his men together, only to have him counter with the indignant reply, "Can't you give me a little time?"

It was 8:00 P.M. before the purser's heroic efforts bore fruit, and the guide was able to round up his far from sober crew. At last our seven scows departed. The only passenger, except myself, was a trader of the Révillon Frères Company, who was booked to leave us at the mouth of some tributary, whence he was to paddle himself to his post in a canoe tied to our boat. He had come aboard in a state of stupefaction, and what with the excitement of getting underway, no one paid attention to him. Suddenly he was no longer with us. We caught sight of him halfway back towards the Landing, paddling the canoe he had furtively cut loose. "I'm just going back for another drink, boys, I'll catch up with you," he shouted, but that was the last we ever saw of him.

It was not only the last saloon we were leaving behind, but in some respects the last outpost of civilization. My goal, Fort Chipewyan, a sort of northern metropolis, received eight mails a year; Fond du Lac, near the Saskatchewan end of the lake, received only two. There was something depressing about this venture into the unknown, and the dirge-like tune struck up by our half-breeds, though doubtless meant to cheer themselves, induced a melancholy mood in me. Moreover, the men seemed to be in an ugly frame of mind, as if ready to break out into open rebellion against the purser at the slightest provocation. Indeed, at one stage it looked as if Kelly, a powerful young man about thirty years of age, would come to blows with the ringleader, but fortunately both of them thought better of it. The reason for starting so late at all after the day's delay was, of course, merely to put a few miles between the crew and the saloon. We soon stopped and the half-breeds tied the boats to trees on the bank. Then we all went to bed—the crew ashore, Kelly and I under an awning aboard our boat. Forewarned that the Hudon's Bay Company provided no bedding, I had bought a roll-up mattress and "four-point" blankets at Edmonton. These were the heaviest coverings available, and I was glad to have them, for in the middle of May the banks of the Athabaska were still rimmed with dirty, weather-beaten ice. Another part of my outfitting that soon justified its existence was a mosquito bar.

There are a few details worth explaining about this means of conveyance in the north country. The scows were absolutely open boats; when it rained, we simply got wet. Their holds were large, for in them the Company forwarded the annual provisions for its many posts in the Mackenzie River basin. There were of course no "sanitary arrangements." Each boat was propelled by several oarsmen, who rose from their seats at every stroke, bracing themselves against bales of goods in the hold, while a steersman handled the heavy sweep. Wherever possible, however, and that meant much of the time, energy was saved by just drifting with the current. The half-breeds improved these free periods by playing the hand-game more or less as I had so often witnessed it at Lemhi. They rowed mainly when making a special effort or when, for some reason, it was desirable to cross over to the opposite bank. For the 437 miles from Athabaska Landing to Fort Chipewyan, one paid thirty-five dollars; for the journey back upstream the charge was forty-five dollars. This price was exclusive of meals, which cost fifty cents each. All baggage was "carried entirely at passenger's risk," the Company's folder announced.

Notwithstanding our inauspicious start, the following morning peace reigned supreme as we kept drifting along. Indeed, the members of the crew were not a bad lot and proved a constant source of amusement. Some of the men were Cree breeds, others Chipewyan breeds, the white strains being mainly Orkney Island and French. Those who spoke English spoke it with a heavy brogue; the French was naturally of the eastern Canadian variety, involving quaint pronunciations and words probably not countenanced by the dictionary of the Academy. A dollar was always a *piastre* for some reason. *Deux fois* sounded like *du fwé*.

The men were full of animal spirits. They would burst into a shout whenever they caught sight of a familiar portage. As a substitute for normal alcoholic liquor they bought cosmetic "Florida water" from the purser. They beat a tin plate to accompany the gambling songs that went with their favorite game and made all the requisite gestures. Everybody called everyone else *Nistau,* which means "brother-in-law" in Cree, the *lingua franca* of the area. With several of these men I struck up a joking relationship, especially with a John McDonald, who occasionally punctuated his God-damn's with relevant conversation.

There is a distinctive flavor, a fascination, about travel in so remote a region as northern Alberta then was, not in miles to be sure, but in point of isolation from the outside world. Sometimes days passed without our meeting a soul. The only description I remember reading that conveyed a similar atmosphere to the one I experienced is Prince Kropotkin's account of his Siberian journeys in *Memoirs of an Anarchist*. Notwithstanding this separation from customary surroundings, our trip was anything but monotonous.

Apart from the antics of the crew, there were wooded islands and abandoned tipi frames with birchbark canoes nearby. In one spot we came upon a jet of natural gas, at another the sight of a moose started Kelly in hot pursuit. Occasionally there would loom up some miserable trading-post—a few shacks with peripheral Indian tents for a suburb.

At first the mornings were excessively cold, but sometimes they brightened into fine, warm days. Dingy masses of ice remained visible on the banks for a long time to come. On the morning of May 19, at Grand Rapids Island, we overtook the eight scows forming the vanguard of our flotilla. At this point we were 165 miles north of Athabaska Landing. Because of the extreme shallowness of the water here and the number of rocks, the crew shifted from rowing to punting. The island, nearly half a mile in length, divided the Athabaska into two channels, of which the western was wholly impassable; during the Alaskan gold rush, I heard, a party of adventurers came to grief there. The eastern channel, however, was a possible pathway—provided the scows were taken through without their cargoes. Therefore every bit of freight and personal baggage was removed from fifteen boats, pushed across in handcarts along a narrow-gauge track, or carried on our backs. A helmsman and a steersman took each empty scow through the shoals of the passage. The current carried the craft possibly a mile beyond the far tip of the island, and each boat had to be towed back; finally, came the reloading. A minor episode at the very start was the running aground of our cook's boat about twenty-five feet from the southern end of the island, whence it had to be pulled in amidst Homeric exultation on the part of the crew. A little later someone caught a wolf whelp that was promptly adopted as a mascot.

The entire operation consumed six days, but they were not so boresome as might have been expected. I helped Kelly sort the cargo and joined the crew in the sports—mainly jumping and shot-putting—with which they beguiled leisure hours. A rendering of the Russian knee dance greatly entertained the men and raised my prestige, for they found it difficult to imitate. Since the New York Academy of Sciences had given me a small grant for getting anthropometric data, I took the stature of our crew, though with so heterogeneous a group, genetically the result would be of little scientific value. Toward the end of our stay a forest fire not far away at times assumed alarming proportions, but afforded a magnificent pyrotechnic spectacle at night. It was virtually extinguished by a heavy downpour.

When we finally left the island, there was an almost continuous stretch of a hundred miles of swift water ahead of us; and on May 26 we had to cope with real rapids, through which each boat was taken by a doubled crew. Fortunately we got through intact and arrived at an uninhabited island opposite Fort McMurray on the following day. Some years subsequently this post, 252 miles north of Athabaska Landing, was made more accessible by a railroad line with trains running once or twice a week from Edmonton. In 1908 the open boats formed the only means of transportation. But paradoxically from here on, that is, beyond the rapids, a steamer plied, so that after twelve days of roughing it in an open boat the traveler once more encountered the luxuries of civilization in the form of a dining room, a toilet, even a berth to sleep in. Of course, the Company provided no bedding, but that did not matter, since it was necessary to carry one's mattress and blankets before reaching McMurray.

We landed on the uninhabited island, and once more the crew dumped out every ounce of the yearly provisions for all the Company's posts as far as Fort Macpherson, which lies within the Arctic Circle, 1,854 miles from Athabaska Landing. The cargo was to be reloaded on the steamer *Grahame,* due within twenty-four hours; and two half-breeds were appointed to guard the goods. Kelly himself had to take his fleet back to the Landing; for good measure he left us enough food for a two-day stay.

I was sorry to see him depart. His formal education was probably not beyond the high school level, but he was intelligent and well-read in the better type of English literature. Indeed, he introduced me to James Barrie and James Stephens, some of whose works he lent me. He took a dim view of my ignorance of such authors, regarding it as a sorry excuse that I had been obliged to concentrate on professional reading. Among nonfiction writers he greatly admired John Ruskin and Thomas Carlyle, the latter especially looming as the embodiment of virility. Altogether Kelly gave me an object lesson in a colonial's "imperialist" psychology. He bitterly resented the term "American" as arrogated by citizens of the United States. What should we call ourselves, then? Why, we were Yankees, of course. He airily dismissed my mild protest that the label would hardly meet with favor south of the Mason and Dixon line. As a true believer in the British Empire, Kelly had only contempt for Gladstone, but great admiration for Disraeli. His was a complex personality; relish of the outdoors life was balanced by his fondness for belles lettres, nor did his stark imperialism and general intransigence exclude an unexpected tenderness of sentiment, as when he spoke of his fiancée in Edmonton. Withal he impressed me favorably.

Waiting for the steamer proved a great strain on my nerves. Instead of appearing on May 29, as Kelly had surmised, she did not arrive before June 5. Worst of all, in the absence of all means of communication, there was no way of finding out when the *Grahame* would arrive. At Grand Rapids I had already had a foretaste of Canadian mosquitoes, but here they made life miserable. For comfort I had to crawl under my mosquito bar. If I stirred about I had to lower the mosquito netting attached to my hat, and with the weather turning warm this was distinctly unpleasant. Even when eating I generally wore gloves for protection.

A major problem was how to kill time. Shortly after Kelly's departure a Captain Shott furnished a minor distraction. He arrived, convoying several priests and nuns bound for some missionary post in the area. Through him I was able to send out mail —a welcome chance in a region where eight postal collections and deliveries a year were all to be hoped for. After he had left, my only company consisted of two half-breed watchmen. One of them had a smattering of Canadian French and sometimes sang a haunting ditty about "la belle patrie." His mate knew neither French nor English. For lack of space in my duffel bags I had brought along only a single volume, Sir George Grey's *Polynesian Myths,* which after a while began to pall on me and was, in any case, soon read. On top of all this, our provisions, designed for at most two days, ran very low. We crossed to Fort McMurray once and got a little sugar and tea as gifts, for the residents were themselves so poorly off that they refused to sell us any food.

One natural phenomenon was for the first time brought home to me through direct experience. At latitude 55° N. the sun still shone brightly late of a June evening, and at whatever time I might wake up at night I had no trouble reading the dial of my watch without having to strike a match.

On June 4, when I had already retired under my mosquito bar, I heard shouts in the distance and presently some newcomers from the north brought glad tidings. They had actually seen the *Grahame*, and she was sure to turn up the next day. The report proved true—exactly one month after my departure from New York. It was one of the most cheering sights of my life when at 2:00 P.M. the steamer's elongated smokestacks hove in sight.

I have already noted the refinements offered aboard ship. They contrasted with the simple fueling arrangements: whenever necessary, we went ashore, and the crew chopped down the timber required. Incidentally, the draught of the boat was only about twenty inches. Pulling out on June 6, with four scows in tow, we slowly jogged along towards the Lake. The river was very wide now, its banks very low. Islands continually sprang up, and whenever one of them was near the wooded bank, the leafy branches from both sides nearly touched, forming a canopy for the *Grahame* to glide under. It was a fascinating experience, of which I was reminded years later in traveling from Göteborg to Stockholm via the Göta Canal.

On this part of the trip an engaging variety of communism came to my notice. Residents of the northern posts would sometimes pool their resources and send a wholesale order to some eastern bookshop. Our steamer was carrying a large chest of literature for general use; the coöperative spirit went so far that anyone was privileged to open the case and peruse whatever suited his fancy. Falling in with this agreeable folkway, I was able to read Sir Walter Scott's *The Bride of Lammermoor* and a story of Marryat's.

Finally, on June 8, we landed at Fort Chipewyan, four hundred and thirty-seven miles north of the Landing and about five hundred and forty from Edmonton. It had taken about five days to get from New York to Edmonton, but about four weeks from there to Lake Athabaska.

The clerk and trader representing the Hudson's Bay Company was a *métis* named Pierre Mercredi, who spoke both English and French; his wife, also a breed, only French. I presented my letter of credit and was hospitably received. Mercredi assigned a room to me, Madame spontaneously prepared a hot bath in a washtub. Before long I met the pillars of local society—the Anglican divine and two officers of the Northwest Mounted Police, Major Routledge and Sergeant Fields. The latter had to patrol a stretch of something like one thousand miles.

Unlike tribes I had previously visited, the Indians at Lake Athabaska, who were a division of the Chipewyan, were not confined to a reservation nor were they even incipient farmers, but for economic reasons were still obliged to scatter over a wide territory as hunters and fishermen. It was sheer good luck that I arrived when they were gathering at the Fort to receive annuities from the Dominion Commissioner. I was also fortunate in getting a tolerable interpreter, a young married breed who usually lived near the post. With his aid I was able to proceed from tent to tent and question potential informants.

The cultural status of these people was curious. Externally they showed even more strongly than the Lemhi Shoshone the influence of white civilization. More easterly bands of the tribe had begun to get firearms from the Hudson's Bay Company not long after 1719, and the post on Lake Athabaska dated back to 1788. Thenceforward the Chipewyan hunted furs for the Company, receiving in return clothing and provisions. In the period of my visit the commissioner brought them every year a stipend of five dollars per head as well as an allotment of ammunition and of twine for nets. Even the old people wore trade clothes and covered their heads with hats or visored caps. Over and above the secular influences of contact with fur traders came the effects of Catholic and Anglican missionary teaching. Elderly women wore crosses on their chests, and on the official rolls there figured such baptismal names as Adam, Catharine, Antoine, and Baptiste. According to the ancient system girls were mostly named after parts of a marten's body, say Marten's-eye; boys were called Rabbit, Rabbit's-head, Wolf's-tail, and the like. That pagan beliefs had not been entirely eradicated by the missionaries seemed certain: within the memory of living men, I learned, a medicine man from the eastern end of the lake had transformed himself into a wolf, the better to hunt moose. But it was not easy to penetrate beneath the veneer of Christianity.

However, even externally, assimilation had not gone so far as a superficial glance at a group of the Indians might indicate. As already suggested, traits intimately connected with the geographical environment, hence with the native economy, persisted. The Chipewyan continued to paddle canoes in the summer, still manufactured toboggans and birchbark vessels, still slept in conical tents, and hung their possessions on tripods outdoors.

In one respect these people were backward as compared with the Indians I had studied previously. Except for a single sophisticate who demanded cold cash for his fee because he got better value at the store with it, all informants asked for payment in kind. One would ask for lard, another for flour, a third for a shirt, and I would hand them orders on Mercredi, who honored them, duly debiting my account with the monetary equivalent and ultimately entering the total on my letter of credit.

It was obvious that these Chipewyan were miserably poor. So far as I can recall, they are the only Indians I ever met that did not consider an offer of food to a visitor a foregone conclusion. Among the Lemhi I once stood outside the tent of a man who had been rather ill-disposed toward me, yet at lunch time he asked me whether I cared to join in the meal. At Fort Chipewyan, my hosts resented my not bringing them food.

In some ways the Chipewyan were highly suspicious. They did not share the Lemhi phobia of being photographed; in fact they were rather eager to get such poor prints as I was able to prepare, though they did not approve of the blue color. But when it came to being measured they were uncompromisingly refractory. Why, an Indian was measured only for a coffin! If anyone were to submit to my tape measure, he would die. That was one favorite argument. Others declared they knew very well what I was up to: the Dominion government had commissioned me to determine the tallest men in order to draft them into the army. When I explained that I had nothing to do with Canadian officialdom and in fact belonged to another country, the reply was, "Well, then, what are you doing around here anyway?" I had to give up anthropometry at Fort Chipewyan, at least for the moment.

As for aboriginal activities, there was of course little to be seen around the Fort—except for the hand-game, which was played by everyone with wholehearted, unremitting enthusiasm. Curiously, this pastime was accompanied not only by singing, but by the beating of a tambourine such as many tribes associate with curing rites and other ceremonies. A player who succeeded in foiling his opponent gave vent demonstratively to his jubilation, exposing the hand holding the button whose position was to have been guessed and disdainfully gesticulating with the other hand before the loser's face.

In the circumstances I did not secure much new information. I did take down a series of myths and tales, discovering that the Chipewyan had adopted a good many stories of a Cree cycle that centered in the adventures of a trickster-hero.

If the Indians were only of moderate interest, the half-breeds and whites of Lake Athabaska would have formed a fascinating object of systematic research; but in those days "community studies" of this kind had not yet become fashionable, and I made only random observations.

The ways of the Hudson's Bay Company alone would have formed a subject worthy of intensive study. Its benevolent, though exacting paternalism toward employees was an obtrusive feature; its history in opening up the country, or its policy toward the Indians would have proved tempting subjects for investigation. All sorts of tales about the Company were told, some of them doubtless apocryphal; one interlocutor said that a recent visitor to the headquarters in London had found the clerks still writing with quill pens. Prince Rupert, the founder of the Hudson's Bay Company in 1670, naturally figured as of heroic proportions; in addition to his creation of the fur-trading company and his military exploits, he was also credited with the invention of "Prince Rupert's Drops," heralded as a panacea for all bodily ills and available at all Company stores. In some respects the organization was certainly conservative; for instance, it deprecated any suggestion of dropping the apostrophe and "s" in its name. So far as I know, it still retains the old spelling for the Bay as well as for its own designation.

Among the phenomena that gave a distinctive flavor to that section of Canada was the Royal Northwest Mounted Police, whose efficiency has always been legendary. I remember hearing that one of Charles Dickens's sons had been a member of the force.

There was certainly no mistaking the fact that around Lake Athabaska, and for that matter in western Canada as a whole, I was not on the soil of the United States. For instance, I heard a company clerk address a Catholic bishop as "My lord." Irrespective of their unquestionable loyalty to the Empire, Canadians referred with contempt to "remittance men" who for reasons of their own had settled in the Dominion, but refused to do a proper pioneer's work, and depended for their income on funds forwarded from England.

Tiny as was the settlement at Fort Chipewyan, it was polyglot and socially many-faceted. I could speak German to an Alsatian priest and hear French, English, Chipewyan, and Cree, the last two being totally diverse forms of Indian speech. The English I heard naturally varied with the speaker's education and provenience; I was shocked once to hear a physician pronounce "case" in unalloyed cockney as "kyse." The Orkney brogue was not uncommon throughout the region; and French was of course usually of the Quebec variety. French folkways and etiquette were not wanting either; and it was entertaining to watch native women seated on the ground bandying polite "messieurs" and "mesdames" with passersby.

About midnight of June 18 or 19, there was a great commotion at the Fort. The store house at the Catholic Mission had caught fire, and the main building was in danger of destruction. Since it was not at all dark at that (or any other) hour, we at the Company's end of the settlement easily made our way to the scene of the fire, which was soon checked, though not without considerable damage. To quote from an account in an Edmonton paper about a month later: "About sixty Indians turned out with kettles and managed to put the fire out with water from the lake." Two days later came a more agreeable break in the routine of life.

The *Grahame* returned from McMurray, bringing my first mail from home. Presently, too, there turned up Agnes Deans Cameron, accompanied by her niece; they were guests of the Company and were gathering materials on "The New North" for a book by Miss Cameron, which was published in 1910.

When I complained to the agent, Mr. Harris, of my trouble in getting Indians who would consent to be measured, he invited me to accompany him to Fond du Lac; there, thanks to his marital connections, he would be able to smooth my path. We headed for Saskatchewan in a York boat and arrived on the evening of June 27. There Harris had an impressive library, not only belles lettres but Darwin and other serious works. His house lacked a guest room, but I had been carrying my roll-up mattress and blankets all the way from Edmonton and was prepared for any eventuality. I simply slept on the floor of Harris's office, which at the time happened to be separated from his bedroom by only an unhinged, leaning door. Harris was a vigorous man in the prime of life and had been away from home for several weeks. Before long the rhythmic swaying of the conjugal bed conveyed an un-equivocal message to the guest nearby.

Hitherto I had not tasted caribou meat, for the Fort Chipewyan country, rich in moose, wood deer, and various species of fish, was not the habitat of the American reindeer. At Fond du Lac, how-ever, its true range began, and I had my initiation to a meal of cari-bou, as delicious a steak as I have ever tasted. Unfortunately, Har-ris's in-laws were camped nearby, and their dogs made off with the bulk of his meat supply. We were thus condemned to a diet of canned goods for the rest of my stay, much to the wrath of Harris, who vehemently cursed all dogs, Indians, and connections by marriage.

True to his promise, Harris exerted himself nobly on behalf of my anthropometric aspirations. It was an uphill job, for we at first met the same stubborn resistance that had thwarted my ef-forts at Fort Chipewyan. However, Harris's status in the com-munity and his relationship with the natives stood him in good stead; and when he publicly presented himself for measurement by me, diffidence waned. I thus managed to get the stature of twenty-six males, a fair sample ranging from 160 cm. (5 ft. 3 in.)

to 188 cm. (6 ft. 2 in.) with an average of 172.35 cm. (something under 5 ft. 8 in.). Like their brethren in the other band, these people offered no objection to being photographed.

On July 1, about 1:00 A.M., I got back to the Fort. Since the mosquitoes seemed in abeyance, and I was very tired, I stretched out on my bed without putting my bar over the four bedposts that are provided for that purpose in all properly equipped northern households. But I was to regret my laziness. There were not many mosquitoes, but just enough to keep me awake. At last I had to get up and fix the netting after all.

The following morning I hoped to resume my ethnographic work, but learned doubly bad news. During my brief absence my interpreter had died, and it would not be easy to get a substitute. Further, almost all the Indians, having received their annuities and rations, had dispersed to pursue their normal economic tasks. I was in a quandary; if I remained at the post, there would be scientifically next to nothing to do and I should have to wait, inactive, to be taken back to the Landing by the next Company transport in the fall. The alternative was to paddle about from one family's haunt to another, with a new interpreter, if one was discoverable, for a guide; and it would be necessary to provide subsistence not only for the two of us but for his household as well. My funds did not permit such expenditure, nor did the prospective yield of either data or museum specimens seem to warrant it. What, then, was to be done?

Fortunately, about that time Colin Fraser, a *métis* "free trader," that is, a fur dealer independent of the Company, was preparing to take his furs to Edmonton, purchase winter supplies for his own establishments and also goods for the Mission, to replenish the stores diminished by the fire. He had already accepted several passengers for his scow and agreed to take me too. Before we left, however, I was able to attend a great social event in honor of Mercredi's eldest son's marriage to a good-looking *métisse*. His father provided sumptuous fare for all and sundry, and the guests were treated to Old World fiddling in the best French-Canadian style.

On July 6, we left the lake, towed by a tug as far as McMurray, which we reached on the ninth. During this otherwise uneventful

stage of the journey it was highly entertaining to watch the gesticu-
lations of our cook who, from the vantage-point of our scow,
managed to carry on a series of long-distance hand-games with
one of the tug's crew.

After Fort McMurray the fun began, for the return trip was
quite different from the inland journey. First of all, there was a
goodly company of passengers, including the one-time captain of
a steamer in the North country, a trapper, a boiler inspector, and
a school inspector of the provincial government. Then there was
not a flotilla of scows, but a single boat, hence a much smaller
crew, only seven or eight "trackers" who, harnessed to a long,
heavy line, were to tow the scow upstream like the "cordellers"
of early days along the upper Missouri.

Fraser was no respecter of persons and felt the obligations of
a common carrier even less than the Company. He was doing us a
favor to transport us at all (which certainly applied to me) ; so
whenever we got to a tough point of the route, we all disembarked
and tramped with the trackers, possibly for a mile and never on
anything suggestive of a towpath. This happened soon after Mc-
Murray near the Mountain Rapids, where for twenty minutes we
trudged in the rain over a slushy, slippery incline. That time we
were at least rewarded by the sight of a beautiful double rainbow.
The following night there was a terrific downpour, which drenched
my canvas tent.

The average routine of travel was to rise early, try to make
twenty miles by our crew's muscular efforts, and go to sleep ashore
at an early hour. It was usually about 5:00 A.M. that the cook
woke us up with a terrific clatter of pans and dishes, and after a
hasty toilette we consumed the first of our four daily meals—four
because our trackers required that number in view of their labors. But what meals! With unvarying monotony we received
bannocks for bread, sowbelly and baked beans for the main course,
and tea. Regarding the beans as by far the least repulsive of the
solid offerings, I went for them "in a big way," with predictable
consequences not unembarrassing in the absence of sanitary facilities, and naturally making me the butt of the crew's merriment.

The enforced walks continued. One day several of us tramped
along for about two miles, now getting a foot bath on a narrow

ledge of limestone by the river, now heaving ourselves up five feet to the next higher shelf, then lowering ourselves again, dodging arrested deadfalls, plunging into mudholes, and running half a dozen thorns into our hands while clinging to bushes for a hold. Even when aboard, travel was not an unmixed joy. When it rained, and it did rain violently at times, we philosophically sat in our waterproofs until the showers passed. After a nocturnal downpour I found myself afflicted with the lumbago. Occasionally the menu improved, through no fault of Fraser's: members of the party shot several ducks, snipes, and partridges, on which we all feasted royally.

On July 23 we were judged to be within striking distance of Athabaska Landing, and everybody was eager to get there on the following day. Accordingly we got up at 3:30 A.M. and actually arrived by noon. We were said to have made very good time between the lake and the Landing. On the evening of the twenty-fifth, the stagecoach deposited me at the Windsor Hotel in Edmonton, where I registered in a hirsute, bedraggled condition, rather ashamed to show myself in public. It was Saturday, the barber shops were closed, and I was unable to get trimmed or to recover my trunk from the Company before Monday. Thus ended my northern excursion.

So far as the remainder of the season was concerned, it was something of an anticlimax in respect to actual work. Since the data I had obtained from the Stoneys in 1907 were decidedly skimpy, Wissler wanted me to eke out the information among another branch of the Assiniboine, living on the Fort Belknap Reservation, in northern Montana. These people had really preserved more of the old customs than their Canadian kinsmen, and though they were less coöperative and less expansive than my beloved Crow, I was able to do a routine job there. However, nothing happened that was of particular human interest. But in trying to reach Fort Belknap from Edmonton via Calgary I had one of the unforgettable adventures of my life.

Railway time tables showed that, taking the direct route from Calgary to my destination, I should have to change trains at the border and undergo a customs inspection at midnight. This idea did not appeal to me, so I decided to save a night's rest by a somewhat devious détour. I would take a sleeper to Fernie, British Columbia, tarry there until midafternoon, then board the train scheduled to leave for Montana at four o'clock. In addition, I would have the satisfaction of seeing a little of British Columbia and the Canadian Rockies.

I did save *that* night's rest, arrived at Fernie in due time, and strolled about, admiring the scenery. Later I went to the station and boarded the train a few minutes before four. However, just as it was to pull out, a forest fire that had gotten out of hand suddenly swept the town and burned down the wooden bridge in front of us. Within a few minutes the townsfolk came streaming out of their homes, mothers crying for missing children, wives frantic over absent husbands. The train, of course, waited to take on the fugitives until it was filled to capacity. Then, since normal egress was blocked we slowly backed for about a mile, where most of the travelers took refuge by the river. With a crippled couple and three other passengers I remained aboard when the train went back for a second load of townspeople. On both sides of the track the timber was burning, and the heat that came through the glass panes was overpowering. We pressed wet handkerchiefs to our noses, but even so we had the sensation of smothering. However, we got through, took on more Fernie residents, and backed about two miles into a relatively unexposed spot. A lawyer from the town showed great coolness and organizing skill at this stage, and a hospital nurse ministered to the needs of invalids; accordingly, though the danger had actually increased, the first excitement yielded to greater calm.

The railroad men suggested a safer place of refuge by a cut bank one and a half miles farther on. Most of us walked there, while the sick and disabled were packed into a wagon. The train was brought along the foot of the cut bank, which extended for about a quarter of a mile. It loomed up from one side of the Elk River, which here flowed around two islands; on its far bank there was more timber burning. The conflagration was gaining on us from the rear with alarming speed, so that at one time the conductors advised fleeing toward Michel, farther east, and herded us into boxcars. But the fire turned out to be cutting off that retreat, so the nearer of the islands in the Elk River seemed safer.

Although some people preferred to remain huddled in the coaches, most of us crossed to this island on logs.

By nightfall we were completely surrounded, the flames seizing upon every bit of vegetation and presenting a gloomy prospect for our future. The lofty trees toppling down on all sides afforded a grandiose sight. A fierce wind, which did not die down until 2:30 A.M., kept fanning the flames and at the same time chilling us. As a protection against it, a man from Missouri, a young lady from Spokane, and I constructed a crude windbreak of rocks. Later on, I was recruited to help keep the terrified children quiet by telling them Indian stories. I also made an effort to sleep, but without overcoat or blankets it was far too cold, and my eyes smarted badly from the smoke. As morning approached, I was fully convinced that we had nothing more to fear, since we had survived that long. However, alarming rumors still circulated: eighty men were said to have perished in a lumber camp nearby, several railroad stations had burned down, there was no hope of relief for us, and so on. All these rumors proved to be untrue. The intermittent booming from oil tanks that blew up in neighboring towns was hardly a cheerful sound. Yet the general spirit was excellent. Apart from the initial flight from Fernie, I recall no panic. Instead, there was a marked feeling of coöperativeness; and a group of jolly Scotsmen made the best of the situation, singing and joking.

Morning broke about five o'clock, and the conductors summoned us to the train, which was still standing intact by the cut bank. They had made reconnaissance to Fernie and found that what was inflammable between us and the town had already burned down. So with a few interruptions en route, we got back in safety. Of the prosperous town, very little remained. We picked our way through devastated streets, stepping over telegraph poles on the ground and over omnipresent dead wires, noting sporadic fires still smoldering. As happens in such catastrophes, a few houses on the outskirts had been spared, and in one of them the residents generously dispensed breakfast to all. It was more than welcome. I, for example, had eaten nothing since lunch the day before, except for a cracker in the evening.

Our plight had not remained unnoticed by the outside world.

Though the Canadian Pacific station had been destroyed and pre-sumably its telegraph instruments also, messages had somehow been sent out, and relief trains arrived to take us to one of two adjacent settlements. I was taken to the hamlet of Elko, which of course was wholly unprepared to accommodate a large caravan of refugees. I shared a room with a Chinese laborer and promptly made up for lost sleep. By a stroke of fortune my duffel bags turned up in the course of time, so I did not even lose the few specimens that I had bought at Fort Chipewyan.

In retrospect the experience was psychologically instructive. According to my recollection and to notes taken soon after the event, I was not so much afraid of dying as I was irritated by the delay in carrying out my plans and worried over the probable anxiety of my family, who would have received my letter telling them I was going via Fernie at just about the time the morning paper informed them of the fire. The episode was in any case a noteworthy by-product of field work, though, of course, in peri-ods of drought corresponding crises may develop anywhere. Thus, I lived unscathed through the conflagration of Berkeley, Cali-fornia, in 1925.

The entire trip to Athabaska took nearly three months. For a philosophically minded, urban youth, it was an exciting and in-teresting experience, and I learned a great deal about my fellow man and his ability to adapt himself to almost anything. Scien-tifically, it was the least fruitful trip I ever made.

CHAPTER 4

BACK
TO THE
CROW

For some reason no field work was planned for me in 1909. In the following year Wissler at last allowed me to return to the Crow for intensive work and to spend the last part of the season among their nearest relatives, the Hidatsa of central North Dakota. What is more, I went out with ampler funds than ever before. The competitive spirit is well developed among big museums. A Mr. Simms of the Field Museum in Chicago had been to the Crow, mainly to buy up valuable old specimens and particularly buffalo-hide shields, of which he procured a magnificent collection, cost being apparently no object. Hence, I, too, was to purchase representative ethnographica and, above all, at least one buffalo-hide shield, even if it took more than a hundred dollars to secure one.

The yield was acceptable, both in specimens and information. As a result, I was allowed to spend at least part of every summer for seven consecutive years—through 1916—on the Crow reservation. The entrance of the United States into the First World War put a stop to these expeditions. In 1917 I was a visiting professor at the University of California; and in 1921 I left the Museum to join the California staff permanently. When I revisited the Crow ten years later, it was under the auspices of the American Council of Learned Societies. Since then, however, I have maintained contacts with the reservation; and, in consequence, the Crow experiences form a continuum in my consciousness. Therefore I shall not give a separate account of each visit, but shall treat them all as constituting a single phenomenon.

Interpreters.—At Lemhi I found out how much an ethnographer's success depends on the caliber of his interpreters; it is, then, worthwhile to expatiate on those I was able to employ among the Crow. Since their reservation is large enough to be split into districts—Reno, Lodge Grass, Bighorn, and Pryor—all of which I visited, I had dealings with at least half a dozen of these assistants in the course of years. Two of them stand out above the rest: Robert Yellowtail and James Carpenter. Although both men proved valuable, they were of totally diverse temperament and character. Both lived at Lodge Grass, my favorite headquarters.

"Bobbie" Yellowtail, now probably between sixty-five and seventy years of age, is the very opposite of the popular notion of the saturnine, pompous Redskin. He is gay, volatile, effervescent, self-assured. When I first saw him in 1910, he had just come home from a long stay at the Indian school in Riverside, California. He was good-looking and spoke excellent English. I imagine he has the equivalent of a high school or junior college education. It seems to me he once said something about having had a fling at the law. At all events, when he called on me once in Berkeley, he astonished my wife no less by his breezy manner than by his flinging about such terms as "a priori" and "prima facie evidence." In years past he was sometimes asked to lecture on old Indian lore and custom to the guests at dude ranches in Wyoming; for these occasions he would bone up by reading such scientific papers of mine as I had from time to time sent him.

When I first knew him, he had steeped himself in radical propaganda literature and expressed a withering disdain for the lying press of the country. Since then he has made a comfortable adjustment to the world about him and risen considerably in the social scale. In the early 'thirties, John Collier, as Commissioner of Indian Affairs, appointed Bobbie superintendent of the Crow Reservation. Though no longer holding that position, he has lately become intensely interested in Montana politics, has appeared in Washington to testify before Congressional committees, has run for Congress on the Republican ticket, and has recently announced his candidacy for the United States Senate.

This seems an appropriate place to mention a curious misunderstanding on the part of Yellowtail's father-in-law, White-man-runs-him, a onetime Custer scout. About 1912 two government officials took a party of Crow, Cheyenne, and Blackfoot to Washington and the East generally. They turned up at the Museum in New York one day, where I showed them the sights, particularly, of course, the Plains Indian exhibits. When White-man-runs-him got back to Montana, he asked his son-in-law, "Do you remember that white man you worked for last summer?" "Of course I do," answered Bobbie. "Well, when he was here, I thought he was just a common white man, but you ought to see the house he lives in in the East!" He apparently thought that the American Museum of Natural History was my residence and that the collections there were my private stock of antiques.

When I returned to the Crow Agency in 1910, I naturally expected to work there with Dave Stewart, the interpreter who had efficiently helped me three years before. But he was otherwise engaged and advised me to make my headquarters at Lodge Grass, twenty miles to the southeast, where Jim Carpenter might be willing to help me. I followed his suggestion and never had reason to regret it. At times, and always in other districts, I had to rely on other assistants, but Jim remained my mainstay.

When I first met him, Jim, then possibly thirty-five years old, was regarded as one of the crack horsemen of Montana. He also had the reputation at the Agency of being one of the worst troublemakers. Actually, he was not a Crow by blood at all, but the son of a white man and a Piegan Blackfoot woman. However, he was brought to the reservation as an infant, grew up there, and developed a convert's love for his adopted tribe. The wrongs suffered by his people deeply stirred him. White ranchers, he insisted, were encroaching on Crow rights; government employees were in collusion with the big cattle ranchers; domineering whites were abusing and cheating the Indians. Jim, never one to mince words, would accuse officials to their faces, irrespective of consequences. He was quick to flare up in defense of his tribe. Once, in an argument, he assaulted a deputy sheriff with his whip and suffered the penalty of the law. As a symbol of defiance he wore his hair long, with little queues dangling over his face.

Typical is the following letter that he once sent me from the county jail in Billings:

Billings, Mont., Jan. 20, 1914.

Robert H. Lowie
Dear Friend:

I am dropping you a few lines in which I am asking you to do me a big favor, should you think it alright. I suppose you will remember I spoke to you about getting myself into a scrape the previous Sept. Well, I was out on bonds, till the 15th of last month, when I had to take my medicine, which is 60 days and one hundred dollars fine. I am very anxious to pay this fine so as to be out and prepare for my spring plowing some time next month. I have tried, and the only way I see is to ask you the favor of advancing me $60.00, sixty dollars, to help pay my fine.

I understand you to say you was coming back the latter part of May and would have me to do the interpreting for you. I will then be able to pay the amount back to you by the work I shall render you. Should you not stay here over three weeks I will pay you the difference as by that time I will have enough money. I hope you will not overlook to help me and send it within the next two weeks. While here I have gone over all of the last book you sent me, and I find some mistakes that would need correction, but I thought I would just mark them on the book, and mention them to you when you come.

I would like you to send me the first book you sent me, as I have lost the other one, some of the boys got away with it. Another thing is if you are coming, you can send me a copy of what you are going to take up, so I can find out the best ones to go to and be prepared for your coming. Hoping you will send what favor I ask you by return mail, I will come to a close.

I am
Your friend,
James Carpenter

P.S. You can send my mail in care of Sheriff, County Jail, Billings, Montana.

Also find out for me where I can get a book entitled *Hell up to date* if you can, send it also, and charge it to me also.

The postscript had an unforeseeable epilogue. I tried hard to get a copy of the book Jim wanted, but since he had forgotten the author's name and had no idea of the publisher, I was stymied. Finally he suggested that if *Hell up to Date* was unprocurable, he would like a life of "Napoleon, the Great." About that there was no difficulty, and Jim read the biography twice during his confinement. However, the unobtainable volume periodically haunted his memory, and on one occasion while chatting with me at Lodge

Grass, he brought up the subject once more. "Too bad, you couldn't get that book," he said, "it had such interesting pictures." Then, for the first time, he began to expatiate on the illustrations, which from his account were lurid indeed. Suddenly a light dawned on me and before my mind's eye appeared hefty tomes illustrated by Gustave Doré. "You don't by any chance mean Dante's Hell, do you?", I asked. "I think Dante was the man's name," Jim answered. On my return to New York I sent him a copy of the *Inferno* with its unforgettable drawings. Except for the decorative epithet of the title, as quoted by Jim, the mystery was solved.

The incident had seemed very funny to me. Some time later, when lunching with the editors of *The Freeman*—Albert Jay Nock was its guiding spirit and Van Wyck Brooks was in charge of reviews—I told them the story along with other reminiscences of my Indian experiences. A week or so later Henry B. Fuller of *The Freeman* staff rang me up, sputtering with excitement. "Do you remember the story you told us about *Hell up to Date?*" "Of course," I said. "Well, that story has a sequel; you must come and have dinner with me and a friend of mine and hear about it." By no stretch of the imagination could I conceive a mysterious friend of Fuller's providing a sequel to the tale, but with my curiosity at maximum pitch, I accepted the invitation.

The friend turned out to be Art Young, the well-known cartoonist, who proved to be a charming conversationalist. He promptly cleared up the residual obscure points in the plot. As a young art student in Paris, primed with the teachings of Robert Ingersoll and other infidels, he had developed the plan of a book irreverently parodying those classics that had theological themes. He had taken Chicago for the contemporary Inferno and had closely patterned his drawings on Doré's. A mid-Western firm had actually published the volume, which had long since gone out of print. By some queer accident Jim had somewhere come across a stray copy and had received an indelible impression. Young had brought a copy to show me, and as I glanced through it, everything was cleared up. The illustrations were clever travesties whose graphic description by Jim naturally evoked my memories of Doré; and since the preface mentioned Dante, his name would sound familiar to Jim when I pronounced it as the putative author's.

In 1910 Jim would still get drunk at times and fail to meet me at the appointed hour, but I soon found out that he was likely to make up for lost time by working during his leisure. At first his suspicions about white people also included me, for at every opportunity he brought up the Indians' good points, contrasting them with the white man's shortcomings. Like many other primitive tribes, the Crow prohibited brother and sister from conversing with each other after childhood. "White people talk about the immorality of Indians," was Jim's comment, "yet they'll speak with their sisters, which no Crow will do." On another occasion we were visiting Medicine-crow, a typical gentleman of the old school. He got up to show me his shield and, instead of making a shortcut across my legs, he stepped around me. "See that?" asked Jim. "There's the politeness of an Indian, no white man would have done that!"

But when once he was convinced of being fairly treated, Jim's dour manner relaxed. After riding about with me for several weeks he threw me a bone of approbation: "The Indians like you," he said, "you're not high-toned." In the same spirit, some years later, he put at ease a half-breed woman too shy to enter his home while the wise man from the East was there. "Why," he explained to me afterwards, "I told her you were as common as she or I." Even so, a paleface had to be cautious in what he said to Jim. Once I exulted over the purchase of a buffalo-hide shield for only seventy-five dollars. Quick as a flash came the comment, "So you've been cheating the Indians!" I appeased him by explaining that I had more than once paid ten dollars for sacred articles that had no commercial value whatsoever in the East. This reply satisfied him. "So it all evens up," he concluded.

Though not without a sense of humor, Jim was the brooding type. The railroad station agent at Lodge Grass, who had lived there for many years, told me that Carpenter was the only Indian of his acquaintance who was constantly worrying. Alas! he had plenty to worry about in his later years, what with a large family to support, frequent and sometimes serious attacks of illness, and trouble with his farm. On top of it all came the death of his oldest son. This note from him is self-explanatory:

Lodge Grass, Mont., Nov. 9, 1934.

Robert H. Lowie
Dear Friend:

It has been quite a while since I heard from you. Ever since last summer I have had hard luck. I lost my crops on account of shortage of water. I did raise a few spuds. The corn was wormy. What the worms did not get the pheasants destroyed. The worst part was when I lost my oldest boy over a month ago. It has been so hard for us to stand, especially on his mother and grandmother. The only relief we get is by going to his grave and weep. We go every day since the accident happened. The strain is such, all we can do is keep alive. I cannot express what we have stood so far. Wishing you in the best of health, I will close.

Your Friend
James Carpenter.

I considered Jim the ideal interpreter. It is true that his English, though fluent and ample in vocabulary, was not quite so smooth as that of some other interpreters. But two qualities made him invaluable—an absorbing interest in old Crow customs, which to the best of his ability he reverently observed; and a meticulousness in obtaining data that rivaled a conscientious scientist's. It mattered little that he might turn up at noon when due at nine in the morning, for by compensation he often worked for me evenings and Sundays on his own. During my last visit to the Crow, we often spent eight hours of a hot summer day, phonetically taking down a text in the original, both of us painfully striving for a correct translation. I discovered that when the day's stint was done, Jim would spontaneously scour the countryside, pumping agemates and old informants as to the true sense of puzzling phrases or vocables. Had we chosen the best possible rendering for the initial expletive in a given sentence? Would it improve the rendering if we made it "Now, then," instead of "Why?"

Invaluable, too, was Jim's combination of absolute loyalty to me personally and his unrelentingly critical attitude toward my attainments as a student of Crow ethnography and linguistics. "You've got a fine pronunciation," he once remarked, "but you talk Crow with a foreign accent." On another occasion I vainly tried to impress him by presenting what I thought to be an idiomatic rendering into Crow of a simple fairy tale from a school reader; he would not allow a single sentence to stand as it was written. His perfectionism, his passion for clearing up the riddles of Crow speech and usage persisted to the last. Smitten with an incurable heart disease and no longer able to take pen in hand, he dictated the following letter from his deathbed:

Crow Hospital, Jan. 27, 1937.

Dear Lowie,

Many, many thanks for the ten dollars you so kindly sent me some time ago. I should have written before this, but have been so ill and weak that I couldn't write myself and did not wish to ask anyone else to do it for me. About as long as I can read or write consecutively is for a few seconds and then I have to quit and rest.

I do not know whether I shall ever completely recover from this ailment. A young man is writing this letter for me as no one else has offered to write for me. I feel that death is steadily approaching.

If you can spare one of your latest publications, I should be glad to receive one, this also applies to your grammar on the Crow language even though it is not finished?

Tepee burial A'wanoo is not a custom, it is only a rich man's burial. Only a chief was accorded this rite.

Another question you have wanted an answer for the last seven or eight years is about Old Man Coyote, the strawberries and the girls, hú·ri koco cá koce ditdik. The word shown above should read hú·rikokoho·cúritdik. This word was taken from the Gros Ventre [Hidatsa] and in the adaption of the story by the Crow the word reached its present usage.

If I survive my last letter to you, I shall clear up the meaning of Absaraka. I'm so weak that I must give up any more effort for the time being.

Sincerely,
James Carpenter
[Signed by himself]

I have mentioned Jim's reverence for traditional Crow ways, a trait constantly manifested, even when it hurt. Most of his age-mates had adjusted to American individualism, no longer recognizing any obligation to assist their remote kin. Not so Jim. A kinsman would never be expected to return a loan he advanced. When a cousin and his aged wife billeted themselves on Jim, ostensibly only for the week's festivities about July Fourth, but lingered on for a month, there was never a hint of remonstrance from their host. Indeed, his hospitality went further: the woman his cousin had married belonged to the old school and no food would satisfy her but beef, the nearest substitute for buffalo flesh. Accordingly, most of the pay Jim earned by interpreting for me went into the butcher's till to gratify the carnivorous guest's palate.

The same trait appeared in his attitude toward the aboriginal faith. I am not sure what Jim's religious convictions may have been. Christened as a boy in the Roman Catholic Church, he had later joined the Baptists, but did not seem to me a communicant in either denomination when I knew him. Quite certainly he did not repudiate the ancient pagan faith. Well aware of an outsider's skepticism when old informants narrated their mystical revelations, he once told me, "When you hear the old people tell of their experiences, you've just *got* to believe them." He behaved in the same spirit toward ceremonial accessories. He and his wife had inherited her father's holy arrow bundle. For the mere privilege of seeing its contents I had had to pay the old man five dollars and a very contemptible price he considered that. When I visited Jim in 1931 the bundle was hanging on the rear porch of his frame house. Why? In former times menstruating women who approached the tipi of the custodian of a medicine bundle would loudly announce their condition, so that the sacred objects could be stowed away. Today's negligent generation failed to observe the old rule, therefore, Jim forestalled defilement by suspending the arrow wrappings at the rear of his house.

He was equally observant of nonreligious rules of etiquette. Many contemporaries no longer heeded the taboo against avoiding speech with their mothers-in-law. Jim faithfully refrained not only from talking to his mother-in-law, but would not even use the native word for a "mark" because it formed part of the old woman's name. He believed in "showing respect" to the old ways, he said.

Much as Carpenter upheld Crow tradition and critical as he was of the white man, he firmly believed in the value of modern education as a means of helping the Indian. His faith in it was attested by the unabridged Webster I found in his home.

A sense of gratitude was another of Jim's most marked characteristics. He keenly appreciated John Collier's championship of Indian rights and strongly defended him when Collier, as Commissioner of Indian Affairs, was under fire. In 1935 he wrote to me:

"I am not going to sit and watch such men as X deceive the incompetent Indians . . . As I have said before, we may not agree with Collier on some questions but that does not mean we do not like him. As I know the man, he is the best friend the incompetents ever had and will have for a long time to come . . . I wish I was in Washington to stand by Mr. Collier."

A year before this I had taken occasion to write Commissioner Collier, explaining why Jim had in the past been *persona non grata* with former agents, and what my own experiences with him had been. When Jim came to Washington with a delegation of Crow, Collier read passages from my letter to him. Deeply moved, he wrote me: "I want to thank you and do not know how to express my thanks to you for the letter you wrote Collier on my behalf. This has cleared [up] a feeling I have always thought the Indian office held against me. Yes, Collier read a part of it to me. Why he did this I am at a loss. He read where I was in trouble with the Indian Bureau and why, according to your opinion; also where you spoke of your dealings with me."

I have had many other interpreters among Indians, some good ones among them; but I have never had another like Jim.

The Old Culture.—In 1907 it was borne in upon me that, if the old Plains culture had in large part disappeared as a tangible phenomenon, it survived very much alive in the Crow and Blackfoot consciousness. The buffalo were gone, and with them the favorite masculine occupation, but not so the most vivid reminiscences of the chase. When the mixed company of Indians mentioned earlier visited the Museum, a colleague and I decided to take them to the zoo in the Bronx. We happened to enter by the gate nearest the buffalo range. One aged Blackfoot bade the rest of the party go on; he sat down to feast his eyes on the unwonted sight, indifferent to the rest of the animal kingdom. An old Crow on the Reservation once began telling me a story. When he got to the episode of a buffalo hunt, he completely lost the thread of the plot, retailing, to my and the interpreter's boredom, all the minutiae of pursuing, killing, and butchering the game.

Of course, the country had long been pacified, but the ideology of warfare had by no means vanished. Medicine-crow, Bell-rock, and Plenty-coups still enjoyed the reputation of great chiefs and recited their deeds at public gatherings. Any tribesman was glad to pay a horse to one of them for giving a name to a newborn child. Informants proudly exposed their bodies to demonstrate wounds from hostile arrows. Many remembered the last braves who had deliberately sought death at the hands of the enemy because life had brought them disappointment and sorrow. Everyone had known or heard of Wraps-up-his-tail who, in 1887, had defied the agent and a troop of United States soldiers.

As for religion, I have already described the a fortiori case of relatively well-educated James Carpenter. With those who were not merely sympathetic, but who had themselves seen visions or heard voices, the sentiment was bound to be stronger still. There was White-arm, technically Christian, whose onetime guardian spirit plagued him at night in punishment of his apostasy. As late as 1931 I met a man, not even a particularly old one, whom I invited to lunch with me at a humble restaurant on the Reservation. All went smoothly until the dessert was served. My friend would not taste it until we had been assured by the cook that no eggs had been used in the preparation: a supernatural patron had once forbidden my Crow to eat birds' eggs, and the taboo still held.

Such was the orientation of these people during the years of my researches. It made work among them incomparably more satisfactory than with the Stoney Assiniboine.

To be sure, the outlook of the Lemhi Shoshone was equally conservative, but there was an unmistakable difference. The aboriginal Crow culture had been much more complex, more colorful; there was far more to get, and it was easier to get one's teeth into what there was. To take a single example, the Shoshone had no fixed subdivisions beside the family within the local group, no definite rule of descent; there were, of course, interpersonal relations as everywhere else, but it was not easy to pry into them. Among the Crow the merest novice could not but stumble on the fact that they were split up into clans within which marriage was forbidden; that every child in the family automatically belonged to its mother's clan; that although an individual owed certain duties to both his paternal and his maternal kin the *kind* of obligations differed for the two sets of relatives. Again, like many other Plains tribes, the Crow had military associations, to one of which nearly every adult male had belonged. Among ethnologists the question had arisen, to what extent Plains Indian membership in a particular organization of this type was a matter of age. The point was easily settled by asking each of the many surviving Crow clubmen, one after another, how and when and why he had entered his onetime organization.

As for direct observation, there was, indeed, little more to be seen in the ordinary routine of everyday life than at Lemhi. But from time to time there were spectacles that eclipsed anything I witnessed among the Shoshone and which recalled the splendor of the Northern Blackfoot. This was notably true during holiday week in July, when even purely social dances were on a much grander scale. Richly decorated men, often of mature years, would perform the "Hot" dance, vehemently executing steps until the perspiration poured from their foreheads, blurring their facial paint. A man eager to shine before his fellows would strip off all his clothes except a perineal band and give them away; others would ride horses into the dance house and present them to poor old people, thus gaining a reputation for generosity. Masked clowns, dressed in the dirtiest rags and riding correspondingly ugly-looking horses, would come dashing into camp and cut their capers, mocking the spectators, disporting themselves as ridiculously as possible, and trying to escape identification. Most impressive of all such sights were initiations of novices into the Tobacco organization, with its solemn procession of women and men in single file from a preparatory shelter to a big ceremonial lodge. There were four stops en route, with four songs at each stop. In the ceremonial lodge the newly initiated danced in position with his sponsors. The tobacco in question was really a species of *Nicotiana,* but in order to have that fact established I had to buy a sample for five dollars at the time of the harvesting. The plant was sacrosanct, for it was the mysterious embodiment of the Morning-star; and according to the origin myth, so long as the Crow planted it, they would remain people of importance.

As I learned to know the culture better, a number of ideas obtruded themselves over and above any concrete information. One of the most obvious of these was the fixed sense of values that held sway among my informants—values that sometimes markedly differed from ours. The point came out forcibly in the case of Bear-crane, whom I regarded as a tiptop authority on practically every phase of native life. In civilized society he might have made a successful lawyer or statesman. Among his own people, however, his stock was so low that I was repeatedly warned against him as a notorious liar. Yet when I compared his statements about so complicated a ceremony as the Sun Dance with what other unexceptionable witnesses said on the subject, there was no noticeable discrepancy. His account differed mainly in being more coherent. At length the mystery was cleared up. Bear-crane was not esteemed because he had never distinguished himself as a fighter; and he gained his reputation for mendacity because he had wrongly laid claim to some deed by way of doctoring his record. His ability in other lines could never make up for his deficiency in valor. And lying about one's exploits was disgraceful.

Generosity was a trait that ranked next to bravery; its lack degraded a man's character and made him an object of mockery. Very strange was the attitude toward a husband who had taken back a divorced or runaway wife: he, too, was ridiculed in satirical songs, even if he was a chief.

Standards for evaluating women were also sharply defined. The paragon of her sex was a good worker at the feminine household chores, especially at skin dressing. Only perfect purity would qualify her for a number of highly honorific ceremonial positions. Such stringency contrasts with the license enjoyed by men, who were rather expected to philander. Yet, curiously enough, the erring female, though perhaps severely dealt with by her husband, was not ostracized by society at large: she was simply regarded as falling short of perfection.

Another point I could not help noting was the clash of theory and practice. That people who esteemed bravery above everything else should teach their boys to die fighting, since old age was a state of misery consistent enough, but the prayers and the biographical memories of the tribesmen unwittingly disclose the reverse of the medal. Ambitious to gain standing by their exploits, the Crow were constantly praying for long life. They heaped honors on a warrior who formally assumed emblems of intrepidity, because by this action he vowed that he would never retreat from the enemy. But the very men who had actually distinguished themselves in this fashion unconsciously revealed in their reminiscences how, when the symbol of bravery was to be awarded, they slunk into the background to evade appointment. Of course it was a fine thing to be lauded as a hero, but for the average tribesman it was also a fine thing to live to a ripe old age until "the skin cracked when one moved about" in the tipi.

Finally, it became obvious that among this handful of human beings there were enormous individual differences. Unquestionably there *had* been madcaps in the past, willing to throw away their lives under the spur of some deep grief or disappointment. In other lines of endeavor differences in ability and temperament could be directly observed if one used his eyes. Thus, one storyteller would relate a myth with vivacity and a wealth of detail, but another merely sketched the main incidents. The Crow themselves were well aware of such differences: they characterized one man as a regular clown and considered another good at topical tales. Yellow-brow figured as a master of the native tongue: he could make up words never heard before, yet which, nevertheless, everyone understood when they were uttered. Jim jocularly called him one of his dictionaries.

Yellow-brow merits special consideration. I first met him in 1910 when he was still in the prime of life. One morning when Jim was sleeping off the effects of a spree, and I was impatiently pacing up and down in front of my shack, a strange Crow suddenly appeared and, in very broken English, made me understand that he had all kinds of specimens to sell. He drove me to his frame house, and a glance at the walls proved that he had not exaggerated. Among other objects I caught sight of one of those buffalo-hide shields that Wissler had ordered me to get. However, the shield was precisely what Yellow-brow refused to part with; lest I tempt him with an offer, he even refused to show it to me. I bided my time buying various articles for a total of more than a hundred dollars. I also noticed some insignia of the Tobacco order, of which my host was a member. These, too, he refused to sell. "I use them all the time," he argued. When I urged him to let me have at least a sample, he set what he considered a forbiddingly high price. Fortunately I hit upon the right response. I said that I did not understand that sort of thing, but that I trusted him and would pay the ten dollars he had asked for. Visibly touched, he laid out his other Tobacco paraphernalia and told me to choose any one of them as a gift. Yet even after that it was not easy to make him change his mind about the shield; only after a great deal of parleying did he let me have it for seventy-five dollars. Then he and his father, Magpie, drove me back, the old man clasping the shield and praying to it with manifest emotion.

Twenty-one years later Yellow-brow became my chief informant. His knowledge of ancient lore seemed inexhaustible, and the versions he gave me of the creation myth and a popular hero saga were far and away the best I was able to collect. Apart from that, his was a reflective mind. For example, this illiterate septuagenarian was quite puzzled about Christian doctrines that prescribed a restraint on sexual indulgence, a principle that has no part in Crow theology. He also worried a good deal about the proper analysis of particular Crow words and over linguistic matters in general. It was never clear to me why such topics should have engaged his interest at all.

My everyday observations thus refuted the hoary dogma that the "savage" man was submerged in his group. The vast differences that exist became as patent in dealings with two of my best informants, Medicine-crow and Gray-bull, as they had in my experiences with interpreters. Both men had been great warriors, enjoying general esteem; both were deeply rooted in the past; yet their total personalities differed greatly.

Of the two, Medicine-crow was the more distinguished. In fact, he was easily the most eminent man of the Lodge Grass settlement. He emanated a certain high seriousness and, though a short man among a tall people, impressed one with the nobility of his bearing. Wholly friendly and willing to impart information, he was not always accessible, for the simple reason that his compatriots were constantly demanding his services. Now he was calling on a tribesman in another section of the reservation to bestow a name on a newborn child; now he was joining a delegation of Indians bound for Washington; or he would be taking an honorific part in a Tobacco ceremonial, for his devotion to old observances was very strong. This did not prevent him from being in a minor way an innovator. He had altered certain details in the Tobacco ritual, had founded a new chapter of the order—but only on the orthodox basis of a personal revelation—and had, by the force of his personality, imposed the change on his own district. The mercenary motives that had enticed others into selling their shields to the Field Museum never swayed him. Accommodating as usual, he consented to show me his shield and even explained the designs on its cover: triangles symbolized a celestial buffalo's eyes and the zigzag lines emanating from them represented its breath. As for parting with the sacred object, that was out of the question. He declined an offer of a hundred dollars; when my interpreter asked whether two hundred dollars would satisfy him, Medicine-crow declared that he would not sell it for a thousand: he wanted to be buried with it.

If Medicine-crow represented the headman's type, Gray-bull was the high grade average citizen, well aware of his worth, yet with no urge or pretension to leadership. He, too, had been blessed with visions in his day, but they were not the starting point of new ceremonial groupings. He was more generally accessible than Medicine-crow and much less solemn. I visited him once when he was suffering from a broken rib and, by way of amusing him, I performed an imitation of the war dance. He rolled over with laughter and yelled, "Tell him to stop or I'll break another rib!" There was no phase of aboriginal life on which Gray-bull could not offer ample information, clearly formulated. Intellectually, I certainly considered him, if anything, superior to Medicine-crow.

In later years the lessons learned among the Crow gained a wider meaning. Distinctive value systems; conflicts between ideals and practice; vast individual differences, assessed according to the regnant ideology—these seemed to be general human phenomena.

The myth of the austere, unbending Indian, so widespread among laymen must have originated with travelers who saw them only at formal councils where, it is true, they are capable of putting on plenty of side. In daily life a very different aspect of native psychology appears, and with the Crow at all events an appeal, conscious or unconscious, to their risibilities rarely missed fire.

At Gray-bull's a dog was barking loudly one day. I turned to it, addressing it with, "*sá·pdak irá·wahu?*" (Why are you barking?). This conversational feat was hailed as a great witticism. As at Lemhi, I assumed absurd relationships with this or that person, calling a little girl "my grandmother" or what not, and almost always provoked merriment. Kinship terms, however, are tricky things. The Crow language has entirely different words for "father" according to whether the speaker is male or female: a boy says *birúpxe* a girl *basá·ka*. Before I had mastered these refinements, I once questioned a girl, "Where is your father," using the wrong word. This implied that I mistook her for a boy, and my error elicited tremendous amusement.

Apart from that, I had to watch my step. In my fictitious identifications with Crow institutions, I had proclaimed myself a member of the extinct Fox society (to which my friend Gray-bull had belonged), an organization that used to compete with the Lumpwoods in warlike feats. In the spring the rival societies had been licensed to kidnap each other's wives. Meeting a strange Indian one day, I found out his and his wife's affiliations and introduced myself as the woman's clansman. Somewhat later in the conversation I asked what military club the husband had belonged to. When he turned out to have been a Lumpwood, I said, "I am a Fox, next spring I'll steal your wife." Quick as a flash came the repartee, "Take her and you marry your sister!" What could have been more disgraceful than suggesting such an incestuous union? I had made myself the butt of laughter.

But there were hours of triumph by means of my buffoonery. I had often heard various men tell about their visionary experiences, how they had gone to a lonely spot, cut off a finger joint to awaken some spirit's pity, and finally seen some supernatural being, who granted certain powers and laid down certain rules of conduct. Though details varied, most accounts conformed to a common pattern. Following this model, I concocted an imaginary vision of my own, which Jim helped me put into acceptable Crow. I made slight alterations from time to time, but approximately it ran as follows: "When I was about eighteen years old, I went up to a mountain top. For four days and nights I fasted and thirsted. I put my finger on a piece of wood and chopped off a joint. At last I saw something approaching. It was a huge bear. He came shaking a rattle and singing a song. (Here I sang the favorite Crow lullaby.) 'I'll adopt you as my child,' he said, 'I'll make you a great chief. But one thing I forbid: You must never eat the flesh of a bear.' I made a raid against the Sioux; I cut loose twenty of the enemy's picketed horses; I struck ten enemies; I snatched away ten guns in hand-to-hand fighting. I became a chief. No Crow ever equaled me. To this day I have never eaten the flesh of a bear." No Indian who heard this affecting tale ever took the parody amiss. Everyone was tremendously entertained, and I had to narrate the story over and over again. Sometimes thereafter I was called "Bear-is-his-medicine"—though my commoner sobriquet was "He-who-regularly-tells-tales."

Equally successful was a topical story of which I was merely the recorder, having taken it down in Crow from the lips of the village wag. It was at the expense of a former policeman who had had his fun with an unsophisticated old couple when they sought his aid in the recovery of some lost money. Instead of proceeding in the routine way of the local constabulary, he pretended to exert supernatural powers on their behalf, mimicking the procedures of a man who had a ghost for his familiar spirit. It generally entertained the Crow to have a phonetically written text read to them, but I did not expect the sensational hit I achieved this time. Men who had just heard the story would bring a chum and remain enthralled, guffawing again over the oft-told tale.

I also scored by learning by heart the favorite tongue-twister, corresponding to our "She sells seashells by the seashore," and rattling it off at top speed to some Crow who had never seen me before.

Even a little knowledge of the native language helps to establish rapport. Once an Indian I was visiting was enlarging on his grievances against white people, when I pompously declared in Crow, "All the whites are bad, I alone am good." On another occasion I met a Crow for the first time and, having learned his name, at once told him what clan he and his wife belonged to. He was naturally amazed at this miraculous feat, but actually it was simple enough. With the aid of some old authorities, I had made a census of the Lodge Grass district, on an earlier field trip, inquiring at the same time for each person's and his or her spouse's clan affiliation. Since I had with me the pamphlet in which these records

had been printed, I merely glanced at my list and furtively read
off my hosts' clan names.

Marginal Men.—Sociologists have a telling phrase for persons
who simultaneously participate in two distinct cultures. The children of immigrants to the United States, for instance, are "marginal men": they do not naïvely live the life of a single society, but
through the circumstances of their descent and residence are marginal to two cultures, learning about one at home, about the other
through school or other outside contacts. This situation holds for
all minority groups and is as noticeable on reservations as anywhere. As might be expected from the manifold individualities
even in a small population, the ways of reacting to the situation
vary from person to person, yet it is possible to distinguish a few
types. The two contrasting orientations of my two principal Crow
interpreters have already been described: on the one hand, there
is enthusiastic acceptance of the new values; on the other, a dogged
resolution to preserve the old. In between there are naturally all
possible shades of difference, in short, varying degrees of compromise.

Marginal men are not always clear about the nature of the two
cultures that concern them, nor are they altogether consistent.
As noted, Jim Carpenter did not reject Caucasian civilization as
a whole, but accepted its educational aspects as beneficial for his
own people. With all his shrewdness within the sphere of his experience, he was capable of curious simplicity in matters beyond
his ken. He once wanted to know whether Shakespeare or George
Washington (it may have been Lincoln) was the greatest of white
men. An older cousin of his had become a devout adherent of the
peyote cult. He assured me vehemently that this was a truly native
Indian faith which owed nothing to white influence. A little later
he declared with equal vigor that the peyote was the tree of knowledge in Genesis and that twelve decorative appendages of a ritualistic object in his cult represented the twelve apostles.

Marginal men could be something of a nuisance. Some of them
had an obsession about the tendency of whites to dupe the Indians and conceived fantastic ideas of the money I would gain by
selling whatever information the old people gave me. One of these
busybodies interrupted an outdoor interview, demanding what

I was writing down. He declared that when he had sent a telegram at the railroad station he had been charged so much per word; therefore I ought to pay my informant at the same rate. Fortunately, the old man was convinced by the literally correct explanation that numerically the words in the translation could not correspond to those in the vernacular. Among the Crow, however, such disturbing episodes were rare.

An exhilarating incident with a more entertaining sequel dates from my early days at Lodge Grass, when I was as yet little known there. A dance had been announced for a certain night, and I made an early appearance on the ground. While I was waiting for the festivities to start, a young man named Wolf-lies-down (as I found out later) accosted me amiably in fair English and was curious about my business. Was I trying to buy horses on the reservation? I bethought myself of what I had once read in Herbert Spencer's essays on education, to wit, that in teaching a child one should always proceed from the concrete to the abstract; and what held for children would surely be appropriate for aborigines. So I answered somewhat as follows: "Well, I am here to talk with your old men to find out how they used to hunt and play and dance. I want to hear them tell the stories of ancient times . . ." But at this point young Wolf-lies-down, who had never been off the reservation, interrupted me with, "Oh, I see, you're an ethnologist!"

Though the experience struck me as comical, its full import was not brought home until the following election day in New York. For some reason, when I appeared at the polling place, the clerk challenged my right to vote, and I was obliged to answer innumerable questions, including incidentally, "Have you ever been convicted of felony?" When I was asked, "What is your occupation?", I innocently said, "I am an ethnologist." The clerk, completely nonplussed, turned to the chairman of the board, declaring, "I hope you know what this man does for a living, I don't!" He evidently lacked the educational advantages of the Crow reservation.

Some marginal men held the dogma that it was impossible to write the Crow language. They were correct so far as their attempts to do so were bound to fail, since English is almost ideally unfit for rendering most native tongues. Italian or Spanish orthography would be a better preparation for the task, though naturally only an adequate phonetic analysis and corresponding alphabet could fully meet the requirements. In 1931 a young Crow who had never seen me before found me taking down a text; he at once declared that it could not be done. He lingered long enough to satisfy himself that he was wrong, since I easily read back to the old informant what I had written, and he, of course, understood it all, as did the challenger. The matter intrigued him no end. He tarried to watch this feat of legerdemain, finally tearing himself away with the remark that he felt as though bewitched.

Two middle-aged cousins, putative quarter-breeds, were contrasting samples of the general type. I say "putative" because so far as their looks went they might have passed as white men; in fact, one of them had had the hair, eyes, and complexion of a Scandinavian. He was admittedly the son of a retired federal official, who according to rumor had fobbed him off on the government as the child of his Indian wife, whereas in reality he was the offspring of a liaison with a Swedish mistress. This maneuver assured the son a title to Indian land, and by his philoprogenitiveness he added a vast acreage for the benefit of his family. In other respects Sam, as I shall call him, displayed less energy, apart from periodic sprees in the saloons and brothels of a neighboring town. However, he was good-natured, fluent in both Crow and English, helpful, and entirely naïve in matters beyond his horizon. "New York City," he kept muttering as we were once talking on his front porch, "I guess you could see a show every night there!"

Cousin Bill, equally good-natured, bi-lingual, and prolific, was otherwise a horse of a different color. Unlike Sam, he was one of the intellectuals of the reservation. He had little formal schooling, but read omnivorously, and was avid for new ideas. The Crow language formed an obvious topic for reflection, and he achieved some weird folk etymologies. Thus, he told me, the word *iró·oce* "my son," was clearly a compound of *iré*, penis, and *ó·oce*, cooking. Was not a son a concoction of one's penis? One winter Bill was struck with the notion of synthesizing the aboriginal vision seeking with modern mysticism. He began attending spiritistic séances in Billings, read up relevant articles in an antediluvian edition of the *Encyclopaedia Britannica,* and began arranging séances on his own. On my arrival at the reservation in the following summer, Bill was eager to demonstrate for my benefit. He, his wife, Sam, Sam's wife, and I assembled in Bill's shanty, sat down about a round table, and laid our hands on it. Indubitably the table began to tilt after a while and moved a few inches; rappings were also to be heard. However, there were none of the spectacular manifestations promised by Bill, who was evidently disappointed. At last he declared that he was going to make the spirit declare his sex: thereafter one rap was to signify a male, two raps a female visitant. Having thus laid down the code, he asked, "Are you male or female?" In response came two raps; before anyone else could say a word, Bill's wife burst out triumphantly: "It's Alexander Upshaw! He always lied!"

At Fort Berthold.—According to their traditions the Crow once lived farther east in what is now North Dakota, forming a single people with the ancestors of the present Hidatsa. They seceded, it is said, because of a quarrel over the distribution of meat, went west, and became the Crow. Much the same story is told by the Hidatsa, except for the motive for the separation. The languages of the two groups are so close as to suggest a separation not more than a few centuries ago. Many words are alike or nearly so, and after a relatively brief residence in the sister tribe a Crow can pick up its tongue sufficiently for easy communication, and vice versa. It is clear that the two dialects form a distinct branch of the great Siouan family, just as Spanish, Italian, and French form the Romance branch of the Indo-European family. The greatest cultural difference is an economic one: instead of being nomadic tipi-dwelling buffalo hunters like the Crow throughout the year, the Hidatsa when first met already grew maize, lived in fixed earth-covered lodges part of the year, and used the tipi only during the months when they were on major hunting trips. They are accordingly described as semisedentary, therein resembling their neighbors, the Mandan, another Siouan people, but speaking a language as different as German is from French. Apart from differences arising from their economic background, both the Hidatsa and the Crow naturally diverged in other respects because of contacts each developed with tribes they had met since the old schism. Nevertheless, there remain notable common traits peculiar to the two in contrast to other Plains Indians.

It was thus an obvious step to extend investigation from the Crow to the sister tribe. Some weeks of three field seasons (1910, 1911, and 1913) were spent on the Fort Berthold Reservation, North Dakota, which the Hidatsa shared with the Mandan and the unrelated Arikara, an offshoot of the Pawnee of Nebraska. A visit to these peoples was especially necessary, because Wissler had decided on a large-scale comparative study of Plains Indian military societies, which were known to have flourished on the upper Missouri.

I was not the first emissary of the Museum to these parts. The Reverend Gilbert L. Wilson, originally a mere amateur, but an exceptionally good observer, had collected specimens and data for Wissler previously and in 1910 personally introduced me to the new setting before leaving the reservation shortly after my arrival.

It was the first time I encountered Indians who had planted corn and lived in villages before the coming of the whites. It is true that they had still largely depended on buffalo and had starved when game was scarce. Yet even partial agricultural activity raised their way of life to a status of greater complexity, and although much had been altered or wiped out by the influence of traders and of the government, much remained to see and to inquire about. Old Hairy-coat still occupied an old-fashioned dome-shaped earth lodge. I saw women climbing stages to dry their corncobs or pounding corn in wooden mortars. For cookery only the metal utensils bought at a store were in use, but the Reverend Wilson and I persuaded an old Mandan squaw to make a pot for us. To be sure, it cracked in the process of firing, but that was because we could not afford the time to let her go to a spot miles away where she could have got the right sort of clay. Quite in the spirit of old times she would not let the teacher's daughters watch her at work; that seemed like an infraction of a copyright.

Occasionally I might see an Indian crossing the Missouri in a bullboat, but more commonly these simple craft—resembling the frame of an opened umbrella with a hide for cover—would be turned upside down over the smoke hole of a lodge.

As for the more elusive aspects of ancient life, I found the old guard at Fort Berthold not more conservative than men like Medicine-crow, but distinctly more reticent about ceremonial matters. The Sun Dance, for example, was regarded here as the peculiar privilege of a few owners of a special bundle with its associated rituals. The one surviving titleholder could not be brought to impart information about it: he was polite, but firm; he said he saw no reason for telling me what I wanted to know. Another man demanded an incredibly large sum, not for a bundle he owned, but for the view of it. In this, we know from Prince Maximilian zu Wied's experiences in 1833, he was merely following a native custom to which Indians as well as white outsiders would have to submit if they wished to inspect sacred articles. Again, the Arikara carefully distinguished between secular and sacred information. They did not object to talking about the military associations, which were essentially of a social nature, but they resolutely forestalled any inquiries concerning esoteric lore.

Given this attitude of the three tribes at Fort Berthold, important phases of native life would have remained unrecorded had it not been for the presence of a number of Christian converts, who had no qualms about retailing what they knew of ancient myth and ritual. Wolf-chief was perfectly willing to describe the Hidatsa Sun Dance, as he had witnessed it in the capacity of a spectator and minor participant. This was not an ideal method of getting relevant data, but it was better than nothing.

On this point Fort Berthold seemed different from anything I experienced among the Crow. There, too, there were converts, but on all those I came to know well, Christianity seemed to sit very lightly; to my mind they were pagans at heart. It was apparently otherwise with their Hidatsa and Mandan counterparts.

Since the Reverend Wilson and I worked for the same institution, I naturally fell heir to his interpreter, Edward Goodbird. Though Goodbird's English was only mediocre, he was unquestionably a valuable aid. Born in 1870, the grandson of a distinguished Hidatsa, Small-ankle, he had been brought up in the old ways and could serve as informant as well as interpreter. Through him it was possible to tap two even better sources, namely, his mother, Buffalo-bird-woman, and her brother, Wolf-chief.

To me Goodbird represented a novel and not very appealing variety of "the marginal man." In reminiscences dictated to the Reverend Wilson in 1913 and printed in the following year, he unwittingly presents, along with some excellent ethnographic details, an objective picture of himself—smug and sanctimonious. Complacently he noted his and his family's ownership of four thousand acres of land; and when asked to become assistant missionary at a post on the reservation, he accepted, feeling that "I was closer to God than I had been when I was baptized." On one occasion Goodbird had worked overtime for possibly a quarter of an hour and painstakingly computed the extra pay that was his due. He rendered good service, but unlike Jim Carpenter, he would not scour the countryside, unbidden and unpaid, to obtain additional information for me. By way of compensation, as might have been expected, he did not miss appointments because of a night's drinking bout.

Of the general configuration of native Hidatsa culture I received a definite impression, one not easily demonstrable, yet worthy of record. In contrast to the Crow, the Hidatsa tended to formulate and crystallize. Whereas the Crow permitted a narrator a great deal of latitude in shuffling the incidents of a plot and in phrasing his sentences, I thought that a Hidatsa storyteller was more strictly bound by convention. Above all, the part-time farmers seemed to have pursued another type of educational policy. A Crow boy grew up, learning from observation that a great warrior enjoyed prestige; from his social environment he absorbed the idea that greatness was the result of a personal revelation and acted accordingly on his own. But a Hidatsa father would prompt a growing son: "It is now time for you to pray to our family's spirits"; and he would supervise the subsequent mystic experiences of his offspring.

The close proximity of three different tribes on the reservation brought with it a good deal of intermarriage between Hidatsa and Mandan, distinctly less between either of them and the alien Arikara. In consequence there was a good deal of cultural exchange, but occasionally also a conflict of principles. An amusing concrete instance of the latter was brought to my attention. Like the Lemhi, Assiniboine, and Crow, the Hidatsa and Mandan practice the mother-in-law taboo, which is not observed, however, by the Arikara. One Joe Packineau, a Hidatsa, had married an Arikara girl, and on one occasion his wife's mother was seen talking to him. His tribesmen were immeasurably shocked. "What's the matter with your mother-in-law?" they asked. "She doesn't seem to respect you at all!"

CHAPTER 5

IN
HOPILAND

In 1914 the English anthropologist, W. H. R. Rivers, wrote a little book on *Kinship and Social Organization,* which created a considerable stir in the United States. It vindicated the theory, long previously broached by the American ethnologist, Lewis H. Morgan, that the terms by which people called their relations by blood and marriage had an intimate connection with social structure and matrimonial customs. When I tried to verify a specific hypothesis of Rivers's for North America, I discovered vast gaps in our knowledge. The Southwestern tribes, about whose ceremonies thousands of pages had been printed, turned out to be among the least known Indians with reference to kinship. With characteristic open-mindedness Wissler, though not himself particularly concerned with the topic, determined to do his bit toward mending the situation: he got A. L. Kroeber, of the University of California, to investigate kinship among the Zuni (New Mexico), and sent me to the Hopi in northern Arizona to clarify the problem there. In this way I spent several weeks in 1915 and 1916 attacking the questions raised by Rivers. After prolonged research in the Plains, and more superficial contacts with Shoshone and Northern Athabaskans, I now had a chance to become acquainted with still another type of aboriginal adaptation to habitat.

Time was too short to make adequate preparation for a comprehensive study of Hopi life, about which a vast literature had accumulated. In accordance with my instructions, I therefore confined my research to matters of clan and kinship terminology; and these were the only topics on which I published anything. Actually, of course, one department of native culture can hardly ever be separated from all others; and among the western Pueblos the clan system pervades much of their life as a whole. Thus, without trying to contribute to scientific knowledge of Hopi ceremonial, to which several scholars had given years of study, I could not help getting object lessons useful for my ethnographical education along various lines.

There were circumstances about the Hopi of forty years ago that made my sojourn with them, brief as it was, forever memorable. They had not only far and away the most complex culture of all the tribes known to me, but also had preserved relatively much more of it. At Lodge Grass the older Indians were inwardly unchanged; but for them the buffalo hunt, the war raids, the military associations, and the Sun Dance were things of the past, enshrined in their memories, no longer tangible realities. In the Hopi villages the realities had survived because their economic basis in large measure remained unshaken. The people were still dry farming, as they had done for centuries.

They did not, of course, live quite as their ancestors had when encountered by the Spanish explorers of the sixteenth century. Even during the twenty-five years that intervened between W. J. Fewkes' visit and mine, innovations had occurred. In his day, for example, the white man's clothes were still rare, native blankets and sashes predominating; there were few wagons and very little tinware. Nevertheless, in essence the aboriginal culture had remained a going concern; for subsistence was still largely gained in the old way, and the people were still living in the old style of houses. I did not have to wait for a special occasion like King Edward's birthday in Canada, or the Fourth of July week in the United States, for a demonstration of native custom. Hopi husbands went to faraway cornfields every morning and in the evening were greeted by the conventional wifely formula on their return. Houses were still invariably owned by women, and the groom followed his bride to her home, which belonged to the corporation of her female matrilineal kin—her mother's mother, her mother and maternal aunts, her sisters and herself, their and her own prospective daughters. A casual stroll through the village, with an occasional peep into the houses, revealed any number of aboriginal activities. Here a woman was making a pot, there an old man was rolling a spindle on his thigh. Women were carrying the water needed from the springs at the foot of the lofty mesas to which the Hopi had retreated two centuries ago as a protection against their enemies. When heavy showers had filled the hollows on a mesa it was amusing to watch housewives exploiting the lucky fluke by dipping up water, while their children splashed in the newly created wading pools. Indoors I saw the girls grinding maize on stone querns with stone mullers, while the lady of the house might be sweeping her floor with a little native broom, presently brushing her hair with the other end of her implement. Outdoors her sister was often to be seen spreading batter over a hot stone slab, withdrawing a sheet after a minute or two, to roll it up into a loaf of wafer bread that tasted like cornflakes.

The very location of the villages, on three flat rocky eminences rising from the desert floor, lent them an air of mystery and romance. As I approached Walpi, on the first mesa, I seemed to be looking up at a series of ruined medieval castles, and the layout of a typical village was a curiosity. Of Walpi, so often photographed and painted, I have never seen a really adequate picture. It consists essentially of one street, that is, of one row of crude flat-roofed sandstone houses, the upper story set back several feet from the wall of the ground floor. This provides a terrace for sundry activities, as well as a grandstand from which to view any ceremonial dances. Residents and visitors climb all the time in a Hopi settlement, reaching upper levels by means of modern ladders; but in a back street I still saw their primeval predecessor, a rungless, notched log. Here and there one can ascend by an unrailed stairway of narrow, crude stone steps. It is perfectly correct etiquette to use adjoining rooftops as a public highway, descending where one pleases. A distinctive flavor is given to the scene by the projecting house-beams, hung with corn in a way rather suggestive of some Italian villages.

A characteristic of every village is the plaza or square for public performances. The more esoteric part of these solemnities mostly takes place in kivas—subterranean chambers reached by climbing down ladders. These rooms also serve for men's spinning bees; I once helped in carding wool in one of them; but when I thoughtlessly fell to whistling I was firmly told that that sort of thing was not done in a kiva.

Ceremonies form a chapter by themselves. If a visitor stays any appreciable time in Hopiland, he can hardly escape seeing some impressive spectacle, for their festivals are arranged by calendar and are spread over most of the year. There is a sharp contrast between the esoteric and the exoteric parts of a religious ceremony; and from the former outsiders, including Hopi who are not of the celebrating fraternity, are excluded. Since my interpreter at Walpi belonged to the Flute society, and because I provided the performers with tobacco, I was allowed to attend the earlier parts of the private rites. Then I was politely told to betake myself elsewhere. Whatever regret I may have felt as an ethnographer, as a human being I was greatly relieved, for anything duller than the proceedings I was permitted to watch cannot readily be imagined. The men were endlessly employed in preparing feather offerings. From time to time someone would take a puff and offer smoke to a fellow performer, one of them muttering the words "My son," to be answered with "My father." By way of contrast the public finale of the nine-day ceremony was vivid and exciting. Possibly twenty members came down the mesa to the spring at its foot, marching in single file, led by a man with a horned headdress, turtle shell rattles tied to his knees, his breast striped with white paint, and his shoulders painted with two big white daubs. During most of the succeeding show, this man remained seated on a rock. Another participant stood to the south, equipped with bow and arrow, quiver, and a bullroarer. A second guard, on the north, carried the same equipment and wore a richly ornamented kilt. All but these three officers went on to the spring. Polluted though it was by domestic beasts, the headman waded into it, filled a bowl with water, and lowered other ceremonial articles into the pool. Two members, one of them standing, the other seated, moistened their instruments, then played them to the accompaniment of other members' chants and rattling. From time to time the guards alternately whirled their bullroarers to symbolize rain and thunder—a form of imitative magic. For, like other Hopi ceremonies, the Flute Dance had just one avowed purpose, namely, to bring on rain, which is the aim of virtually all Hopi ritualism. While I was at Walpi, rumors reached the Indians that the government was planning to suppress the native ceremonials. My interpreter, Lehungwa, was greatly disturbed. The Hopi, he explained to me, were not like other Indians who had plenty of water with which to irrigate. They had little water; therefore, they had to keep on performing their rain-bringing ceremonies. This is an excellent sample of what has been called the instrumentalism of Hopi religion.

In all sorts of ways the Hopi proved different from other tribes I had known. For instance, there was a division of labor between the sexes new to me. The Hidatsa also planted maize, but it was women's work. Among the Hopi, wives might keep little gardens, but the main task of cultivation in the cornfields devolved on their husbands. Elsewhere in North America skin-dressing and the manufacture of clothing were peculiar to the female sex; in the Southwest these were strictly sex-limited masculine activities. I saw a man measuring his wife's feet for moccasins, attended a men's spinning bee, photographed an elder twirling a spindle on his thigh. Plains Indian husbands occasionally expelled their wives from a lodge; that could not happen in Hopi society, for the house invariably belonged to the wife and her kinswomen. If she wished a divorce, she would simply bid her spouse begone. Again, practically everywhere else a noted tribesman used to have two or more wives; not so among the Hopi, where monogamy was imperative. This was not, as might be supposed, a simple corollary of feminine house ownership. Like any number of fellow Americans, the Hopi might have permitted a man to marry simultaneously two or more sisters, yet such unions were unheard of. As for the mother-in-law taboo, the Hopi did not practice it, though they knew it to be a Navaho custom.

No less sharp were the differences in the religious sphere. A Blackfoot or Crow ascribed all notable skills, all rescue from apparently unescapable predicaments, all major blessings in life, to a revelation by a patron spirit. This attitude was foreign to the

Hopi, who were more concerned with correct ritualistic formal-
ism than with mystic thrills.

This contrast between Pueblo and Plains dwellers profoundly
impressed me. When I later visited two colleagues who were working among the Zuni of New Mexico, I could not help harping on
this difference, not merely in details, but in what has since been
called the total "configuration" of the cultures.

Ethnographically and aesthetically the Hopi trips were highly
satisfactory, and I succeeded in solving the particular problem I
set out to attack. On both the mesas where I worked I had acceptable interpreters and developed friendly relations with their families. On the side I managed to see the public parts of two Snake
Dances, a Flute Dance, a women's ceremony, masqueraders' performances, and the antics of clowns. In short, considering also all
that I witnessed as a daily visitor in Hopi households, my education
in North American ethnography was greatly enhanced, even
though I contributed to knowledge of only a single aspect of Hopi
ethnography.

Moreover, my Hopi observations bore on some points of general interest. The language was unmistakably related to that of
the Lemhi and of my juvenile idols, the Comanche, which meant
that it fell into the Shoshonean group along with the Ute and
Paiute. Indeed, my fellow student, Edward Sapir, had just proved
that the affinities of these peoples were even wider, including the
Aztec of southern Mexico. It was thus brought home to me that,
in the New World as in the Old, unquestionable linguistic relationship could accompany vast differences in cultural advancement.
Just as the extremely primitive North Albanians belong to the
same linguistic family as the French and the British, so the starved
Paviotso of Nevada, with their stunted cultural development, were
in speech relatively close to some of the most advanced peoples of
North America. Speculating on how this could have come about,
I visualized the ancestors of the Hopi living in a desert-like environment, but being raised in status by waves of influence from
the south.

There was another general conclusion. The three mesas are separated from one another by only trifling distances, and the same
language is spoken on all. Even in Hano, a village occupied by de-

scendants of immigrants from another stock, the residents, although maintaining their original tongue, have long since become bilingual. In short, there were neither geographical nor linguistic barriers to communication, and naturally, there have been many intermarriages between the villages. Conditions thus seem ideal for a complete leveling of cultural differences. Yet among this small population, about two thousand in 1915, there was local specialization of crafts, so that baskets were made on the second and third mesas and traded for pottery manufactured on the first. Some clans were common to several villages, but others were distinctive. There were local variations in the performance of the same festivals, such deviations being commented on with proper hauteur in the neighboring settlements.

Still more remarkable was the extraordinary separatism, the complete lack of tribal unity. There was no chief over all the Hopi, little sense of kinship beyond the narrower ties of family and matrilineal household. As a matter of fact, we know from direct historical evidence that the Hopi, notwithstanding their stress on the necessity for complete harmony, have been perennially bickering, with the result that families have seceded to settle in new spots. One cause of friction, dating from Spanish times, has been the varying attitude toward white civilization. For instance, in 1700 the other Hopi destroyed the village of Awatobi for tolerating a friar in search of converts.

White visitors to the Hopi, including some justly esteemed ethnologists, have voiced veritable paeans of praise of the Hopi way of life and their attitude toward the universe. I was never able to share this enthusiasm. Natively, of course, these people are neither better nor worse than other human beings; but from what I saw, and subsequently read in more detailed accounts by later investigators, they seemed incomparably less attractive than the Plains Indians or even than their much simpler fellow Shoshoneans of the Plateau and Basin. This is, of course, admittedly a subjective reaction, not a scientific judgment. It does seem to me, however, that no more glaring discrepancy can be found anywhere between theory and practice than among these Pueblos. On the one hand, they exalt sweetness and light: tribesmen must collaborate, they must suppress urges toward self-assertion, must refrain from quarreling, lest the gods in disapproval of dissension withhold the all-important rain. A Shipaulovi chief declared that the tranquillity reigning in his village brought heavy rains during a festival, whereas clouds stayed away from the discord-cleft Walpi. On the other hand, there is an undeniable record of constant gossiping, altercation, and literal schism. An ill-disposed observer might speak of hypocrisy. At all events, there are undesirable aspects to the traditionally prescribed hiding of one's light under a bushel, as when an office essential from the Hopi point of view goes begging because no one dares thrust himself foreward to assume the responsibility. Such things occur elsewhere too, but not so obtrusively as in Pueblo society.

If there were nothing else to dismay the outsider in these "harmonious" communities, it is the residents' abiding fear of witchcraft. This obsession dominates behavior, for who can be sure that he is not offending an evil sorcerer, ever ready to visit punishment for the affront? It is not merely strangers who inspire this dread, but also one's nearest and dearest relatives. Some years ago Sun-chief, a sophisticated Hopi, wrote out his reminiscences at length. He records that his mother was the most dearly beloved person he knew; yet after her death he wondered whether perchance she had been a witch.

Progress as we conceive it must of course be checked at the source by the prevalent Hopi orientation. The reformer, the individualist, the person of exceptional ability at once becomes suspect of witchcraft. Not that sorcery is absent in other parts of North America; in fact, often enough, there is a personal union between witchcraft and supernatural curing. However, there is no such monomania: if a medicine man had repeatedly failed as a practitioner, the conclusion was that he had deliberately abused his powers, for which he was promptly killed by the victim's kin. When I was among the Ute of Ignacio, Colorado, in 1912, a medicine man from the Navaho Springs division of the tribe came driving up posthaste one evening, seeking asylum: he had been unsuccessfully treating a patient and was trying to elude the vengeance of the aggrieved relatives. Long after this incident newspapers reported similar occurrences, with deadly issue, among California Indians.

The contrast between Pueblo and Plains Indian mentality seems to me further illustrated by the way in which violent resentment expresses itself. The Plainsman sometimes acted like a savage, as when a Blackfoot cuckold cut off the tip of an adulteress's nose; yet the reaction, repulsive as it was (incidentally to the Crow, too) is humanly intelligible. Compare with this the reactions of a legendary Zuni who does nothing to either his wife or to her paramour, but revenges himself upon the community at large. The disgruntled village chief in a Hopi myth causes a flood or earthquake or even encourages the enemy to demolish his pueblo.

Even on short acquaintance such contrasts made a deep impression. About the same time the late K. G. Haeberlin made a related point. The Pueblo Indians and the Navaho, he found, shared many items of culture, notably in ritual, yet the spirit animating them was essentially different. Where a Navaho stressed curative values, a Pueblo was forever compulsively associating the same procedures with rain and fertility. Thus both of us, without using the term, had a strong feeling for the existence of different "configurations."

CHAPTER 6

SURVEY
WORK

Because there were so few trained
workers and so many tribes hardly known at all from a scientific
point of view, museum ethnographers were rarely permitted to
stay for a long period with any one people or to revisit them for
intensive study. Moreover, a museum was concerned with expanding its collection from as many sections of the world as
possible. I was fortunate to have been sent to the Crow for re-
peated investigations, but much of my remaining time was spent
jumping from one reservation to another. Such "survey work," as
it has been called, can be very fruitful, notwithstanding its obvious
drawbacks. For example, I paid scouting visits to a good many
Shoshonean groups in Idaho, Wyoming, Utah, and Nevada, sometimes not tarrying more than a few days in any one spot. Though
I never attached great importance to these efforts, they provided
preliminary data which later researchers have found useful.

Sometimes even a brief survey might settle significant problems.
As already explained, ethnologists were concerned to know to what
extent the military or police organizations of Plains Indian tribes
were graded according to the age of the members. With willing
informants who had lived the old life, such a question could be
settled for any given group in very short order.

But whether the reconnaissance led to definite results or not,
it could prove valuable for a young ethnographer who had often
read about things without being able to form a clear picture of

them. On the coast of Peru and on the lakes of the Andean high-lands the Spanish conquerors had found native fishermen poling curious cigar-shaped reed rafts, which the invaders called "balsas," a name that has stuck in ethnographic usage, being also applied to similar craft manipulated by the now extinct Tasmanians. I had the unexpected pleasure of seeing such a raft made and poled around a pond by a Paviotso Indian near Fallon, Nevada, in 1914. His tribesmen used this conveyance when hunting ducks and mud hens in the fall. It took only two hours to tie together two bundles of tule rushes ready for use.

But it is never possible to predict with assurance what native trait or aptitude has lingered and which has disappeared. While among the Paviotso I obtained a model of an ancient fire-making apparatus, but the combined efforts of two Paviotso men failed to make it work, and a third man had no idea what to do with the thing. My interpreter naïvely suggested that it would take from half an hour to an hour to drill fire, proving that his people had long since lost the skill, for in practiced hands the task can be performed in less than a minute.

It was easy enough a generation ago to get circumstantial ac-counts of how a medicine man worked, yet a white man rarely had the opportunity to see one in action. As it turned out, neither did I. During one of my stays among the Hopi I learned that a native healer was going to treat a sick child. Through my inter-preter I obtained both the parents' and the doctor's consent to my attending the performance. But an unforeseen difficulty arose. An old woman suddenly declared that no such thing had ever been permitted before, and at once public opinion asserted itself. Irre-spective of his earlier complaisance, the medicine man simply re-fused to enter the home so long as I was about. There was thus nothing for me to do but to withdraw.

Among the Crow I heard much about wonder workers whom my informants had seen conjuring forth cherries in mid-winter, trans-forming buffalo droppings into a skunk, and producing tobacco out of the bark of a tree. Cut-ear, whom I knew, was credited with being able to make flannel come out of his mouth and then to roll it back again. He promised to give me a private exhibition, but did not appear at the time stipulated.

However, during a very brief sojourn in southwestern Arizona during the Christmas vacation of 1921–1922, fortune favored me without the slightest solicitation on my part. I was accompanying E. W. Gifford to the Indian settlement near Somerton, where he was pumping a Cocopa informant with the aid of a Yuma interpreter—both languages belong to the Yuman family. Somehow Gifford discovered that a medicine man, whose name turned out to be Jackrabbit, was staying a short distance beyond the international boundary, so we decided to go across and lure him to the Cocopa settlement. Jackrabbit readily consented to come with us, but a difficulty arose. Our Yuma interpreter could not communicate with the newcomer, who spoke Akwaala, which was too distantly related to his own tongue for mutual intelligibility. It was as if a Frenchman knowing only French and English tried to interpret an Italian's speech. Fortunately Cocopa and Akwaala were comparatively close, so that at least our Cocopa informant could translate what Jackrabbit told us—but he could translate it only into his own tongue, and his renderings had to be englished by our Yuma friend. Using two interpreters is a nerve-racking procedure, and the sources of error are inevitably doubled. Nevertheless, much of the material we obtained in this way proved trustworthy in the light of what was known about cognate tribes of the same stock.

To turn to my lucky fluke, one day, at about two o'clock, while Gifford was resting after our lunch, the interpreter called my attention to Jackrabbit's strange antics. The old man was pacing up and down in front of our host's shed, trying to drive away the lowering clouds. After a few minutes, he got his bunch of feathers and began walking on the other side of the shed, waving the feathers, singing, and at the same time blowing the air as if to shoo away the clouds. Occasionally he moved into a slow dance step. Later, he took off a red waist sash and waved it also. As a matter of fact, no rain fell.

Subsequently Jackrabbit offered us the following explanation. Once, when a young man, he was staying in the mountains of his native country, Lower California. He squeezed some jimson weed (*Datura*) leaves and mixed them with water; he drank the liquid in the morning and continued, taking a very little at a time, all day and all night. In the morning he walked a short distance and thought he had become insane, presumably because the poison was giving him feelings of strangeness. At this point a coyote approached him from the east; it walked once around Jackrabbit, then turned away and lay down. To quote Jackrabbit's own words:

> I looked at him, and asked about it: "What do you want to see me for?" He said, "I just came here to show you what you can do. If at any time the rain clouds are coming toward you, you must turn your face toward the clouds, twist your neck and turn one way and the other, then there won't be any rain; the rain will stop."

The coyote did not give our Akwaala absolute power over rain, although he gave him more power in the summer than in the winter. Still our friend was quite confident that he had stopped the rain that day and night. The coyote exhorted Jackrabbit not to forget about the gift granted to him, so he soon began to exercise his newly gained power. Four Indians once hired him to stop the rain, one of them paying him two dollars, and the others, half a dollar each. The reason Jackrabbit had used crow feathers to shoo the clouds away when I saw him was that the coyote had so instructed him. I asked whether perchance his benefactor was actually a spirit transformed into a coyote, and was told that it was really the animal itself, which went back east where it had come from, and was never again seen by Jackrabbit.

Incidentally, our shaman was blessed with other supernatural favors. The same coyote taught him to cure arrow wounds, and a snake showed him how to treat people bitten by snakes; for such treatment he had received as much as fifteen dollars.

Thus, despite great difficulties of communication, even a very brief stay could prove profitable, provided only that one could obtain a willing and knowledgeable informant. Indeed, a lucky chance may throw all sorts of firsthand observations in the ethnographer's way. As Gifford and I were driving along one day, we met a gaily dressed Indian wayfarer, wearing hawk and jay feathers on his head and carrying a shinny stick. We offered him a ride in our auto and learned that he was the survivor of a pair of twins. Like all twins, he had the privilege of always dressing in gala clothing.

To take another instance, in the summer of 1926 I spent several weeks with the Washo, who live on both sides of Lake Tahoe, partly in Nevada, partly in California. Again I was treated to an ocular demonstration of something I had read about—a girls' puberty dance. In California, a girl's coming of age is celebrated as a great ceremonial, whereas among Plains' tribes its significance—when there is any rite at all—is negligible. Therefore, I had never witnessed this type of performance. The custom had evidently been so important among the Washo that an attenuated version persisted, though hardly in spectacular form. In front of an Indian shack a tiny fire was kept up, the only other illumination coming from a lantern hung outside the hut. A few women began to sing, faced by two adolescents, each of whom was holding a long stick. The girls would jump two steps to the left, resume their position, then jump to the left again. A little later, the performance was shifted to a darker site, where women and girls formed a ring, facing its center, and walked or leaped in a clockwise direction. After a considerable lapse of time boys and men joined in the performance but rarely jumped; instead, they would take two quick steps to the left. This kind of action, accompanied by singing, went on for hours. All participants were dressed in trade clothes. The whole affair was a rather sorry spectacle compared to the dances I had seen among the Crow and Blackfoot. However, it did give me a clearer idea of what a puberty ceremony had been like in these parts than I could have derived from a written report.

Among the Washo I also ran into a curious sample of the "marginal man." A young Indian who had worked in a printer's shop was, nevertheless, a mystic with shamanistic aspirations. He had seen a man step on fire without being hurt, thanks to his "mental power"; and he apparently believed the story of a woman who had walked up the perpendicular side of a cliff.

I also learned how the Washo assimilated their experiences with white civilization to their own conditions. Like many other American Indians, they were divided into two permanent major groups, distinguished by their body paint, when playing athletic games. Informants tried to make the situation clear to me by comparing the opposing teams to Republicans and Democrats. Sometimes, however, these people recognized a third group, which was much smaller than the others. The mystic explained to me that this minor subdivision corresponded to American pacifists or neutrals.

Robert and Risa Lowie about 1895

Crow couple

The Crow White-hip and his wife

Hidatsa interpreter and his wife

Assiniboine dog travois

Crow tobacco ceremony

Horn lodge

The Crow chief Bell-rock

Mandan woman

Assiniboine clown

The Bear Lodge of the Bloods

Hopi women's society dance at Mishongnovi

Hopi spinner at Mishongnovi

Hopi interpreter in Walpi kiva

Taken about 1915

Taken about 1922

Taken about 1930

Taken about 1933

Taken about 1950

With Mrs. Lowie in Venice, 1953

In his Tirolerhut

A trip down the Rhine, 1953

Titisee in the Black Forest, 1956

In the course of my wanderings hither and yon I was impressed with the great differences in attitude displayed by different tribes and subtribes. I am not now referring to the matter of cultural configuration, though possibly that exerted its influence, but rather to the varying ways in which the groups—not merely individuals—responded to me in my interviews or to white people generally.

For example, Plains Indians, notwithstanding their frequent hostilities against whites, proved as a rule to be the most satisfactory informants. As I have explained, they too would now and then appear suspicious of an ethnographer's motives and would not always fall in with his wishes, especially if he sought esoteric information or wanted to buy objects of religious value. But by and large they were genial in their attitude and, when once launched on an exposition of a particular subject, would discourse fully and expansively. There was no difficulty about getting an old Crow to talk for six to eight hours a day on topics of scientific interest. At the same time there was never the slightest indication of obsequiousness. An eminent British ethnologist, the late W. H. R. Rivers, once suggested that aborigines were so overawed by the superior material equipment of the white man that they kowtowed to him and were ready to adopt the whole of his culture, abandoning, for one thing, their native cults. This assumption is not supported in the least by my experiences among Plains Indians, who, man to man, regard themselves as in no way inferior to whites. In this respect I consider an observation of Clark Wissler's highly illuminating. He had procured some phonograph records from the lips of an aged Blackfoot and, by way of making conversation, enlarged on the wonderful ability of the man who had invented this remarkable apparatus. The old Indian would have none of this; the "inventor" was not a whit abler than anyone else, he contended; he had merely had the good fortune of having the machine, with all its details, revealed to him by a supernatural being.

Within my experience such was not the attitude of most of the Indians I encountered outside the plains. If they were not actually deferential to a white man, they nevertheless did not have a Plains Indian's self-assurance. As informants they were less satisfactory: they tired easily and would not spontaneously discuss a given topic, answering each question laconically and then falling silent. Getting information was like pulling teeth. The Basin Shoshoneans were conspicuous in these respects, the Northern Ute proved worst of all—exorbitant in their demands and at the same time chary of dispensing more than a minimum of knowledge. A Bannock woman who had agreed to work for me on the subject of kinship grew restive after about an hour's talk. She was not exactly disagreeable, but she said if she had realized how hard and how long she would have to work, she would not have promised to give information at all. After that pronouncement it was of course unprofitable to continue much longer.

What could be the causes underlying such tribal differences? To a certain extent they can plausibly be accounted for in terms of a people's culture. Since the Plains Indians explain all extraordinary success as the result of supernatural aid, it is natural for them to ascribe the technological superiority of the whites along the same lines instead of being dazzled by the users' or inventors' native ability. Wherever this premise was lacking, on the other hand, the attitude might well be what Rivers supposed. It is not so easy to explain the group differences concerning the ability to give a lengthy and coherent account of native custom. We can guess that some tribes were, and others were not, prone to expound such matters in aboriginal days, but this surmise is of course an unproved conjecture. As to the degree of reticence in talking with whites, past experiences with government agents, traders, and missionaries doubtless varied appreciably, hence produced varying responses. Prejudices are more easily aroused than banished. In 1916 it had been a long time since the Hopi had had anything to fear from Spanish invaders, but the chief of one of the villages would not talk to me until I convinced him that I was not a "Castila." The episode parallels the statements of a departmental factotum at the American Museum of Natural History at the outbreak of the First World War. "The other employees," he told me, "think I'm for the Allies, but I can't forget the War of 1812!"

In any case it is quite clear that the observed group differences I am discussing cannot be interpreted on a genetic basis, for not infrequently tribes very closely related display marked contrasts in their behavior and attitudes toward outsiders.

CHAPTER 7

EXTRACURRICULAR EDUCATION

I learned, then, about a goodly number of American Indian tribes, some so markedly different from others that I had visual demonstration of the variation possible among aborigines of a single race and occupying a single continent. But my wanderings from Lake Athabaska to Arizona and from Nebraska to Lake Tahoe taught me something quite as valuable from both the human and the ethnological points of view. For ethnology means more than the study of "savage" tribes; it involves an insight into human culture in all its reaches, not excluding that highly specialized sample of it found in the central and western states of this country and Canada.

Now, in the abstract, New York may seem as good a place as any for studying American life, for over and above its numerous foreign colonies and the native New Yorkers, it harbors people from all over the country. In reality, however, almost every inhabitant moves in a small circle of those similar to himself and has a restricted outlook upon the national scene. Such a "marginal man" as myself, living in a middle class, German-speaking, German-Austrian milieu, had the doubtless broadening experience of discovering by firsthand observation the world outside this narrow range.

The process began in my early years. Public School 83 on East 110th Street was markedly different from the Cherninschule in

Vienna. There was, for instance, the early morning assembly of classes in a large hall, the pupils singing "Onward Marching We Come," while a teacher played the piano, after which the principal read a passage from the Bible. Textbooks were distributed gratis. And, oddly enough, there was no separate atlas but a single volume containing the text and the maps bound together. We each had an assigned seat in which we could keep our books and papers, so we did not need to carry everything home with us every night in the knapsack that is so inevitable an accompaniment of European education. We did not get report cards in those days, although one fellow pupil had heard of such a thing as a "stifficate," for the meaning of which I searched through the dictionary in vain. As strange as anything were the teachers; except in the two higher grades of grammar school they were all women! This fact was a recurrent cause of unfavorable comment from the impoverished Austrian immigrants who made up the circle of my parents' acquaintance, and in articles in the German-American press. How could a woman, apart from her intellectual inferiority, keep unruly boys in order? Here direct observation clashed with what I heard and read. It was a simple, daily demonstrated fact that an emaciated, elderly spinster could and did, without apparent effort, control a tough class of male youngsters in a tough school.

Other prejudices were not so easily corrected. In 1895 Theodore Roosevelt was appointed president of the police board of New York City and promptly began enforcing the "blue" laws against the sale of liquor on Sundays. His argument was irrefutable: if the laws were bad, it was the task of the legislature to amend them; the business of a police department was to enforce them as long as they remained on the books. But in German-American circles such reasoning was violently attacked. The blue laws were ridiculous in themselves and were a sample of Anglo-Saxon hypocrisy. They were also undemocratic; a Union League clubman could guzzle all he wanted on the Sabbath, but a poor citizen was deprived of innocent pleasure on his one free day. Of course, liquor vendors had their methods of circumventing the law. I recollect with what exhilaration I accompanied an Austrian friend of the family to a room, in the basement of a building, into which hiding place an Irish saloonkeeper had piped beer for the benefit of his trusted customers. At fourteen, or thereabouts, I thought I was striking a blow for civic liberty and delighted in getting the better of Anglo-American Pecksniffs. The German press naturally reflected the sentiments of its subscribers, both in its editorials and in its literary sections. A South German friend once wrote a typical story for the *Staatszeitung,* the plot of which revolved about a sanctimonious *Mucker* who denounced harmless drinking but was ultimately exposed as a clandestine toper.

The boys whom I met in school did give me whiffs of a new atmosphere. They played baseball and football and were greatly concerned about the heavyweight boxing championship of the world. Here I attained a quite mistaken position as an authority because the boys confused Austria with Australia and thought I came from the same country as their idol of the moment. An Irish boy, who for some reason spoke better German than any German-American lad in the school, was my best friend for the first two or three years, but a coolness developed between us over—of all things—the candidacy of Seth Low for mayor of New York. I knew nothing about Mr. Low except that he was president of Columbia University, hence a representative of education and a person to sympathize with; for John Augustus Cornelius, however, he was merely the tool of Protestant nativism. Even my subsequent attendance at the College of the City of New York did little to widen my horizons, because almost all my friends came from the same background as myself.

A generation ago the melting pot theory still reigned supreme, and there was general faith in the power of the public schools to transform foreigners into average Americans. Not that my four years in Public School 83 had had more than a superficial effect upon me! Subsequently, I discovered that there were native-born Americans upon whom the effect had been still less, although they had presumably attended American schools until they reached the legal age for leaving. In New Mexico, for instance, I found many adult men and women, born and raised within our borders, whose sole medium of communication was Spanish. In both Milwaukee and Cincinnati, I met American-born natives who spoke only German. In these numerous instances, the melting pot had not succeeded in "melting" either the language or the attitudes of natives. In my own home I had further proof of this situation. The language spoken there was exclusively German, except as I might exchange a few words with my younger sister, who became Americanized sooner and much more thoroughly than I. As a result, after my marriage, my wife had to teach me the English names of the simplest household objects. For example, the only word I knew for "saucepan" was the Austrian "Reindl," and one morning, when the faucet in my bathroom would not quite turn off, I had to take a surreptitious peep into the German-American half of the dictionary to determine the proper word for "Wasserhahn," in order to tell my wife what was amiss. In German I use spontaneously the many idiomatic expressions that one picks up in childhood but is rarely if ever taught. It is precisely this natural phraseology that is lacking in my English. Any good observer who has heard me speak both languages can note the difference, although I speak both without error.

It is, of course, true that a bilingual person enjoys certain advantages, but he also suffers from handicaps. As my wife has often spontaneously noted, after I have been speaking German for a few hours, I become a different person, with different values and attitudes. It is the fate of the bilingual to be forever a split personality. However, there are compensations. The "marginal man" starts with at least two modes of thinking and acting and is, therefore, likely to be more perceptive of additional differences between groups than the average American who has had firsthand experience with only one mode. But as far as this benefit was concerned, it was potential rather than actual, until after I set out on my travels. It was doubtless my own marginality to typical American culture that led to the deep impression made upon me by the non-Indian individuals whom I met in the course of my wanderings in those parts of the United States that lie west of New Jersey.

Travel had always seemed to me a *summum bonum*. Indeed, I was ever a geographical mystic, investing with an intense emotional aura any place that I spontaneously located on a map, becoming hypnotized by its presumed charm, and feeling an almost overpowering urge to drop whatever I was doing and rush off to visit it. In my grandfather's library in Vienna I had read the story of Alexander von Humboldt's researches in South America, also accounts of David Livingstone's missionary labors, and of Paul du Chaillu's journeys to the haunts of pygmies and gorillas. In my childhood Sir Henry M. Stanley's name was on everyone's lips, and as a birthday gift I received juvenile versions of Emin Pasha's and Herrmann von Wissmann's travels. By the time I was ten, my burning desire was to become an *Afrikaforscher*. I grew quite sentimental over the subject and burst into tears at the news of Emin's death.

At ten the urge to see foreign parts had been temporarily gratified. A farewell excursion was made to Budapest to visit my father's relatives there, followed by the journey from Vienna to Hamburg and the voyage to New York. During this period I kept a diary that reflects my passionate interest in travel. However, that long journey seemed to have been the last. Henceforth there loomed no prospect of sating my thirst for foreign scenes. Wistfully I would sometimes cross the Hudson on the Fort Lee ferry, and then take the Hackensack trolley as far as it went, in order to visit at least another state; a week in the Catskills seemed like a sojourn in a far country. With this sort of emotional background, my numerous field trips took on meaning that they do not have for the investigator who merely puts up with the inconveniences of travel in order to reach his objective. However, the pilgrimages to the Indians gave me more than mere emotional satisfaction; they furnished me with an invaluable perspective concerning the folkways and types of inhabitants to be found in my adopted country.

The reservations of the period would have formed a rewarding subject for sociological study, perhaps also for a sketch by some American Dickens. No two were alike, and although they were microcosmic worlds, their personnel certainly yielded a fair sample of American humanity; for the employees came from all over the United States and represented widely different levels of intelligence and social standing.

The most extended observations of American customs, manners, and personalities, I naturally made on or near the Indian reservations or settlements that I visited. I shall describe what I learned, beginning with government officials. These men were almost invariably courteous and well-meaning in their attitudes toward

me, but it seemed only by accident that one of them possessed the
particular information that I needed. On my first trip it was impossible to discover where the Indians I was to visit could be found
until I was in the same state with them. Even then, the powers-
that-be only "thought" the Shoshone were still in Lemhi. Before
my next trip I exchanged letters with representatives of the Hudson's Bay Company. The letters had an old world charm of phraseology and they were signed "Your obedient servant," but they told
me precisely nothing. This kind of thing happened frequently.

In order to judge fairly the white officials on the reservations
and their relation to the Indians, it is necessary to consider the traditional policies imposed on them by the Bureau of Indian Affairs.
It was a foregone conclusion of the superiors in Washington that
the Indians were to assimilate the ways of their white neighbors.
To put it concretely, they were to become farmers, to own their
land individually, to send their children to schools that conformed
to the American pattern, and to forsake their heathen beliefs and
practices. This basic principle was adhered to until about 1930,
when John Collier—a crusader on behalf of Indian rights—became Commissioner of Indian Affairs and introduced a policy of
preserving as far as possible the aboriginal ideals, customs, and in-
dustries. The older governmental policy was of course in effect
from 1906 to 1916, the years when I made most of my field
trips.

One fact made guidance of the acculturation process especially
hard for the officials: the Indians who were to be made over into
replicas of white men had been, and were, completely different
from one another in speech, economy, and customs. It was one
thing to teach progressive farming techniques to the Hopi of
Arizona, but quite another to make agriculturists out of the seed-
gathering, grass-hopper-hunting tribelets of Nevada or the roving
buffalo hunters of the high plains. It was easy to pacify the ever-
docile indigenes of, say eastern Washington, but very difficult to
ban war among the Sioux or Cheyenne, who esteemed men precisely according to their deeds of bravery in battle. Again, some
of the tribes had been in fairly close contact with white traders
and settlers for two or three hundred years, whereas other groups

lived far off the beaten track and had rarely seen whites, aside from federal employees.

In evaluating the work of these officials one must consider not only the enormous diversity of conditions among the Indians but also the shifts that an agent might have to make in the course of his official career. For instance, an agent who had become well adjusted to his duties at Lemhi, seventy miles or more from the nearest railway point, might be transferred to a Minnesota band of Ojibwa who had intermarried with French and Scots for two hundred years. On some reservations an official could communicate freely in English with even the oldest Indians; elsewhere an interpreter was required to talk with all but the youngest generation. Indeed, unbelievable as it may seem, in 1912, when I came to the Ute of Navaho Springs, thirty-eight miles from Mancos, Colorado, I had to leave after a few days for want of a single person who spoke intelligible English. Finally, it should not be forgotten that the maximum salary of these bonded officials was three thousand dollars, and some of them received only one thousand dollars a year.

As might be expected, the agents I met varied widely in character, education, and attitude toward their charges. At least one of them fancied himself an author and had produced a book on southwestern Indians. On the average they were doubtless not of very high intellectual caliber. It would be unfair to compare these men with, say, the Dutch civil service officials in the East Indies, who had undergone five years of university training to qualify for their positions. There was, indeed, no practical reason why the United States government should require parallel training of prospective officials in the Indian Service, as comparison of the situations will show. The native population of Java alone was twenty-seven million; in America all the aborigines north of Mexico numbered only 400,000 at the time of which I am writing. In the Dutch East Indies moreover, a form of Malay served as a *lingua franca*. It was sound policy therefore, that Dutch civil servants should have a solid knowledge of Malay before going to their posts. But in the United States, it would have been folly to train a man in, for instance, Navaho, when four years later he might be transferred to the Pawnee, whose language shared not a single word with Navaho. And what held for American languages held equally for the associated cultures. When I once described to my Crow friends a ceremony that I had witnessed among the Hopi of Arizona, they listened without the slightest consciousness of kinship with this tribe, as if I had spoken about inhabitants from another planet. Even the white man's ways were far more familiar to them than those of the Hopi.

Everything considered, then, the agents of the system could hardly be blamed for not entering understandingly into the aboriginal ways, or for not making scholarly studies of Indian culture. Nor did government agents greet with enthusiasm an ethnographer who not only wanted to preserve precisely what they were supposed to destroy but might conceivably upset what at best was a precarious equilibrium between themselves and the Indians. Even if the visitor did not actually stimulate revival of ancient ceremonial, his interested queries about pagan cults tended to foster them. An ethnographer was thus a potential enemy, and he had to behave warily, lest he be legitimately ordered off the reservation. It was not easy to strike the golden mean. The Indians had real or fancied grievances. They would pour out their hearts to a sympathetic listener from the outside, who might be hard put to it, especially when ignorant of local affairs, to give satisfactory answers. He could not know, for example, whether or not the superintendent of the reservation was really in league with Montana Livestock barons and defrauding his wards. At Lemhi the Indians were averse to their contemplated removal to Fort Hall, and it was difficult to avoid taking sides on the issue without giving offense either to the natives or to the officials.

Here and there one came upon suggestive reminders of the period when Indians were under army control. Many agency compounds bore the names of forts, and the buildings had the bleak aspect of barracks grouped around a central square. Often the most unmilitary looking agents were still unofficially hailed with the courtesy title of "Major." Altogether there was an air of bureaucracy about a superintendent's premises, and I was glad to keep my relations with him correct, but aloof.

In the discharge of their executive functions the agent and his subordinates were aided by Indian policemen, whose obvious duties of maintaining order included the specific obligations connected with reservation life. They checked illegal liquor traffic, supervised the issuance of annuities and rations by the government, and compelled parents to send their children to school. Fifty years ago they received from ten to fifteen dollars a month and usually lodgings and extra rations also. Their position was not an enviable one, for their association with the agency was bound to alienate them from their own people—no small matter considering the intense sense of kinship in which they had been brought up. Their job might be a trying one even in the ordinary routine of life, say, when truant pupils had to be herded back to their classes. During armed uprisings their duties precipitated a conflict of loyalties. In view of this fact it is amazing to what lengths these men carried their fidelity to the federal authorities. The most notable case occurred in December, 1890, when Sitting-bull, Sioux fomenter of the Ghost Dance rebellion, was to be arrested. When his followers tried to rescue him, forty-three native policemen held off more than a hundred assailants. Two of the policemen killed their recalcitrant prisoner; six of them were killed in the fight.

Of course, not all Indian policemen were heroes. I do not doubt that some of them used their office to exploit their tribesmen or to wreak vengeance on a personal enemy. Thus, it is hard to understand on any but personal grounds the killing of the Crow "prophet" Wraps-up-his-tail in 1887. To be sure, he had defied the agent and the U. S. soldiers sent against him, but he had caused little damage and was in flight when a Crow policeman, Fire-bear, deliberately shot and killed him. Twenty years later my informants still bitterly resented the act, and some said that the victim's brothers would have long ago avenged his death, but for the fact that they were never able to catch the murderer unawares.

The government provided medical care for its protégés, and its physicians naturally were on the average better educated than other officials. On the other hand, they hardly represented the cream of the profession. Why would a competent doctor accept a possibly isolated post in the Far West and the burden of constantly coping with aboriginal prejudices and superstitions and misunderstandings in return for a mere pittance? A doctor could rarely oversee the carrying out of his instructions, and there was no knowing how the Indians would interpret them; the one sure thing was that they would blame him if something went wrong. If a doctor prescribed three tablespoonfuls a day of a cough medicine, his patient might convince himself that since three tablespoonfuls were good for him, then the whole bottle would be better—a form of reasoning that more than once had serious consequences. Moreover, the mere survival of the native medicine man created a problem, and any criticism of his skills evoked enmity. One shrewd government doctor whom I met solved the problem by compromise. He agreed on a sort of consultation with his Indian competitor, allowing him to chant and manipulate according to ancient wont, provided the medicine man then permitted him to minister to the patient in the white man's way. But of course it was only an exceptional man who would display such tact and resourcefulness.

Notwithstanding the poor prospects of government doctors, I met several who inspired me with respect and whose reasons for entering the service were intelligible. One, for instance, had been an alcoholic and wished to escape to a place where spiritous beverages were hard to come by. Another was tubercular and required the type of climate afforded by some of the reservations. The agency physician who treated my dysentery was a manifestly able man, whose clear-cut, independent thinking stood out in sharp relief against a visiting colleague's good-natured fuzziness. Dogging his footsteps, and causing me no little amusement, was a very articulate half-Crow, half-Negro youth who proclaimed that he was learning the "doctor's trade." Rather close to the lower end of the scale was a burly doctor in charge of medical affairs at a Southwestern reservation. According to his own story, he was the son of a wealthy westerner who had wanted him to study medicine. He, however, had quite different tastes and aspired to become a heavyweight prizefighter. After being knocked out at a fairly early stage, he was willing to compromise, providing his father would send him to Vienna. "Vienna!" he cried rapturously to me, "Wien!." I divined his mind's eye roving to Grinzing, with glasses of new wine before him and an arm around a complaisant grisette.

It was a more convincing picture than Dr. X as either an M. D. or a Ph. D.—for he claimed to have won both degrees.

With lesser officials—farmers and teachers—it was possible to maintain more genial relations, and I often got on fairly close terms with them. Both these functionaries had their problems. It was not easy to make farmers out of warriors who regarded all agriculture as "women's work" of an especially menial sort. One farmer complained to me that the Crow took more pains in raising their utterly useless ceremonial tobacco (which they did not even smoke) than in cultivating market crops. Moreover, the government farmer might come from a state with an annual rainfall of forty or fifty inches a year and then find himself in the Arizona desert trying to teach farming to the Hopi who, through centuries of experience, knew a great deal more than he did about growing maize on a yearly precipitation of only ten inches. The teachers on some reservations were still combating old prejudices and superstitions, and at best they could make little progress with children who spent most of their time with illiterate kinfolk and spoke English only when in school. Notwithstanding such difficulties, some of these employees took a genial interest in the Indians, and to several of them I owe worthwhile observations on native customs and photographs of Indian dances, in addition to hospitable entertainment at their hands. Some of these minor officials were themselves full-blooded Indians, though often from other tribes than those who lived on the reservation. After an eight-hour workday with native informants it was pleasant to relax in the home of a middle-aged couple and to sing "Sleep, Baby, Sleep" and other sentimental ditties accompanied by the half-breed wife on the piano. In the year of the dance mania started by the Castles, I amused myself by initiating several Indian women employees on a Nevada reservation into the mysteries of the tango, whistling or humming "Maurice Irrésistable" for want of proper accompaniment.

Traders and missionaries, though not part of the agent's official family, belonged to the fixtures of a reservation. As the accounts of Far Western exploration show, traders played a significant part in inter-racial relations. Many of them married squaws, learned the native languages, and even took part in native life. Traders were often helpful to me in packing specimens for shipment to the Museum and in cashing checks. I generally arranged with the storekeeper to pay out money according to the drafts I gave my informants and to settle my total indebtedness to him at the end of my stay.

The traders themselves extended credit to the Indians, expecting to be paid on annuity days—periods of great excitement about the stores. At the time of which I am writing the older Indians were not yet adept at handling money, and I heard of some curious consequences of their lack of familiarity with it. The Navaho, I was told, insisted upon being paid for services or goods exclusively in silver dollars, so that anyone doing business with them had to go to the expense of shipping in heavy cases of silver. Elsewhere an Indian buying goods would not trust either his own arithmetic or the storekeeper's honesty; if he bought five articles, he would not have the total amount computed, but would insist upon paying for each item separately. At Lemhi I met with an amusing case of suspiciousness. I tried to pay an old Shoshonean with a two dollar bill that I had found in a vest pocket and thought I might as well get rid of. He had never seen such a bill before, and it was amusing to watch the alternations of his obvious anxiety lest he be cheated and his unwillingness to accuse me of fraud. After a bit, I solved the problem for him by proffering two silver dollars instead.

Like the physicians, the traders were of varying backgrounds, and to some of them we owe, directly or indirectly, excellent data on the tribes with which they had settled. I cannot remember meeting anyone of this caliber, but, as already indicated, many of them proved helpful and at least one of them was a character. He was the son of a onetime agent in the upper Missouri country; his wife, who bore him a large brood of children, was a half-breed, educated at an eastern school and long befriended by a wealthy New England family that continued for years to send her the *Atlantic Monthly* and other literary periodicals. I knew her as an amiable, middle-aged woman of dignified bearing, who did not chide her husband for his peccadilloes but endured them with exemplary, if somewhat bovine, forbearance. He had periodical lapses from grace, during which he would befuddle himself in the nearest town and frequent its brothels. He certainly made no pretense of immersing himself in her reading materials as a means of entertaining himself. Burlesque shows were more in his line.

Not all the interesting people that I met on reservations were in the federal service. There were squaw men and innkeepers, veterans of the wars against hostile Indians who had decided to settle near the scenes of their past adventures, painters, photographers, traders, and missionaries. The keeper of the very modest hotel in Lodge Grass was an old frontiersman in the Little Big Horn country, who had risen to a sergeant's rank under General Miles. He would wax expansive over the Sioux-fighting days, tracing the campaigns in detail, but also throwing in some personal yarns. I recall especially one about his narrow escape from a bigamous marriage into a Mormon household. If not all the tales were true, they at least served to pass the time and to keep life from becoming dull. Incidentally, I picked up from the old Crow warriors some "inside dope" on Custer's last stand. The Custer battlefield lies in Crow territory, and many of the old men had been Custer scouts. They told me that they had gone to the general the night before the battle and had warned him that his position was absolutely untenable. Custer refused to withdraw to a defensible position, so the Crows, seeing no point in dying for a stupid white man, left en masse and prudently went home. History has proved them right and Custer wrong.

Among the strange assembly of souls at one government mess was a German dentist who drove his one-horse carriage about the Lemhi reservation with more speed than control; an agency trader who had sat in the state legislature; a farmer's assistant who told me that I was an "absolutely typical Yankee"; an enormous Canadian who thought me the spit and image of a German crony and insisted upon treating me to a drink on the basis of the likeness; and a gaunt, saturnine white functionary who was given to serious reading and embarrassingly prodded me as to my views on evolution. He was willing to concede that some species had died out but never that new ones had arisen. On one of my later trips I reached the town of Lawton, Oklahoma, where prohibition was strictly enforced. There I ran into a stout, middle-aged German, originally from Berlin, but long resident in Chicago, who invited me to join a party in his room. To my surprise I found a group feasting on various kinds of sausage and guzzling beer. The German was to all appearances a substantial businessman, but he represented a type I had never met before. He made no bones about being part owner of a Chicago brothel ("of course, my wife doesn't know about it"), and he grew ecstatic about the merits of Negro wenches as sexual partners.

Among these assorted characters I was able to observe some odd folkways. For instance, there was the matter of how one government teacher and his wife addressed each other. Since I had read *Dombey and Son*, I knew that in Dickens' day, husbands and wives might address (not merely refer to) each other as Mr. and Mrs. Smith, but it took a stay with a teacher on the Hidatsa reservation to observe the custom in everyday life. It never ceased to intrigue me when he would say at the table, "Mrs. Smith, would you please pass the salt." In another family that lived on a ranch, the entire household, including the hired men, was called together just before breakfast, and while the pleasant odor of bacon drifted in from the kitchen, we all knelt in prayer, led by the head of the house, who prayed for each person separately and by name. He always asked the Lord to keep me from leading the Indians astray by my inquiries into their native life, although he never mentioned astray from just what.

When I visited the Stoney Assiniboine I at first had a room at the trader's. He was the son of a famous missionary, long since dead. His older brother, a recently superannuated preacher of the gospel, was likewise a well-known figure in those parts, who had, I believe, something to do with the Cree translation of the Bible. At all events, at a gathering of Stoneys which I attended, he certainly preached in very fluent Cree. He was extraordinarily cordial to me, but neither he nor his kin were exactly shrinking violets. The two brothers would pooh-pooh the then world's marathon record as something they had often outdone in their youth. The missionary brother was fond of enlarging on his physical toughness—how of a freezing night he would make shift with a single blanket, wade across streams with hefty wives of less puissant fellow clerics in his arms, and so on. Later I heard it said that there were just three liars in Alberta: the trader was reckoned as one and his reverend brother as the other two. The deceased father was still held in high esteem, however.

Canada was a revelation—so near to the United States, yet so far. The Union Jack that floated over the Blackfoot camp circle at Gleichen was no empty symbol of British sovereignty. There was a tincture of malice in many of the comments on the United States. I read in an Edmonton newspaper that a Negro had been recently condemned for some felony, but by due process of law, "not lynched as he would have been south of the line." Yet the Dominion, imperialistic enough in the sections I visited, was perceptibly differentiated from the mother country. In spite of the pinpricks aimed at the "Yankees," Alberta seemed in many ways far closer to Montana than to Ontario, let alone Quebec, where I got lost in a French quarter, and had to keep on wandering until I found my way out because all replies to my requests for guidance were couched in archaic French. On one occasion the Indians I was supposed to visit took it into their heads to decamp en masse for the Provincial fair, leaving me for several days in idleness until their return. I beguiled the time in browsing through the trader's books. To my astonishment I found that Canadian historians had their own ideas about the American Revolution, quite different from the version I had been taught in the schools of New York City. It seemed that our Tories were the true heroes of the Revolution. These intrepid, loyal men did everything within their power to put down the impudent rebellion of the upstart "patriots" and their failure to prevent a separation from England did not reflect upon their heroism. Particular commendation was given to Sir William Howe, who turned out to be a direct ancestor of my wife, about whom she generally kept silent!

In Alberta I encountered a kaleidoscopic range of human types. Stock breeders and prospectors, Indian agents and Royal Northwest Mounted Police, Orkney Islanders and their half-breed progeny, squat Indian women, Catholic and Anglican missionaries from humble fathers to bishops, Hudson's Bay factors and *métis* guides, fur traders and Canadian versions of cowboys.

The reader will recall that at Lake Athabaska I made the acquaintance of Mr. Harris, the Company's representative at Fond du Lac, Saskatchewan. Harris's had been a checkered career. He came from the eastern provinces originally and had been destined for the priesthood, but his major foible—fondness for drink—eliminated him during his probationary period. Then he had turned to law, taking his degree at the University of Acadia. But once more liquor proved too strong a lure. He drifted west, spent a few years in the Royal Northwest Mounted Police, married a full-blood Chipewyan woman, and finally wound up at his present post, where the priest was the only other white inhabitant and where mail from the outside world came twice a year. Characteristically, Harris became keenly interested as soon as he heard that I had a museum connection. But his was not a purely altruistic concern: he surmised that I would be carrying alcohol for the preservation of specimens and seemed gravely disappointed at my inability to minister to his spirituous wants.

Naturally of an alert mind, a colorful personality, saturated with years of varied experiences, Harris was a delightful raconteur. He had almost inevitably become a legend in the country. There were stories galore about his failing in its amusing aspects, and some of them he told himself with verve and gusto. Obliged to get a license for every quart of liquor he imported north of Athabaska Landing, he had made his Indian wife obtain one also, to double the household supply. But even that did not suffice, so once he hit upon the ingenious plan of going to the Mission at Chipewyan, pretending that the priest at Fond du Lac needed sacramental wine. It was naturally given as requested, but never reached Fond du Lac. Then there was the episode of the red ink. Harris would order huge quantities from the headquarters in Winnipeg and gulp down the supplies that came as a substitute for liquor. "You can get a jag just as well on red ink as on anything else," he explained to me. At last, however, the recurrent requisitions roused the officials' suspicion. "We cannot understand how in your tiny post you can use such amounts of red ink," they wrote. Harris knew the ruse had run its course. "I don't use it," he replied, "I abuse it."

There was one other person at Chipewyan quite as interesting in his way as Harris. When the handle of my suitcase came off and I despaired of having it fixed, Mme. Mercredi sent me to "Father" Wylie: "Il arrange tout." Wylie was an Orkney Islander, whom the Hudson's Bay Company had taken into their employ as a youth of twenty, originally on a five-year contract. Major Routledge and I inspected the document, in which Wylie obligated himself to serve the interests of the Company by day and by night, at the risk of his life, to obey unquestioningly the commands of his superiors, etc., all for the noble stipend of twenty pounds a year. Wylie had married, raised a family, extended his contract, and stayed on indefinitely. He was now approaching seventy and was entitled to be taken back to his native land. What piqued his curiosity above all was the sight of a railroad train. He had never seen one, because in the old days the Company shipped in their Orkney Islanders via Hudson's Bay and inland waterways exclusively. Wylie had not only a knack at everything mechanical and technical, but a keen theoretical bent along those lines. He had imported relevant treatises, teaching himself enough to rig up an effective telephone line from one northern post to another. He knew all about the principle of a steam engine and craved the sight of a locomotive. From what I heard later, he never returned to the Orkneys, but if I remember correctly his favorite wish was fulfilled and he did get to Winnipeg.

Possibly there was no aspect of American life about which I learned more during my travels than about religion. People regularly said grace at their meals. Even one of my interpreters, who was a catechist of sorts, stared at me in austere rebuke when I began to eat a picnic lunch without first bowing my head in thanksgiving. I had not known that so many people spontaneously gathered in prayer meetings—which I attended, singing "He Leadeth Me" as lustily as anyone else—or that whole families knelt night and morning in prayer. I was likewise impressed with the diversity of Christian denominations in the country. On the Crow reservation there were at least three missions—Catholic, Baptist, and Episcopalian. Somewhere in Utah I lodged with a Moravian couple, although my memory retains only one nonecclesiastical feature of their lives; the husband was inordinately fond of pumpkin pie and, accordingly, his wife presented us with a sample of his favorite food at every meal. I attended revivals, testimonial prayer-meetings, Catholic masses, and even received communion administered by the Episcopal bishop of Utah. One Baptist lady, returning after a few weeks' respite from reservation duties, grew expansive over her wonderful vacation, which had consisted of flitting from church conference to church conference. This frivolous vacationer grated terribly on my rationalistic sensibilities, especially when she tabooed the playing of some German student songs on the doubtless correct surmise that they were "not nice" —that is, they were drinking songs—but there was no doubting her sincerity. These people were religious, but they did not in the least resemble the sanctimonious *Mucker* stigmatized by my freethinking German associates in the East. Nor were any of these religious manifestations likely to have fallen under my observation in my normal round of activities in New York City. I was learning, but had not yet learned, that it takes many kinds of people to make a world.

With the Mormons I had very pleasant, if casual relations, and I was glad to hear both Moravian and Episcopalian neighbors commend these simple, kindly folk, especially for their attitude toward the Indians. There was one Mormon, the son of a patriarch, whose lapses from grace were many, but who remained steadfastly devoted to his faith. He was keenly grateful when I listened sympathetically to his outpourings and in a maudlin moment all but embraced me, crying, "*You* were *born* a Mormon." Another member of the church—let me noncommittally dub him Young— stands out above all others in my memory. An attractive, intelligent man of possibly thirty, he was a state engineer by profession and was working at Moapa while I was studying a subdivision of the Paiute there. Like most of his educated coreligionists, he had been sent to missionize the heathen soon after his graduation. The French part of Switzerland was his chosen destination, and soon after arrival he found himself booked for a lecture. Seated on the platform, Young was listening to the chairman's introductory words when to his horror he recalled that he knew no French. In this emergency he fervently prayed for the gift of tongues. Forthwith the Holy Ghost possessed him, and for an hour he spoke in French—perfect French, as his audience afterwards assured him in congratulatory speeches. After adjournment of the meeting the Holy Ghost departed, and Young began learning the language of the country from scratch. Not less curious was an experience of my friend's uncle while proselytizing the South Seas. In strict consonance with the Lord's injunction he carried "neither purse, nor scrip," living wholly on the natives' bounty. On one occasion he had planned to go by steamer to the next island on his itinerary, but was quite destitute of means. He was standing at the landing-place in silent prayer just before the scheduled departure of the boat when an utter stranger came down a hillside and presented him with the exact amount required for the passage.

These stories, told in obvious good faith, reminded me of my Indians' reminiscences of visions. One did not need to descend to the savage plane, then, to find souls deeply and sincerely religious; even an engineer ostensibly no different from other educated persons could believe in the literal efficacy of prayer and be divinely inspired in the twentieth century.

Some of the missionaries among the Indians were men of ability and training. Science owes to them some of the very best reports on aboriginal customs and language. The Reverend J. Owen Dorsey among the Omaha is a shining example. Such missionaries resided for years among the same tribes, acquired their language—which they often were the first to reduce to writing—and painstakingly recorded what they could learn of ancient custom and belief. They proceeded on the sound principle that it was well to discover what manner of men were to be dealt with before attempting to convert them to Christianity. Unfortunately, not all ministers who tried to carry the gospel to the Redskins adopted this view.

Indeed, some of the missionaries and other clerics whom I met represented the opposite extreme, and were extremely narrow in their views. They had a phobia of anything that smacked of "paganism" and refused sternly to so much as attend an Indian religious ceremony. They did not propose to lend the weight of their tacit sanction by witnessing pagan rites. On one occasion I saw an elderly male missionary have veritable tantrums because he noticed a group of Indians—some of them his parishioners—driving off to a purely social dance in a near-by town. Such narrow-minded and rigid men were trying to convert their wards without the slightest knowledge of what these were to be converted from, without using their unique opportunities as permanent residents to discover whether the pagan system might not contain fragments that would make conversion to Christianity easier, and without even trying to see Indian psychology against its own background, but rather viewing it through a screen of their own prejudices.

But if the narrowness of some missionaries passed the bounds of reason, others inspired me with genuine esteem. In fact, even the stupid ones taught me a lesson, and forced me to recant from my previous ideas, gained early from European writings of an anti-clerical character. These men were not knaves trying to exploit their dupes. What gain, material or social, could one extract from heading a mission in southeastern Montana, let alone in the Athabaska country? The Crow, quite articulate about their grievances against whites, were still reverently extolling a priest who had tended their sick during an epidemic and himself fallen a victim to his altruism. On the Athabaska River I saw two frail young Belgian fathers painfully handling the sweep of their boat which was destined for some spot in the wilderness. Were they being lured on by prospects of high living? Was the priest at Fond du Lac with his solitary white parishioner and two mails a year a specimen of Voltaire's courtly abbés with their 200,000 livres of income? Were men of science willing to undergo like privations and sacrifices? Undoubtedly there were such, but not many, I thought to myself. No, the old formula of the eighteenth-century *philosophes* might require some mending.

Somewhat to my surprise I found that the old spirit of the frontier, even though obsolescent, was still cherished in odd sports. At the Hubbells' trading posts on Southwestern reservations the traveler was lodged and boarded scot-free. Various Westerners showed from time to time a most attractive and unexpected trust in human nature. When the First World War broke out, I found myself in Reno en route from one Paiute band to another and extremely short of cash. The bank seemed paralyzed by the news and, though I presented more than adequate credentials, I could not prevail upon the manager to give me any money. I had to telegraph to the Museum and ask Wissler to wire me some in care of Western Union. While waiting for a reply, I met my landlady from the reservation that I had just left. She waved at me the check I had given her, which she had been unable to cash. Since

I had been lodging with her for some time, the check was for a fairly sizable amount, and she wanted her money. In this emergency I turned, without much hope, to the manager of my hotel in Reno—a bluff Westerner of the old school. He cast one glance at the check and said, "I never had any use for a man who wouldn't honor my checks," and paid out the entire amount at once. In New York City that sort of thing simply was not done. Still more remarkable was an episode in Garrison, a tiny town in North Dakota. A colleague, instructed to transfer the residue of his own appropriation to me, had foolishly sent me a single check for two hundred and fifty dollars—an amount equal to nearly a thousand dollars now. This sum was far beyond the contents of the local trader's till. Yet without the money I would not be able to get home. With little hope I went to the railroad town of Garrison, where I was a total stranger, and approached the keeper of the general store. He looked at the check, said, "It looks all right to me," and paid out the entire amount. On my first trip to the Shoshone I was given change from a ten dollar bill in the form of nine silver dollars, and indeed I rarely saw a dollar bill west of Omaha. In San Francisco, a bank teller cashed a hundred dollar check for me entirely in gold coins, most of which I had never even seen before.

One salutary effect of a new environment is to teach the traveler humility. The New Yorker is notoriously superior in his attitude toward the rest of the universe, and I had my share of this Gothamite superciliousness. But you cannot very well put on airs when you have never before sat on a horse and simply have to ride one in a place where the very babes are expert equestrians. You look rather silly when all your incipient efforts at kindling firewood prove abortive; or when your ever so fine tent from Abercrombie and Fitch comes tumbling down about your ears for lack of such simple supports as the stupidest native—white or Indian—would have known enough to provide; or when on a fowling expedition the only target you manage to hit is the Missouri River. Still more galling was the versatility of the better educated frontiersmen. They knew their woodcraft, they were fine horsemen, they could cook a respectable meal, and they almost never got lost. In no respect could I compete with them.

It was mortifying, too, that laymen were in some instances ahead of me at my own game. Of course, I could hardly be expected in a short period to learn a particular native tongue as well as the missionaries or traders or squaw men knew it after years of daily conversation with the Indians. But the fact remained that these outsiders could and did converse freely and fluently, whereas I, the specialist, could not. Among the Hidatsa I was taken down another peg. The Reverend Gilbert L. Wilson was neither particularly cultivated nor in any sense intellectual, but he was a superb observer. In the recording of ethnographic detail—about house building or pottery making or farming customs or the care of infants, for example—I, the trained ethnologist, could not begin to compete with him. As von Helmholtz once remarked, it prevents excessive conceit to observe your fellow man doing what you cannot do yourself, or doing it better. I received many such lessons in humility, and often from unexpected sources.

The ethnographer of thirty-five or forty years ago was not merely "roughing it," in the usual sense of taking a short vacation from modern conditions with an easy return to them whenever desired. He had, for instance, a series of object lessons in what transportation meant in ruder periods. At times he might have to choose between sharing a bed with another wayfarer or spreading his roll-up mattress on the floor of the barn, surrounded by half a dozen fellow travelers. Often he slept on the ground. For short trips he either walked or rode a horse. He ate what the country provided and if he could not digest this food, he went without. In three weeks I once lost seventeen pounds because I could not eat beans and had to live primarily on tea. Nor could the investigator jump into a car and leave for a weekend respite in a reasonably comfortable hotel a hundred and fifty miles away. He was "stuck" with whatever he found, and there was no escape.

The resulting gain on the human side, and in the development of unexpected skills, was considerable. The city boy had to learn how to cook his own meals, to wash his own clothes, and to find his own way through woods and across prairie land. He had to hire and fire interpreters, to learn how to sit on a horse, and how to make fire without matches. It was something new to live at a distance of a hundred miles from the nearest railroad, to fall asleep on the floor of an Indian boarding school to the nocturne of coyote howls, or to go unshorn and unshaved for lack of a barber—for I was so steeped in European culture that at the age of twenty-five it had never occurred to me that I might learn to shave myself. I had always followed the European model of visiting the barber every morning. The beard I wore for a decade was one more by-product of my field work. Incidentally, upon my return from Lake Athabaska, although I had had the wildness of my appearance somewhat subdued by a barber in Chicago, my mother and sister, who came to meet my train, did not recognize me, although I must have walked right past them.

Thus I learned that there were white people in the United States with interests altogether different from those of my friends at home. These new acquaintances were not concerned with the latest books or plays, but they had a lot to say about horses and alfalfa crops and cattle breeding and prospecting, and especially about the amount of rainfall in recent months. This subject was discussed daily with infinite ramifications. A prospect of rain was clearly a matter of life and death to them and not, as I had always assumed, merely a question of whether or not one set out equipped with umbrella and rubbers. It was extremely educational for a young ethnologist with a metropolitan background to discover what the people of his country were like, what they were thinking about, and what values they placed upon different things.

CHAPTER 8

A
BUSMAN'S
HOLIDAYS

There are several ways of approaching the study of culture, all of them potentially profitable. Some scholars get absorbed in the life of a particular primitive people and ignore everything else. At times they produce enviably full records, which provide a sound foundation for the thinking of other ethnologists, but they themselves are content with presenting their descriptive data. About the turn of the century there were investigators of a different type, possibly willing and even eager to interpret and compare, but bent above all on reconstructing native life as it existed before the impact of Western civilization. Generally there has been an aversion to studying any but truly primitive, that is, preliterate people; indeed, some ethnologists *exclude* literate culture altogether in defining their science.

Much can be said in justification of these several attitudes. Aboriginal life has been vanishing at an alarming rate, and science profits if enthusiastic reporters rescue what can still be procured in the way of information. Further, it is important to "peel off," so to speak, western accretions in a native culture. It makes a great difference, therefore, in our view of Plains Indians whether they rode horses before or only after the coming of the Spanish conquerors—just as it is important for an economic historian to know that Europeans did not cultivate the potato until after the discovery of the New World.

However, there are other, equally defensible ways of looking at the issues. The best observer cannot spontaneously see everything in an alien society. If he concentrates on one favorite tribe, he is bound to miss noteworthy traits that he might have discovered if he had asked about them on the analogy of other groups visited or read about. As for studying an aboriginal way of life only with the aim of finding out what it was like before "higher" civilizations influenced it, this goal is inadmissible. Borrowings from a complex civilization do not differ in principle from other loans, and every people has at one time or another adopted features from the outside. If we concern ourselves solely with what a given culture was like in a supposedly simon-pure state, we ignore some of the most interesting of ethnological problems; namely, what happens to traits when they are taken over, why some are taken over and others rejected, and what role in diffusion is played by individuals and by pre-existing native institutions. Thus it is easy to understand that Christianity spread rapidly among a people ruled by "divine" chiefs who had somehow been converted by missionaries. Finally, no sane ethnologist would attempt to compete with such specialists as Sinologues or Egyptologists in their own field. But, as Sir Edward Tylor, the great leader of British cultural anthropology, realized long ago, human culture is one grand whole and any thorough study of its regional manifestations may illuminate the rest, irrespective of time and place. The documented history of "higher" civilizations may yield a direct answer to questions that have troubled ethnologists. Admittedly a higher culture is more likely to transmit its inventions and customs to a lower than vice versa. But is that uniformly so? The spread of the potato and of tobacco conclusively refute the universal validity of the generalization, and Chinese records show that these instances are not exceptional: felting, for example, was borrowed by the Chinese from "barbarian" nomads. On the other hand, the Sinologue may well profit from the ethnologist's broader perspective. A scholar who is merely wrapped up in his texts misses vital points for a scientific knowledge of human development. To take a concrete case, he may study Chinese kinship terms solely in the light of ancient writings, whose authors scorned peasant life altogether and therefore neglected regional differences and actual usages among the common folk.

Altogether there is no logical warrant, whatever expediency may dictate in particular cases, for separating the literate and the illiterate populations of the globe. In 1920 Spain, notwithstanding the past achievements of her poets and painters, had nearly forty per cent male and fifty-three per cent female illiterates; and the figures for Italy were roughly comparable. Those for Turkey, let alone Albania, were even more startling. Granting that the mere proximity of literate compatriots causes a seepage of "advanced" ideas to the lower strata in such areas, the fact remains that in many respects the mentality of an unschooled Gheg or Sicilian is not vastly different from a Papuan's or Crow's. That is surely the import of folkloristic research. Ethnology, therefore, cannot logically be restricted to the primitives, but must envisage a study of culture throughout the range of human history.

For the ethnologist who has once grasped this idea, every experience of foreign travel, every bit of cultural information gained from reading, is grist for the mill. In this respect he differs from the ordinary tourist. He has what was once called an "apperceptive mass" for the interpretation of what he sees or reads into general or even philosophical terms. At home in his study or abroad on his leisure travels, he is on a perpetual busman's holiday. There is no observation, however trivial in appearance, that cannot potentially assume grand proportions. For instance, many years ago I asked a four-year-old Crow boy, "Where is your daughter?" He at once puckered his lips and protruded them toward a little girl, still younger than himself. She was actually his mother's brother's daughter, but since the Crow designate a maternal uncle as an elder brother, they consider the brother's child as their own, so my little friend was quite correct by tribal standards. But I was interested in his method of pointing. Not long ago, I read in a book by Francis Huxley that Brazilian natives point out a person by "a pouting thrust of the lower lip." And I think I once read that the same custom occurs in Tibet, although I cannot at the moment confirm this impression. These observations—which might have been noted by any tourist—at once raise a series of questions in the mind of the ethnologist, even if he is on a vacation or merely reading for his own pleasure. Are we dealing with a pan-American aboriginal tradition? Or is lip-pointing perhaps a widespread and ancient practice of the Mongoloid peoples? How is its distribution to be accounted for? Since it does not appear all over the world, one cannot assume it to be an instinctive trait of all peoples. We must rather regard it as a simple motor habit determined by a definite cultural tradition or—to take nothing for granted—by a series of independent cultural traditions. The phenomenon falls into the wide category of learned, not genetically determined, motor habits, whose study was stimulated by Boas, and also by the French sociologist, Marcel Mauss, in his little-known but immensely valuable essay on "*Les techniques du corps.*" The apparently trivial observation with which this discussion started merges into a basic problem of ethnology and human biology: what is, and what is not, part of man's original nature?

Sometimes it may be reading in a totally different field that calls to mind ethnological principles. Many years ago I ran across a book on Leonardo da Vinci by the Swedish art historian, Osvald Sirén. I found the discussion of "The Lord's Supper" a revelation. From numerous illustrations it became obvious that not only had the theme been a very popular one in earlier and contemporary art, but that its treatment likewise illustrated the ethnological concept of a "pattern"—just as did the variations of Plains Indian military societies or the forms of Blackfoot medicine bundles. But beyond that the critic demonstrated why Leonardo's treatment was supreme: he had introduced a novel, dramatic formulation of the Biblical incident used by his predecessors. Sirén showed the artist's originality within a given cultural frame, emphasizing how genius differed from mere competence. Patterns and individual differences were illustrated as convincingly as, on a lesser scale, among a primitive people.

No matter to what aspects of his own civilization the ethnologist turns, he will find close parallels to the phenomena familiar from the study of aborigines and will fit them into familiar categories. The economists investigating entrepreneurship in the United States —Arthur H. Cole, Clarence H. Danhof, and their associates— come face to face with the significance of individual variability in business. Further, just as Crow men were not all either heroes or cowards, either profoundly religious or irreverently skeptical, so businessmen cannot be dichotomized into bold innovators and unimaginative followers of routine. "There is a 'spectrum' rather than a 'dichotomy' among such individuals." When an economist recognizes the "considerable amount of imitativeness among companies in the matter of official organization," he is noting what Boas found in his study of Kwakiutl secret societies—the compulsive force of a pattern. More significantly, when economists stress "the non-rational as well as the rational components in economic action," they independently arrive at the conclusion borne in upon ethnologists at every stage of their professional inquiries.

Travel, no matter where, offers endless food for reflection if one sees culture as a whole. In 1925 I paid a purely recreational visit to Tahiti and Moorea (Eimeo), but I could not help making some professional observations on the side. How greatly things had changed since Captain Cook called there in 1769 or even since Darwin's stay in 1835! A stroll through Papeete, the capital, with its 5,500 residents, at once revealed that I was in a French colony. The very names of the streets—Rue de Rivoli or Boulevard des Champs Elysées—recalled Paris, even though very little resembling their metropolitan namesakes; here was a Cercle de Bougainville, there a Club Loti. Later came other indications of Gallic impact on this marginal area. Government officials openly lived with Tahitian mistresses, yet the better class of natives conformed strictly, so far as appearances went, to bourgeois standards of etiquette. At dances, for instance, fat dowagers carefully chaperoned daughters and nieces. When I once ventured to ask a young Polynesian lady, whom I had not formally met, to dance with me, she at once referred the matter to her guardian, whose negative advice led to a polite refusal. One afternoon at the Club Loti the hostess welcomed me in her bare feet, but with all the refinements of French courtesy. She apologized for not being able to entertain me because of pressure of work, but urged me to stay in the lounge, where she propped up some cushions for my comfort, and finally departed with an "Estimez-vous chez vous," accompanied by a graceful gesture.

But France was not the only alien molder of modern Tahiti. English and American missionaries, planters, and traders had been long established there, and, in consequence, the island—or at least Papeete—was trilingual. Important announcements were nailed to trees along main thoroughfares in French, English, and Tahitian; this last the missionaries had reduced to writing. Christianity had left its mark—Mother Hubbards and churches. In Moorea I ran across the same quaint dichotomy I found in Hopiland: when I asked my guide whether the church in some locality was Catholic, he answered, "No, Christian!" Schools, too, had made their appearance; one of those I passed bore on its outside the simple symbolic formula: "$2 + 2 = 4$." Another, run by a Protestant missionary couple, had a blackboard covered with geometrical and arithmetical exercises, and in the courtyard the boys were playing leap frog. Europeans not content with such educational facilities might send their half-breed daughters to French boarding or convent schools, where they learned to read Racine and Molière.

Notoriously, the island of Cytherea had long attracted artists, literati, and other intellectuals longing for freedom from the conventions of the Western world. Whether they exerted any perceptible influence on the natives or not, their presence lent a certain flavor to the character of Papeete. I do not recall any successor to Gaugin, but there were James Norman Hall, who had already begun to write; Frank Stimson, amateur ethnographer proficient in the Polynesian tongues—a brother-in-law of Van Wyck Brooks, who has given us an engaging sketch of him in *Days of the Phoenix*; and Jean Ably, the owner of the Club Loti, a highly cultivated Frenchman who had moved in the literary circles of Paris and London. Four years later he sent me a copy of his book, *Tahiti, aller et retour*. There, also, was Kenneth Emory, doing archaeological research for the Bishop Museum in Honolulu. Papeete itself had a museum, though a meager one that was generally locked up; and it could boast of a Société des Études Océaniennes that published "Bulletins," sometimes containing information on ethnography, Polynesian languages, and natural history.

Cook and Darwin would certainly have been startled by the ultra-modern refinements that had invaded the capital since their day. The tourist could hire a Citröen, or Ford, or Buick, and deal with an agent for Dodge Brothers. A light and telephone company advertised a complete stock of electrical goods; and the Mariposa Café served "fancy sundaes" and "iced beverages." From diary entries and receipted bills still in my possession I infer that I consumed respectable amounts of champagne, cocktails, and gin fizzes in one or the other of the clubs and cafés. Trilingual posters gave notice of a *Grand Assault de Boxe* in which the champion of Tahiti was to be pitted against his Rarotongan counterpart. The cinemas, of which Papeete had three, were quite remarkable. Those were the days of the silent films, mostly American—with subtitles in English—including Charlie Chaplin's "The Pilgrim." At first I was taken aback by the terrific noise emanating from two persons who stood at one side of the theater on a slightly raised platform. It turned out that for the benefit of the mixed population these two interpreters were bawling out renderings of the English titles into French and Tahitian. The shouted translations went on simultaneously and continually throughout the running of the films.

With all these innovations an ethnologist might well ask what was left of the aboriginal life. As a matter of fact there was precious little. Native huts at best roughly corresponded to the old type; on the shore I watched boys spearing fish; in a side street I once came upon youngsters on aboriginal stilts; on Bastille Day an effort was made to revive the ancient dances. In Moorea I was once paddled to my destination in an outrigger canoe. But, on the whole, the first impression ethnographically was disappointing, and to a lesser extent this applied even to the countryside. Yet points of interest abounded on a closer view.

Of the several foreign strains—Chinese, Melanesians from New Caledonia, Annamites from southeastern Asia—the Chinese were the most conspicuous and so numerous as to warrant the existence of an Association Philanthropique Chinoise de l'Océanie Fran-çaise. As everywhere, they were indefatigable workers and seemed to have a monopoly of certain callings. In Papeete they made tropical suits for Europeans and in Moorea controlled most of the little general stores; they alone grew rice. In Papeete the Chin Foo Bank was in Chinese hands.

Such random observations suggest a number of questions to the professional even if he is unable to answer them. There is, for instance, the apparently nonsignificant cultivation of rice by the Chinese. The point about this is that, though rice is a superior food and can be grown in Tahiti, the natives stick to their aboriginal crops—bananas, plantains, taro, and the like. This interests the ethnologist, for the fact disproves a once common assumption that if two peoples were living side by side they would readily borrow each other's cultural traits, especially when a practical consideration entered. My Tahitian experience illustrates the principle, now generally accepted, that there is no such automatic transfer; on the contrary, diffusion works in a highly selective way. Why some features are eagerly embraced and others spurned, has never been explained by a generally valid formula. We can say with great assurance that the processes sometimes involved rational, but very often, as in the present case, nonrational motives.

Why, we ask further, do some features survive when any number of others have disappeared? Here Tahiti invites comparison with otherwise so utterly different Fort Chipewyan. In both instances some obvious adaptations to the physical environment have persisted; the Polynesians grow bananas and breadfruit, the Chipewyan hunt caribou or moose and catch fish, and so on. But it would not be correct to assert that the material culture *in toto* has remained, for Tahitian women parade in unsightly Mother Hubbards and the Athabaskans wear clothes furnished by the Hudson's Bay Company. Superficially, the native supernaturalism seemed to be dead in both places. Christian chants could be heard in the *himene* (hymn) houses of Tahiti, and the Chipewyan, apart from a knowledge of old myths, were apparently Christianized. Yet in both places I came across survivals: I heard that Tahitians would not pluck flowers from the remnants of holy platforms (*marae*) for fear of being smitten with leprosy; and the Chipewyan still had a lingering belief in the forces of medicine men. It is indeed a knotty problem why some fragments of old arts, customs, and beliefs survive, but awareness of the issue on the part of ethnologists may sometime lead to a solution.

The attitude of the Polynesians toward the Chinese also gave food for thought. Here were indefatigably industrious, thrifty folk, but their virtues did not endear them to the natives. My

Moorean guide complained that they made lots of money and later returned to China; in short, they were just "no good." And a Tahitian woman concluded a similar diatribe with the words, "Je n'aime pas cette race." The ethnologist thinks of corresponding reactions—of the Irish toward the Scots, the Bavarians toward the Prussians, Southerners toward the damned Yankees. Crudely summing up, we might say that whenever austerely frugal, capable people come in contact with comparatively feckless folk they make the impression of being an unnatural, inhuman lot, their very virtues taking on the character of unpardonable vices. It is amusing to recall that a disgruntled German immigrant described the Americans as being, even more than the English, nothing but "Protestant Jews."

It is difficult for the ethnological traveler to remain nothing but a tourist; even improbable starting points will bring him back to his professional ponderings.

During a brief visit to Spain I gained some familiarity with Goya. What has ever since haunted me is the diversity of his work. How could the artist of the graceful, delicate cartoons for Gobelin tapestries have produced the stark pictures of the Peninsular War, the portraits of the royal Spanish family, and the macabre etchings of his later period? A priori we must assume that there was some bond linking these manifestations, but who could have predicted the *Caprichos* from the painting of executed Spanish rebels? If it is impossible to reduce a single personality to a simple formula, it certainly seems hopeless to characterize adequately a whole culture by a neat phrase, as some of the guild have tried to do. Surely there are highly distinctive emphases that tend to integrate large areas in a people's attitudes and behavior. I had already seen how sharply the Hopi way of life contrasts with that of the Plains; and K. G. Haeberlin, Ruth Benedict, and Cora DuBois have expounded some of the integrative factors that operate. But the rich manifoldness of reality is never exhausted by these integrators: just as we cannot deduce Goya's war scenes from his drawings of a picnic along the Manzanares, so we cannot deduce from the Dakota men's unremitting lust for military glory that their wives would organize craft societies for skilled tipi makers and porcupine quill embroiderers.

This leads us to the problem, much discussed by ethnologists of recent years, of national character, which essentially coincides with that of configuration. The ethnologist who has read what was written a century or two ago about a particular culture and compares these earlier records with later ones and with his own contemporary findings as a traveler will be very cautious about broad generalizations. It was in 1810 that Mme de Staël published her work on Germany, depicting that country's natives as feeble-minded in practical affairs, but devoted to metaphysical speculation. Sixty years later no one could conceivably have passed the same judgment; and in 1907 a British fellow traveler in Canada who had been to the Continent told me that the Germans were "the Yankees of Europe." Again, Mme de Staël stressed the contrast between the Germans' boldness in abstract thought and their servile submissiveness to authoritarian orders. The latter, indeed, continued to loom large in both German and foreign comments on the German fatherland: an apocryphal, though characteristic, anecdote had it that a revolutionary German Communist mob carefully stepped aside when confronted with a tablet inscribed "Betreten verboten." During and since the Hitler régime this acceptance of authority by Germans has again and again been the target of savage criticism from without. Yet in 1956 the newspapers of Germany bristled with accounts of juvenile delinquency of precisely the same nature that we are familiar with in the United States. In Hanover some three hundred young rowdies fought the police, who were obliged to use their clubs. In Hamburg youthful vandals broke into the Händel-Archiv, wantonly destroying irreplaceable notes; in Munich a hundred youngsters attempted to storm a police station in order to liberate one of their fellows. In the district of Cologne nineteen inmates of a corrective institution attacked the guards with iron poles, and wrought damage on windows, doors, and furniture; two police squads were required to reëstablish order.

It is clear that what ethnologists have been preaching in recent times—the need to consider primitive peoples dynamically—applies with at least as much force to civilized nations. A characterization that holds for one period may be quite incorrect for an earlier or later one.

In 1924 I spent a long time in Europe—my first return since I left Vienna as a child. As I traveled about, I was enormously impressed by the differences among groups that I visited, as well as by the distribution of traits that I observed. One does not need to be long in Hamburg and Munich in order to notice variation in the usages and attitudes of the populace. These differences are presumably in large measure due to the geographical position of the two cities—not through a direct influence of physical environment, but through the different contacts that each area has made with its neighbors. In Munich my broadest Austrian dialect could be understood, but in Hamburg the people on the streets spoke a type of *Plattdeutsch* of which I could make nothing. In dialect, in folk custom, in general orientation (including religion) the South Bavarian is incomparably closer to the Austrian than to the Hanseat. A traveler who scans the daily papers is sure to discover that Hamburg is definitely in the Anglo-Saxon culture sphere. That summer I went as far east as Budapest, and it was interesting to note how the "typical" German traits petered out, almost mile by mile, and those of an oriental nature began to appear.

It is often not even necessary to travel. Not long ago I became interested in reading about certain attitudes in Russia, and I was struck by the similarity of the underlying psychology to that of the Hopi and of certain other Indian groups. In all cases, it was a matter of values. Among the Hopi, government officials have long recognized a "friendly" or "progressive" faction and a "hostile" faction. Many in the latter group do not reject all the useful things brought in by white people; they merely attach a low value to them and subordinate them to aboriginal values. Dorothy Eggan, whose contacts with these pueblos have been exceptionally close, reports, for instance, the remarks of an old man who told her: "I pity you and I don't envy you. You have more goods than we have, but you don't have peace ever. It is better to die in famine than in war." Other Hopi groups have been receptive to the white man's values as well as to his ways, and the clashes between the antithetical tendencies have caused much dissension. Or again, similar dual reactions appeared whenever an Indian prophet set himself up as a messiah to lead his people back to their ancestral ways. Although some of the tribesmen were captivated by the prophet, others continued to accept the white man's inventions and additions, with resulting dissension. The conflicts of which I read between the Russian Slavophiles and the groups in favor of transplanting Western civilization in Russia reminded me strongly of the above mentioned cases. Dostoevski and his friend Pobedonostsev, Procurator of the Holy Synod, did not deny the technical advantages enjoyed by Western peoples, but by their own scale neither industrialization nor its sociopolitical concomitants had the slightest value. What did they signify as compared with the fathomless depths of the Russian soul? Beside Holy Russia, the effete West, which men like Turgenev wanted their countrymen to emulate, was a pitiable phenomenon.

Still another parallel appears in nineteenth-century Japan. The polar antithesis just noted can be traced in the reports of European visitors for the period when foreigners were first welcomed. From Ernest Satow, a British diplomat, we learn that from 1864 to 1868 nativists repeatedly ran amok and slew foreigners in protest against their admission. If condemned to execution by their own government for fear of punitive measures by the European power involved, these patriots would indulge in high-flown bravado: "Though reproaches may be cast upon me, those who can fathom the depths of a warrior's heart will appreciate my motives." "I do not regret being taken and put to death, for to kill barbarians is the true spirit of a Japanese." Newspapers of the time deprecated the Mikado's granting audiences to the European diplomats.

A. M. Mitford, second secretary to the British Legation, who witnessed hara-kiri in 1868, narrates that the Japanese parliament of the following year, by the overwhelming majority of 200 out of 209, voted to preserve self-disembowelment, which subversive innovators were trying to abolish. In the debate the ancient custom was grandiloquently eulogized as "a pillar of religion and a spur to virtue," as "the very shrine of the Japanese national spirit and the embodiment in practice of devotion to principle."

In the diaries and letters of Erwin Baelz, a German doctor who was called to a professorship of internal medicine in Tokyo in 1876 and who married a Japanese lady, the fluctuating sentiments of the Japanese public appear very clearly. As a newcomer, he found many tone-setting Japanese ashamed of their past; ancient sports like jujitsu and archery had fallen into desuetude; there was widespread aping of European dress; intellectuals read John Stuart Mill and asked the advice of Herbert Spencer; some even advocated a republican form of government. But within fifteen or twenty years Baelz noted a marked change, which was fostered by the successful war against China. Thereafter there set in a deliberate restoration of indigenous ways.

For the ethnologist the data from Russia, Japan, the Hopi, and the messianic cults are all of a piece. He sees in them the independent development of contrasting attitudes arising from similar conditions, the pitting of new values against old. Such investigations of higher cultures prove especially rewarding because the material from literate peoples is likely to be ampler and can usually be dated. These insights come to the ethnologist because he is already familiar with such problems through his study of simpler peoples; he sees what the specialist in the area may miss. Hence, his busman's holidays can prove profitable, increasing as they can his understanding of the unity of culture; they may also be of equal profit to others.

CHAPTER 9

FIELD
WORK IN
ABSENTIA

Undoubtedly the least strenuous of my "field trips" were those that lead me into developing an interest in certain primitive tribes in Brazil. All my share of the work was done at home, comfortably seated before a desk of mammoth proportions.

As early as 1925 the late Baron Erland Nordensköld told me something of a certain Nimuendajú in Belém de Pará and praised him as an acute observer of native customs. "Nimuendajú" was a name given him by natives and invariably used by him. He was a German named Kurt Onkel, who had spent most of his adult life in Brazil, except for a year's study in Sweden at Uppsala. His formal training was meagre, but his natural talents were exceptional. In 1925 I had no interest in South America, so I merely filed this odd name away among my neurons, where it lay for a decade, until Karl G. Izikowitz, a student of Baron Nordenskiöld's, asked me if something could not be done for Nimuendajú, who, ultimately, wrote me a letter himself and sent a sample manuscript. In 1935 I was able to get him a grant for field work from the Institute of Social Sciences of the University of California and to have this renewed for a number of years, sometimes eked out or superseded by grants from other institutions or foundations. I also translated his reports and arranged for their publication. In this way I unexpectedly found myself "in business" in Brazil, although the actual sweating was done by an alter ego.

The close association lasted for a decade, until Nimuendajú's death at the end of the Second World War. We wrote each other regularly, interrupting our communications only when he was in the field. For the first six years we wrote in German, and he sent his manuscripts in that language, but the outbreak of the war introduced difficulties, because all letters in German were held up by the censors. So we had to pursue a roundabout method of communication, which slowed our joint work and maintained a constant and irritating state of confusion. He wrote to me in Portuguese, through which I waded with the aid of a dictionary; and I wrote to him in English, through which he had to plod in similar fashion. His last manuscript was also written in Portuguese. Although I could extract some meaning from a short letter in the language, I knew I could do nothing with two hundred and fifty pages of manuscript. It therefore just had to wait for translation until one of my students, William D. Hohenthal, returned from his army service. He had spent much of his childhood in Brazil and had a thorough knowledge of Portuguese.

During our decade of joint research, Nimuendajú visited or revisited a number of Gê tribes, notably the Apinayé, the Šerénte, and the Timbira, and later on, the non-Gê Tukuna. His last trip to them was made against his doctor's advice, and he died, fittingly enough, among the Tukuna. His work was widely appreciated in the United States. His report on the Apinayé was published by the Catholic University (1939), his Šerénte monograph by the Frederick Webb Hodge Anniversary Fund (1942), and the remaining two by the University of California Press (1946 and 1952).

The extraordinary accuracy of Nimuendajú's observations, which revealed unexpected phenomena in the sociological and religious culture of South American tribes, stimulated me into producing a number of brief papers setting forth the theoretical import of his work for the reconstruction of American culture history or for the problems of culture growth generally. The point I especially emphasized was the remarkable tendency of the simple Gê tribes to strike out along independent paths from an obviously common cultural base.

In order to give some faint idea of the abilities of Nimuendajú and of the wide range of problems with which we dealt, I am inserting a few excerpts from interchanges of our letters. Some of his better efforts occupied six to ten single spaced pages. When I asked him a simple question, I received practically a master's thesis in reply. Sometimes it seemed to me unfair that I should be sitting comfortably at home while he was going up dangerous rivers, plodding through tropical forests, or fruitlessly visiting tribes that had been almost wiped out by epidemics of measles. But he asked nothing better than to go among the Indians; all he wanted out of life was enough financial support to make his journeys. I could guide him to some extent, since I had had more formal training; and I could interpret his results, adding comparisons with data from other regions. I consider my own difficulties of travel as nothing in comparison to his.

From Nimuendajú to R. H. Lowie, October 5, 1936

Day before yesterday I finally got back to Belém do Pará. I certainly hope that it will not be necessary any more to wait for weeks in the state of Maranhao for motorboats, trucks, railroad trains, and steamboats. It would really have been better if these things did not exist. Then one could depend upon rowboats and pack animals and would reach one's goal sooner. However, in spite of the great loss of time, I did have a bit of luck. I had hardly left Maranhao when a little revolution broke out there, and if that had happened while I was there I would still be stuck fast in Maranhao. . . .

In December I will begin to make preparations for the trip to the Šerénte, that I must visit in January, so that I can travel on the Tocantins River while it is at low water. Then the danger from the swift current is at a minimum, and I would not like to lose my luggage and equipment before I even reach my working fields.

You understand that . . . it is not possible to have money or goods sent into the field after me, nor can I return for new equipment, if the supplies I take with me from Belém become exhausted. It is therefore absolutely essential that I should have the means well before the beginning of the journey for buying what I shall need. It would be best to send two checks for $500 each and one for $200, but of course I don't know if this would be administratively possible.

I am asking you once again to call my attention to any shortcomings in my methods of work to date and tell me how I can improve them; also that you should look again at the list of relationships among the Šerénte and tell me if there are lacunae or items that are not clear.

From R. H. Lowie to Nimuendajú, October 21, 1936

I received with great joy your letter telling me that in spite of all obstructions you were safely back in Belém, and that you are ready to undertake the difficult trip to the Šerénte.

Today I can write only briefly, but I want to tell you first that I have persuaded the administration to send you the first check for $500 at once. The balance I shall, if possible, send in accordance with your suggestion. When must the third check leave here, in order to reach you in time?

For some time I have wanted to ask you a question: whether you have the chance—aside from your collection of origin legends—to collect myths. The legends from Tierra del Fuego by Koppers and Gusinde contain some extremely remarkable parallels to North American, and even Californian, episodes, which naturally tempts one into finding further parallels. Also I should like to ask for information about the original housetype of the Ramkókamekra. If I have understood the matter correctly, you consider the square houses as neo-Brazilian loans. How did the Ramkokámekra live in earlier times, especially during the rainy seasons?

Now as to the table of relationships among the Šerénte. I believe that the diagrams that you recently constructed certainly help one to an understanding. I should like to suggest first the splitting of the designations of relationships into two parts (a) blood relationships and (b) relationships by marriage. In this way I can mark what does not fit. [Here follows some technical material.] In this way the total picture of the separate items will appear, and then will arise the usual questions, for instance: Why is the child of the father's brother reckoned as a brother? Has it something to do with the livirate? and so on.

In your list for the Šerénte it strikes me that there are two inconsistencies. Namely: that the children of the mother's sister are called i-zdekwa and i-pna but *also* i-kumre and i-nori. If it is remarkable in and of itself that the children of the mother's sister are otherwise indicated than the children of the father's brother, then it is obvious that i-nori and i-kumre are correlative concepts that complement each other. It is also puzzling in what relationship the pair of terms i-zdekwa and i-pna stand to the other pair, i-nori and i-kumre.

Extremely interesting also is the cutting across of generations in the case of cross-cousins. In North America the equation of mother's-brother's-son equals mother's brother appears primarily, if not exclusively, among tribes with patrilineal descent, such as the Omaha. But it is different from the North American parallels that also the corresponding aunt should be reckoned as a mother.

It is remarkable that the wife of the father's brother is equated to the mother, but in spite of this, the children of the brother-in-law are not considered as son and daughter. One would expect at least a restrictive suffix, as exists in the case of the nephew of the mother's sister. The same point applies naturally to the nephew of the husband of the mother's sister; if this man counts as a father, then is there a special word for the nephew instead of the usual indication for a son?

I certainly do not wish by these remarks to cast doubts upon your sketch, because I know that complete consistency hardly ever appears. However, there is always the possibility of a misunderstanding, as I know well from my own experiences.

From Nimuendajú to R. H. Lowie, November 30, 1936

I was not able to determine the type of original rainy season house among the Ramkókamekra. The Indians always insisted that they had from long ago lived in square, gabled houses, just as they do today. This is possibly right, but I hardly believe it. Even yet round temporary houses are built that generally have the form of half a ball or half an egg. The diameter is about nine and a half feet. There are neither materials nor skill for making them any larger. The women build them. In spite of what they say, the Ramkókamekra must once have built much larger houses because, as you know from my sociological data, community houses for celebrations or age classes played an important role among them. In 1933 the Western age-class consisted of 57 men, and earlier it was certainly not smaller. It is out of the question that such a number of men could get into one of the dome-shaped huts of today. . . . The Eastern Bororó whom von den Steinen visited in 1888 . . . already had square gabled houses. It is therefore not surprising that the Ramkókamekra . . . cannot today remember the old form of their big houses. Major Francisco de Paula Ribiero speaks to be sure of the little round houses, but perhaps he never saw a rainy season community. The question must therefore remain open.

From R. H. Lowie to Nimuendajú, October 11, 1937

As far as religion is concerned, I am trying to put the matter in order for myself, so I am asking you a question: How does the native behave in a crisis, such as a serious illness or when he is passionately striving for some particular outcome? . . . Among my Crow Indians, almost every human problem was solved by means of a vision. The Trobriand Islander in New Guinea use[s] mainly magic formulae. The Bantu makes an offering to his ancestors, and so on. For a similar point of view it would perhaps be easiest for you to explain briefly to me how your Gê Indians behave in the face of serious illness.

One special question: Do you have the impression that among the Tupí a medium is possessed by a spirit in a literal sense, so that, for instance, the spirit itself speaks from the mouth of the medium? In North America this sort of thing occurs rarely . . . Many field workers doubt an actual possession. Therefore the facts from South America would be important.

When you speak of the Gê "stone-cooking" should this not be equated in meaning to Tylor's "stone-boiling"? (when, for example, heated stones are dropped into a water-filled vessel or a watertight basket, in order to boil food)

Or does your term refer only to the use of stones in an earth oven? Or am I completely mistaken?

From Nimuendajú to R. H. Lowie, October 20, 1937

I want to answer immediately your letter of October 11th, which I received yesterday.

1. How the Gê behave when they have a serious illness:

a) The Ramkókamekra. These Indians always try under such circumstances to make contact with the souls of their dead relatives. Not with the souls of their ancestors in general but with the souls of particular individuals whom they knew personally and in whom, when alive, they had confidence. . . . I myself saw a sick man go into a sort of seclusion hut, so that the souls of the dead could appear and help him, for the condition of seclusion makes it easier for the souls to approach.

b) The Apinayé, with their theory that all illness is caused by the "shades" of plants or animals which have served the sick man as food and have thus gotten into the body, seek first to determine the hidden cause of the illness through the pulse rate or through external symptoms (a fast pulse betokens a deer; a slow one, a turtle, etc.). Then they seek through the plant kingdom for a specific that can be considered as having some external similarity to the cause of the illness (against a deer's shadow, one uses a decoction of the root of a plant, the fruits of which look like the horns of a deer). From this therapeutic theory they depart only if they believe it is a matter of some person bewitching the sick man.

c) Among the Šerénte, visions seem to stand in the foreground, less for the healing of illness from case to case than for the obtaining of a general magic power to prevent natural phenomena such as eclipses of the sun, drought, floods, etc. I have never heard or seen anything among the Šerénte about seeking help from the souls of the dead in a case of serious illness. One Indian told me that he had died twice, but each time the planet Jupiter, his protector, had taken him by his hand and brought him back again.

2. Possession occurs undoubtedly oftener than the usual form of traffic with dead souls, as among the Ramkókamekra. Among the Palikur the demons not only take possession of the body of the medicine man, but also the demons of animal go into certain carved wooden benches and are there treated with hospitality. Among the Mura I saw the medicine man as he was treating a sick man first fall into a sleeplike condition, then rise suddenly, and give with a changed voice the directions for the medicine to be used, whereat he sank down again. It was very clear that it was not himself speaking in a dream but a trusted demon who spoke through him, and so those present understood the matter.

3. Stone-cooking: I have used "cook" in the sense of preparing food. It is not only steamed by means of stones in earth ovens but I have myself seen how the natives make a hole in the bank of a brook, in which they let water gather; then they line the hole with leaves and make the water hot by dropping in hot

stones from a nearby fire. Further, I have been told that in earlier times the women cooked with hot stones in their wooden mortars. On the other hand, woven baskets seem never to have been so used.

And so it went—question and answer—for nearly ten years. Then Nimuendajú went to the Tukuna and died among them. But characteristically, he first wrote up his notes.

My acquaintance with Baron Nordenskiöld led to another successful bit of promoting. When I was in Sweden in 1924, he and Paul Rivet had told me of a handbook of South American Indians which they had in mind as a joint venture. This idea did not result in anything definite, however. In 1932, when hard put to it to justify to my conscience my salary as Chairman of the Division of Anthropology and Psychology of the National Research Council, I proposed that the Council foster a handbook of the kind Nordenskiöld and Rivet had suggested. I even asked Nordenskiöld to edit it, and although he agreed to do so, he died before any definite plans could be made. For years nothing whatever happened, except that the Division continued to appoint a committee to consider the project. During this latent period, the Smithsonian Institution assumed leadership and moral sponsorship, but there were no funds available from any source; so the whole plan lay fallow and showed no signs of sprouting. However, when Latin-American relations assumed political importance, the United States Congress was persuaded to make an appropriation, and the Department of State actually came to take a lively interest in the work as tending to promote pan-American amity. Julian H. Steward of the Smithsonian Institution, one of my former students and also one of Nordenskiöld's during the Baron's semester with the Department in California, became the editor of what turned out to be an impressive six-volume handbook.

In the fall semester of 1941, since I had to be in the east for summer school teaching at Columbia and again in late September in order to receive an honorary degree from the University of Chicago, I arranged to take a leave of absence and to work in Washington until early January, 1942. I then planned to visit Mexico for about six weeks. Many of my colleagues and former students were in love *jusqu' à la folie* with this country, and I wanted to find out why. In Washington I worked with Julian

Steward and Alfred Métraux on plans for the handbook and wrote certain sections of it. This pleasant interlude came to an abrupt end on December 7, 1941. I lingered on in Washington until the day after Christmas, finishing my commitments there. Since our tickets were already arranged for return by the southern route, we substituted a week's stopover in New Orleans for our intended jaunt to Mexico. I still do not know of my own experience, as the lawyers say, wherein lies the lure of our neighbor to the south.

This chapter has presented two accounts of good teamwork, although most of it was unplanned. Nimuendajú and I found each other by sheer accident, but we made a good team, partly because each excelled precisely where the other was weakest and partly because of our common German heritage and our common thirst for facts and objective proofs. In "Operation Handbook" each of us contributed something, and each of us carried the ball a few yards farther toward our goal. I was in the midst of the effort only at the beginning and toward the end, being thoroughly content to spend most of the time on the fringes. The main result to me of these two undertakings in absentee research in South America was to distract my attention from work I should have been doing among the Plains Indians in North America. The Brazilian interlude was intensely interesting to me, but whether or not this deflection, from what my wife, who was brought up on *Pilgrim's Progress,* would undoubtedly call the straight and narrow way, was justified, only the future can tell.

CHAPTER 10

SUCCESS
AND FAILURE
IN WRITING

In the course of the last forty years I have produced ten books of various types in the field of anthropology. Their fate, both financially and professionally, will never cease to surprise, annoy, and bewilder me. I would like to characterize these books briefly, because they are reflections of the period almost as much as of my own thought. Also, some of them have been criticized for not being what they were never intended to be, and I should like to put the record straight. Any young anthropologist who is planning to write a book might well take to heart the lessons that may be deduced from my efforts at authorship. For want of a better plan, I will discuss the books in chronological order.

Culture and Ethnology.—In the days when I was at the American Museum of Natural History, the Department of Anthropology gave a course of popular lectures each winter. In 1917 I gave the series, choosing as my topics, "Culture and Psychology," "Culture and Race," "Culture and Environment," and "The Determinants of Culture." During the preparation for these maiden efforts at lecturing, my abysmal ignorance was forceably brought home to me, for instead of having at my fingertips a number of appropriate illustrations for ideas that I shared with everyone else, I had to search high and low for suitable material. In the first three lectures, I at least knew what I wanted to prove; but when I came to the fourth I was a bit flabbergasted to discover that I did not even know what the determinants were, and it required a long talk with Pliny Goddard to clarify my notions sufficiently to make "diffusion" the hero of the plot. Also, feeling that prehistory ought not to be wholly neglected, I read an article by Oscar Montelius and peeped into Hugo Obermaier.

Believing fervently that I was aiding the work of popular enlightenment, I spoke forcibly and found a responsive audience. Elsie Clews Parsons, I remember, appeared at the lectures. By chance I saw a letter of hers to another staff member, in which she wrote, "Didn't Lowie do well?" By leaning heavily on Berthold Laufer's writings on Asia I even conveyed a sense of wide ethnographic knowledge, which was certainly far from the truth.

Wissler strongly—and, as it proved, wisely—advised me to publish the lectures, even at my own expense if necessary. In order to make the material long enough for even a little book, I was obliged to double its length by throwing in an extra chapter, for which I chose the subject that most interested me at the moment, "Terms of Relationship." This addition was not exactly felicitous; it was far more technical than the other essays, and was in subject matter quite out of keeping with the first four sections.

Having some personal contacts with Douglas C. McMurtrie, the printer, who also did a little publishing, I got him to undertake the job, assuming part of the costs myself. He did a very nice piece of typography and binding, but he had no facilities for publicity, and presently he got into financial difficulties of his own. As a result, I temporarily took over what remained of the edition and ultimately turned it over to Boni and Liveright, losing several hundred dollars on the whole transaction.

Nevertheless, *Culture and Ethnology* gave me a certain prestige when I arrived on the Berkeley campus in the fall of 1917. Professor Henry Morse Stephens, still a power at the University, was favorably impressed by it—as well as by my knowledge of Gilbert and Sullivan operas. When, some months later, he became one of three rulers of the University, he strongly urged me to accept permanent appointment, which, however, I declined. I also refused a call to the University of Washington from President Suzzalo, who was doubtless aided and abetted by my good friend Will Ogburn, at that time his righthand man. Of course, I did not know then that the Museum was planning to drop me.

In view of its lopsidedness, if nothing else, the welcome given my little book was very strange. The reason must have been that the problems dealt with are vital and that from sheer ignorance I presented them in extremely simple form. Further, except for Franz Boas' *Mind of Primitive Man* there was at the time no book that expounded the methods of American field workers. Among the blind, the one-eyed is king; but I hope it is not true, as some of my friends have told me, that *Culture and Ethnology* is the best book I have ever written. There is certainly no reason why it should be and quite a number why it should not.

Primitive Society.—This book, in spite of various defects, which will presently be pointed out, will remain forever green in my memory, because it was the first one that ever earned me any money—not a great deal, of course, but enough to pay for a European trip. Since its publication in 1920, nearly seven thousand copies have been sold (exceeding Wissler's initial guess by two thousand). There was a British edition not long after the American; the rights to publish a Japanese version were granted some years ago, with what results I do not know; and as late as 1935 Payot in Paris still found it worth while to issue a French translation.

The reception accorded the book on its appearance was on the whole gratifying and encouraging. The two most authoritative reviews in English were, to be sure, less so. Kroeber, then still in his psychoanalytic period, found the book honest and sound, but unilluminating; and W. H. R. Rivers chided me for its lack of diffusionist fervor. But other critics were more appreciative. Boas almost knocked me over by telling me, "I think you've written an awfully good book." Edward Sapir—not sparing of criticism in other comments on my publications—wrote that he was "fairly enthusiastic" about it. Elsie Clews Parsons printed a highly favorable review in the *New Republic*. Father Schmidt paid his respects in *Anthropos*, wrote me in even more complimentary terms, and suggested a German translation which, however, the Austrian financial situation rendered impossible. Wissler orally called it a great book, E. A. Goldenweiser a "good" one—with his customary reservation as to my work, which he honestly assigned to a lower plane than his own, Paul Radin's, or Sapir's. J. L. Giddings soon cited me with approval in his Columbia lectures and in some of his publications. Chief Justice Oliver Wendell Holmes also had something to say. He wrote: "Recently I read Lowie's work on *Primitive Society* with unqualified admiration. It seemed to me to unite an extraordinary way practical experience, learning, and insight, and so far as one not a specialist on the subject could judge, to represent a most characteristically modern and real advance from earlier and too easy generalizations. The book convinced me at once that Mr. Lowie is a real force in the present world of thought." In short, I woke up one morning to find that I had become a small celebrity.

Years later Father J. L. Cooper gave the book unremitting praise in issues of *Primitive Man,* calling it "our best study of social culture" and a "masterpiece." He wrote further: "Thoroughness, sanity, cautious interpretation, closeness to factual evidence, and discriminating judgment mark every page." In another context he refers to the book as a "classic study of facts and interpretation of sib organization." It was also credited with being "one of the best treatments in English of the status of women in primitive society." In discussing Hilde Thurnwald's *Die menschliche Gesellschaft,* Cooper says that it is in a sense indispensable "but, while much more voluminous than Lowie's *Primitive Society,* appears to fall short in many respects as regards interpretation." Writing on the early history of the family, he remarks: "The casual reader is impressed by Westermarck's and Briffault's enormous three-volume works. In reality there is more real science at the back of the one-chapter treatment by Lowie than in all of Westermarck's or Briffault's *opera magna.*" Certainly, no author could possibly ask for more.

All of the above remarks convincingly proved to me that the fate of a book depends largely upon the circumstances of its appearance. The circumstances that led to the publication of this particular book are the following. In my early postgraduate days I was as yet little interested in social organization, least of all in its technical aspects, which I gladly left to Goldenweiser. As late as about 1911 I had to ask his advice about recording kinship terms, and my first exposition of the subject in the "Social Life of the Crow Indians" (1912)—apart from actual errors—was certainly no model. In January, 1914, I gave two lectures on social organization at the American Museum of Natural History, which were published soon after in *The American Journal of Sociology,* but I was mainly interested in popularizing the "American" point of view in ethnology rather than in the specific phenomena of social structure. The paper however involved a critique of Lewis H. Morgan. And at about the same time I broached similar views in popular articles and lectures. But to consider myself in any sense a specialist in this field was wholly outside my thought. Theoretically, I was still absorbed in Plains Indian military associations and, more generally, ceremonialism. It was W. H. R. Rivers' *Kinship and Social Organization* that first made me attack relevant problems in a serious way, as witnessed by my article on "Exogamy and the Classificatory Systems of Relationship" in the *American Anthropologist* (1916), and the paper on "Historical and Sociological Interpretations of Kinship Terminologies," which I contributed to the Holmes Anniversary Volume (1916). Fired by Rivers' theories, I began pestering my colleagues with queries about kinship lines, with the result that a good deal of material was collected in what for many years had become a neglected field in this country.

By 1917, when I became Visiting Associate Professor at the University of California, I had developed sufficient interest in the wider ramifications of the subject to offer a one semester course on "Primitive Society." On my return to New York I conceived the idea of a book based on the systematization of the ideas inevitable in such a series of lectures. I was beginning in the spring of 1919, in a very leisurely fashion, to write the first chapter on "Marriage" and decided to ask Elsie Clews Parsons to use her good offices with Putnam's, who had published some of her writings. It was then that Harold Stearns pounced on me with the proposal to do a book for Horace Liveright, whose secretary was Stearns' fiancée—later, his wife—Alice McDougall. I met Liveright and soon had a contract and an advance on royalties. But I was to deliver the manuscript in four months! I worked feverishly all summer and in the fall delivered the manuscript a week or so in advance of the deadline—somewhat to Liveright's astonishment, I think. The book appeared a few months later.

These circumstances explain a number of facts. In the first place, the smoothness of the exposition and the style were bound to suffer from my haste. Second, having given the corresponding course only once, I was most inadequately aware of all the difficulties that confront the student—let alone, the general reader— who first attacks that knottiest of departments in ethnology, social organization. More important, I was lamentably unprepared. Museum experience had, indeed, enlarged my ethnographic horizon, but along other than sociological lines. My ignorance, then, remained crass. That single term of teaching in California had been wholly insufficient to remedy it. What is more, even gaining a comprehensive general survey of the main areas of the world was not at all easy in 1919. Most of the works to which I would now go had not yet been published. For some notion of Polynesian political life, for instance, in its regionally varying forms, I had to go back to Waitz-Gerland (1872)! There simply was not time to do all the dirty work required, and modern *Vorarbeiten* were completely lacking.

Equally disastrous was my unfamiliarity with more than a few of the obvious topics. I knew the status of the clan and kinship controversy, of course; and my study of Plains Indians had precipitated some investigation of associations. But now I had to deal with all sorts of problems—the sexual division of labor, property, law, government. Moreover, having always had an aversion to reading general books (though not to writing them) and a horror of sociology proper, I was further handicapped through ignorance of the positions taken by my predecessors. This, too, was not a situation curable in four months, even if I did for the first time make the acquaintance of Sir Henry Maine.

In view of these autobiographical conditions the comparative success of my volume would be unintelligible if the course of scientific progress were not as irrational as all history. The point simply is that there had not been any modern work by a trained ethnographer that surveyed the facts of comparative sociology.

In other words, I happened to be the first to apply the critical anti-evolutionist position of American ethnologists not merely to the clan problem in North America, as John R. Swanton had already done years before, but in principle, at least, to all phases of social organization and to the entire world, which implied a survey of both the kin groups dealt with by Morgan in 1877 and the associations treated by Heinrich Schurtz in 1902. The volume thus became a convenient text and also a convenient work of reference for sociologists, jurists, and other social scientists. Crystallizing views widely held, though not yet generally expressed in print, on the family, clan, castes, and so forth, *Primitive Society* acquired typical value even for the Socialist adherents of Morgan, who at once raised me to the proud eminence of a sort of anti-Christ.

From the foregoing remarks it is clear that I am not a one-sided admirer of this strange book. Unfortunately the rapid publication of the French translation prevented a thorough revision: I was able to correct only a few positive errors and to include a lecture on the family, delivered in 1932. In the preface to that edition I outlined a proposed revision. There ought to be a series of vividly sketched samples of social organization; there should be an indefinite number of demonstrated correlations; and there should be a historical reconstruction for each major area. Correlations are, indeed, already adumbrated in the book, but neither in sufficient number nor with adequate demonstration. Nearly three decades later I got a chance to follow my own advice in the production of a "sequel" to *Primitive Society*.

Primitive Religion.—My next book, *Primitive Religion,* met with a cold reception and I doubt whether it has exerted any influence. Several colleagues—C. C. Uhlenbeck, Elsie Clews Parsons, Father Schmidt—printed nice things about it; R. R. Marett wrote me a highly appreciative letter; and Leslie Spier expressed his satisfaction orally. But all Boas had to tell me was that the best chapter was that on "Individual Variability"; and the American super-intelligentsia—Goldenweiser, Radin, Benedict, Sapir—had already decreed years before that I was devoid of imagination, hence incapable of dealing with the religious consciousness. Archbishop

Söderblom of Sweden has, indeed, expressed the reverse statement about my discussion of Crow religion; nor did Father Schmidt ever urge this particular criticism.

Actually, the book marked a revolution in my general outlook. Advancing beyond my earlier eighteenth-century rationalism, I had come to view sincere believers with sympathy, although not receding an inch from my own freethinking. I thus came to call for a reëxamination of "liberal" dogmas and specifically challenged the axiom that liberals must support the state against the church. I asked "whether the perverse adoration of brute force is a preferable substitute for a faith and a Church never wholly devoid of spiritual elements." There may be equally tolerant freethinking anthropologists, but I have not met them. I recall Boas' declining to contribute to *Anthropos,* Laufer's refusal to vote for a Catholic, Radin's recent relapse into the most naïve explanation of religion on the basis of economic interest. However, the point is not what the book signified in my mental progress to a serene attitude toward human faith, but what it contributed to an understanding of religion by others. This is a matter on which I am still not at all clear.

I am, however, certain that the book includes discussion of certain topics that had been greatly neglected in previous works. In fact, even raw data was lamentably scarce. I asked Boas, I wrote Sapir, for reports of visionary experiences from the Northwest Coast. They had none to offer. I scanned Radin's monograph on the Winnebago and was astonished at how few firsthand statements it contained. I tried to avoid emphasis on my own work, but I was in the end driven to using Crow records almost exclusively, for the simple reason that I could find no others.

The aspect of religion that required emphasis, because so little was known about it, was the psychological one. Had I kept abreast of psychological studies, including those on personality, I should have been more successful—and my distaste for psychoanalytical literature was doubtless carried too far. However, I did analyze the meager material on the Ghost Dance and indicated that there was a whole gamut of religious responses there expressed, showing also that "leadership" itself hinged upon an interplay of subjective and social conditions.

In short, I was hampered by both my individual ignorance and by the state of ethnographic knowledge on the more elusive facets of native mentality. But I approached the psychological phenomena of religion as a scientist, frequently unable to give solutions but propounding questions rarely if ever asked before, yet capable of being answered in the future. Here, then, was the core of my book. Naturally, those to whom the subject matter of religion offers only exercise for dialectics or vague literary pronouncements cannot but scorn the mentality that regards subjective manifestations objectively and tries to define them in intelligible terms. However contemptuous these critics may be of my position, I feel that they cannot possibly approach my contempt for theirs.

Primitive Religion, which unlike its predecessor expressed not the "American school" but myself, left little impression—so far as I can see. However, it was in sufficient demand to warrant a revised edition in 1948. [This book was also published as a paperback in 1958.] It was certainly a much better written book than *Primitive Society.*

The Origin of the State.—Naturally I did not lose my interest in the subject of primitive society after the publication of my book, and when I became acquainted with Oppenheimer's work I felt impelled to formulate anew my ideas on the origin of the state. Because of my friendly relations with *The Freeman,* I wrote an article for it in 1922 on that subject, utilizing certain African data that seemed especially suggestive. The essay continued to be quoted, but was soon out of print, so that I was tempted to enlarge it and to offer it to Harcourt, who published it as a small volume in 1927.

Being essentially an appendix to *Primitive Society,* this booklet was unsuited for use as an independent text, and the sales were small. Since I had received seventy-five dollars from *The Freeman* and a honorarium of, I think, fifty dollars at Michigan for a lecture on the subject, I probably was not out of pocket in the end. From a noncommercial angle, however, *The Origin of the State* was successful, especially with social scientists outside of anthropology. Harold Laski wrote a highly appreciative review in *The Nation,* as did Harold Lasswell in the *American Anthropologist.* The small edition was soon exhausted, and copies have become a rarity. Sporadically I am asked where they can be secured, but the sales do not encourage the publisher to venture a second printing.

Are We Civilized?—Since my experience at the American Museum of Natural History, which discharged me with a two years' notice, I intensely resented the idea of dependence on institutions. Before the depression set in, a number of writers had made money by writing popular books. I was confident of my ability to do likewise and once more felt the urge to appear as an *Aufklärer*. The result was *Are We Civilized?*, which Alfred Harcourt published in 1929. He was very enthusiastic about the manuscript, but for some reason lost all interest after publication, so that there was a minimum of advertising, and the sales remained relatively low. Incidentally, the pessimism that disturbed some readers has since been amply justified by subsequent events in Europe. For years the book remained out of print. In 1937 a teacher in Hunter College, where it was used for collateral reading, persuaded Harcourt to reprint it in a cheap edition. The first half year about one thousand copies were sold, but since then—with secondhand ones becoming available—the annual sales have dropped to half that figure. However, the book continues to sell in small quantities.

A characteristic feature of the book—apart from its critique of the Nordic myth—is the critical attitude toward scientists themselves as subject to irrational impulses. As compared with my earlier writings, it shows a more intensive concern with the culture history of Europe. I utilized especially Alfred Franklin's volumes on France and T. F. Troels-Lund's work on Scandinavia. The style was certainly at the opposite pole from the ponderousness of *Primitive Society*.

The reception of this book varied, especially among anthropologists. Boas, surprisingly, told me it was a very good book; Elsie Clews Parsons approved of this inculcation of the comparative method with modern examples; and several younger colleagues found the examples fresh and in part piquant. Berthold Laufer's review in the *American Anthropologist* was all I could have wished in my wildest dreams: "It is at once the production of mature scholarship coupled with wide reading and keen thinking, and more than that—it is the book of a man of culture and a philosopher who has seen and observed much of life and who has his own ideas about men, things, and events. Besides, he is an eminent teacher, and he is amply endowed with that faculty which makes the real scholar, but which is growing rarer and rarer among modern scholars—the faculty of thinking objectively, without bias, without newspaper and mob psychology. . . . As an introduction into modern anthropological thought, as a guide into the workshop of a clear-minded and honest thinker, this book is excellent . . ."

However, A. M. Tozzer wrote me the book, although perhaps useful for "pepping up" introductory courses, was not equal to my previous books—as though its aim were at all comparable! Others, like Leslie Spier, thought it a waste of time to write such a book; and Radin was scornful on general principles, not being on particularly good terms with me at the moment.

In any case, the book did not put me in a more secure financial position, and altogether I doubt whether it netted me five hundred dollars over the expenses for typing.

Introduction to Cultural Anthropology.—Nothing, I have always felt, was more detrimental to my anthropological education than the lack in my graduate years of any up-to-date summary of the elements of culture history in a systematic topical survey. Boas could have supplied the need but never dreamed of doing so, even in his lectures; it was only in his eightieth year that *General Anthropology* appeared under his editorship, and even then there were eight collaborators. In my student days there was no good, topical treatise outside of Tylor's *Anthropology,* which was by then out of date.

In 1933 there was still no treatment that would have suited my needs in my student days. A decade earlier Kroeber had published his *Anthropology,* but he had made no effort to make it a systematic survey; rather, he had selected topics on which he could hang illuminating discussions of principles. For our elementary class in Berkeley, this type of organization was no particular handicap, for the lectures gave precisely the topical exposition that the book lacked. Elsewhere, however, teachers were at times perplexed because of the lack of system, as I was told on several occasions. This text, although excellent of its kind, did not provide the systematic exposition that I had craved as a student.

My ever-smouldering resentment at Boas's failure to provide that solid basis of elementary fact, without which all one's ideas must be awry, no matter how one may advance knowledge in particular directions, was bound to precipitate a prophylactic text for the young—one that would, as stated in my preface, forestall "wasteful confusion" and "needless floundering." James van Toor, who had just become head of Farrar and Rinehart's college department, wanted such a book as I had envisioned for years, and a contract was soon arranged. This text has proved the one financially successful book I have ever published. Since the fall of 1934, when it appeared, nearly ten thousand copies have been sold in America; there has been an English edition; and in 1936 Payot published a French translation prepared by Rhoda Métraux, under the title, *Manuel d'anthropologie culturelle*.

A revision appeared a few years later, as a result of comments secured by Farrar and Rinehart from the users of the text. Of course, there were a number of completely silly suggestions, like the request for a "fuller" treatment of physical anthropology—in a text entitled *Introduction to Cultural Anthropology*, in which there was no treatment of the subject at all. To my great surprise, almost everyone wanted a chapter on language, a topic I had deliberately avoided as too technical for undergraduates. The more sensible of the remaining suggestions fell into two categories. Some teachers were not content with a factual presentation that incidentally brought out the principles of culture growth; they insisted upon an explicit labeling of these principles in a special section on theory. I had purposely kept the theories close to the facts upon which they rested, that being where I thought they belonged, but the teachers evidently either did not notice them or else preferred to have them separated from their basis—for what reason, I cannot imagine. Other users of the text missed the presentation of synthetic sketches of tribal cultures as units. They wanted their students to read such materials, and it was inconvenient to send a large group of students to the library to read selections from, say, G. P. Murdoch's *Our Primitive Contemporaries*. Since students could then buy only one book per course, they wanted a few such sketches in the text itself. These suggestions obviously represented the teaching experience of various people who desired within the covers of a single volume the subject matter for a whole year rather than for a semester. Since my publishers were willing to add two hundred pages or so without any notable increase in cost, I acceded to these wishes. The new edition proved even more successful than the first, presumably because it met the specific needs of those who wanted to use it.

For this book I had a "good press." F. G. Speck and W. F. Ogburn in the United States, Sayce in England, Wilhelm Koppers in Austria published favorable reviews; R. B. Dixon wrote me an appreciative letter, others expressed their satisfaction orally. The *Science News Letter,* for November 17, 1934, said that the text offered "an orderly and clear-cut exposition of essentials" and added: "It is not a 'heavy' book. Casual readers, merely curious to know how the other half of the world lives, will find it full of striking and thought-provoking facts about the human race." I feel that I have done what I set out to do.

The Crow Indians.—My sundry technical publications on the Crow Indians are the basis for my reputation as a field worker. Bronislaw Malinowski told me in 1926 that he rated them above my books; and Wissler in *Man and Culture* cited them with Waldemar Bogoras' *The Chukchee* and two other monographs as exemplifying "approximately complete data" on a tribal culture. William I. Thomas, searching as a sociologist for samples of human behavior, was delighted to find in my paper on Crow military societies what he wanted and strongly urged me to make the material more generally available. Lloyd Warner subsequently impressed upon me the desirability of giving a total picture of the tribe in a compact volume. After my supplementary field trip in 1931 I was powerfully stimulated by some of the new material obtained, and the result was *The Crow Indians* (1935).

The anthropological reviewers of the book were at best halfhearted in their praise. A British reviewer in *Man* found the facts interesting enough, but clearly did not know what to make of a book that tried to describe a people without labeling the account as "functional" or "historical," and this same lack seems to have perplexed a German reviewer in *Anthropos,* although I still do not know what such an orientation has to do with a simple description of a given culture. Wissler in essence said that I had not given a balanced and intimate picture of Crow life; Bernhard J. Stearn in the *New Republic* described the treatment as "conspicuously uneven," though declaring that as a whole it "teems with descriptions of human behavior that will delight and enlighten persons interested in the relativity of morals and customs." A lay review by Florence Finch Kelly in the *New York Times Book Review* was more gratifying. She found the book "a real treat" and continued as follows: ". . . its outstanding virtue is that in simple, lucid style it not only enables the reader to see intimately the colorful daily life of these Indian folk but also throws open the doors into their minds and hearts and souls and reveals their basic quality." There were also several anthropologists who, in letters or by word of mouth, expressed their appreciation—Kroeber and the Spiers, for example. Anna Gayton Spier particularly liked what I myself regarded as perhaps the most noteworthy contribution of this volume—the discussion of literary values. Boas was genuinely pleased by the dedication.

I was not certain, however, whether or not the volume had served its purpose until quite recently. Within the past two years Frederika de Laguna has persuaded my publisher to reprint the book in a paper-bound edition, because she used it regularly as an introductory text for her students and found it better in arousing interest and understanding than any topical discussion. Now that the book is again available, possibly others will find a similar use for it. Financially, it was only a moderate success. I recovered my expenses of production, but am only now (1956) beginning to get a small but regular income from it.

History of Ethnological Theory.—For several years toward the end of my teaching career, I conducted a seminar on this subject, and in 1937 these discussions culminated in a book, which appeared a day or two before Christmas. Actually, I wrote it for the French publisher, Gallimard, with whom Alfred Métraux had connections, and expected it to be translated from my English typescript; but I had reserved the rights of publication in English. However, Gallimard has proved dilatory, so that I still have not seen a translation of the script for correction. Farrar and Rinehart were somewhat dubious about such a venture, since they could not see any "course" in which it would be used as a text. This book has, however, not been a financial failure. It will never make a fortune, but the returns are steady and rather better than I had expected.

The reactions in print have been decidedly encouraging. Alfred C. Haddon wrote me a most cordial letter, which was soon followed by a favorable review in *Nature*. Father J. L. Cooper called the volume the "anthropological book of the year" and wrote a flattering review in the *American Anthropologist*. In the *Journal of Social Philosophy* the sociologist Henry Alpert found it more a series of analytical essays on theorists than a history, but was most complimentary concerning its judgment and taste. Elsie Clews Parsons wrote me that I set "all of us" a model of fairness, except in my treatment of Margaret Mead. C. Daryll Forde was enthusiastic, stressing two points in his letter—the fact that I had for the first time given an intelligible picture of Boas's influence and that I had deflated A. R. Radcliffe-Brown's pretentiousness. Several younger colleagues were wholeheartedly enthusiastic. Boas, characteristically, disliked being limned *in toto* and would not reveal to Elsie Clews Parsons whether he regarded my portrait as a fair likeness, but it was clear that he did not actively dislike anything in it. Equally characteristic was Goldenweiser's reaction. He thought it was a good book, but he clearly preferred the discussion of ideas and theories apart from the men who held them. He also was not happy over my insistence on distinguishing sharply what men did from what men said should be done. As he rightly remarked, his own achievement was not conspicuous in my presentation, but he heartily concurred in the idea that mine was a history of ethnological theory from the ethnographer's point of view.

Radcliffe-Brown wrote me an intemperate, petulant letter. Malinowski, writing about another matter, signed himself "Yours as always," adding in the margin: "And that in spite of the wonderful caricature silhouette drawn of me—which I hugely enjoyed and appreciated. Not so R-B, whose pedestal shook under the blows of the chisel."

My own feeling is that this is my most mature book, formulating the scientific position in ethnology; that it is on the whole eminently fair and wise; and that pages in it attain literary distinction.

Social Organization.—Early in the 1940's there was some talk of getting out a new edition of *Primitive Society,* but I sensed that there was no real enthusiasm for a new edition; Liveright seemed mainly to be tired of telling people that the book was out of print. And I had no greater interest than they had, because the book seemed to me to be "dated" and never to have been as good as some critics said it was. However, I was led to think a bit about the situation, and in the end I decided to write an entirely new book for a different publisher on the same general subject but with a different organization and title, with every chapter written anew, so that there would be no question about an infringement of copyright. I felt that with twenty years of teaching behind me I could do a better job. Also, I had far more material from which to draw and enough time to develop ideas in a clearer manner than before. I tried to use fresh examples also, so that this book is really a new production, not a rehash of the former volume. Twenty years of living and working had given me greater maturity, and twenty years of anthropological research on the part of many people had furnished adequate material for my needs. The resulting book is much superior to its predecessor.

The reviews were, on the whole, good, and I was glad to note that the points most stressed were precisely those that had been introduced to make the book more readable and more generally useful than its predecessor. Reviewers seemed especially pleased with the short sketches of primitive cultures intended to illustrate and to illuminate the more general discussion of the earlier chapters. Curiously enough, two reviewers saw in the book political connotations that certainly must have wandered in by mistake. As one reviewer wrote, "He has a point of view which, strangely enough, has a political aspect, though he makes no reference to it." At least, I am not accused of deliberate propaganda! The review ends: "What it all has to do with the advantages or disadvantages of communism as an economico-political regime it is hard to say, but there it is, and it means that Professor Lowie's book will be read not only by those who merely want to weigh the evidence . . . it will also provide the infidel with ammunition and the believer with yet another heretical document to take a 'line' about."

If the above comments approximate the truth, I must have builded either better or worse than I knew.

Indians of the Plains.—This small book was written at the request of Harry Shapiro of the American Museum of Natural History and published by the McGraw-Hill Book Company in 1954. What was wanted was a small book of not too technical a character for the average reader. Wissler's book on the American Indian, wholly aside from its original unevenness, had been out of date for years, and Shapiro wanted a summary of modern studies, so presented as to be of interest to the general public. I was very glad to accede to his wishes, because the writing gave me a chance to organize the work of many others in the field, in which my chief interest lay. The Museum put at my disposal its own collections of illustrations, and I was able to include many more pictures than would have been possible in a strictly commercial venture.

The reviews of this book have not been numerous, but they have been uniformly good. Two excerpts should suffice:

Dr. Lowie's book, well worth reading for its own sake, is particularly valuable because it presents, for the first time in such detail for popular reading, an account of those Plains Indians who have so molded our Indian stereotype. He analyses their material culture, examines their social organization, looks at their notions of recreation, art, supernaturalism. He tells something of their prehistory and their history, carrying the latter until their almost complete assimilation by the white man.

In a letter to me, Waldo Wedell in Nebraska wrote:

I should say that your handbook on the Plains Indians is an interesting and highly useful volume. We shall be taking and using suggestions from it for a long time to come. Those of us who have long been interested in the Plains area are indebted to you for a forthright and lucid statement, written after years of experience and reflection on the many problems there presented. I commend you again on a job well done.

Toward Understanding Germany.—My most recent production is a book dealing with the social structure of modern Germany, published by the University of Chicago Press. Since the next chapter will describe the underlying research, I will not go into the matter here. My intention in this book was to give both a historical and a psychological explanation of German social life and attitudes.

I was brought up in the German tradition, and I think I have a better insight into German character than many who have written books of similar nature. Moreover, between them and me there is no barrier of language. My linguistic handicaps are in English —a language I learned from a book—not in German, in which I do much of my thinking, all my arithmetic, most of my first writing of papers or important letters, as well as much of my nightly dreaming.

This book on modern Germany has had a peculiar reception, that perhaps I should have expected. American reviewers had kind things to say about it, or about parts of it, but they seem to have misinterpreted my intentions in many cases. Some of them I judge to be victims of their own prejudices, because they take me to task for not condemning the entire Nazi regime. Some have even gone so far as to accuse me of having written an apology for the Germans; this notion is absurd, if for no other reason than that the Nazi regime liquidated almost all my European relatives. Although I was not especially close to them, I was certainly not amiably disposed toward a government that sent them to be destroyed in Polish furnaces. I could set aside my personal feelings, but evidently several of the American reviewers could not. Others objected because I did not come to sufficiently detailed, definite, black and white conclusions. I did not intend to, because the whole picture presents itself in a series of grays. Nor did I wish to lay down the law about anything. The reviewers in this class seem to have confused scientific inquiry with propaganda. However, a reviewer here and there did understand what I was talking about, as the following quotation indicates:

"The last part of the book, dealing with the position of the Jews in Germany, the Hitlerjugend, Nazism and the prospects of democracy in postwar Germany, is most interesting and well-written. One cannot read this book without modifying or at least re-evaluating some of his conceptions regarding, for example, German love of military glory, fondness for abstract principles, or paternalism. For this accomplishment we must welcome the book as a valuable contribution to better international understanding."

The German reviewers, of whom I expected little, surprised

me by their uniform approval of my work. Of these I will quote only one:

Other foreign mirrors have been held before us more than once, and by no means all were distortions. But among them there were hardly any that were presented with such care or so rightly drawn as the picture in this book of the seventy-year-old American anthropologist. The book can be described as an absolutely classic contribution to international understanding. This book could, if it came into the hands of enough German readers, perform an invaluable service of giving our people self-recognition and self-understanding. . . . This book, the fruit of a six-month stay in Germany, grew in the soil of a scientific experience that spans half a century. It was therefore not to be expected that it would contain snap judgments or one-sided views. Nevertheless, the reader stands completely overcome with admiration before such a fulfillment of learning, before such mastery in the handling of so much and such varied material.

Other German reviews are in the same vein. At least the subjects of my inquiries seem to have understood what I was trying to do.

This book, while great fun to write, has proved only a moderate success, partly because it appeared too late after the war. To make money, I should probably have tossed off something in 1945, but the handicap of being a scholar led me into waiting until after I had spent several months in the field in 1950. It has satisfied a real personal need to formulate in my own mind the nature of my own heritage, to investigate from an objective point of view something I had always known. I am glad that I wrote it. The returns have reimbursed me for the expenses of typing, plus a small amount over. It is possibly a curious book for an anthropologist to have written, but I feel that it presents a good study of a modern culture—a field that is coming every day more and more into the focus of attention.

I omit from this list my very latest effort, since it is even more distant from my usual field than the book on Germany. With my wife I recently (1957) published a small book on how to get ready for a trip to Europe. In this last year I have also edited and written a fair share of a UNESCO publication on the nature of compromise.

As may be appreciated from the above accounts, the motives for writing a book are varied. So, also, are the financial returns from books of equal merit. It is clear that the success of any given book depends upon a number of factors, of which its value is only one. Its sales are influenced by the extent to which it crystallizes the most widely held points of view at the moment of its publication, by its possible usefulness as a text in large courses, by the extent to which it covers all phases of a subject, by the competition it receives from other books of similar nature, and by the attitudes of the particular colleagues who happened to be asked to write the reviews. Sales are not likely to be great if the book is off the beaten path, or if it will be used primarily as collateral reading—which means sales to libraries rather than to students— or if it is conspicuously one-sided or uneven. The book not to write is the one on a narrow topic in which you happen to be interested but few other people are, at least not until you have a reputation that may be a substitute for immediate usefulness. Thus, I am content with my *Crow Indians,* although it has not made great contributions to my income, because I could afford to indulge an interest in between two texts that were reasonably successful. On the whole, I have probably done as well as I should have expected to do, although I have certainly fallen far short of my dreams on many occasions and have not established as large an independent income as I had once hoped, although in some years I have almost doubled my salary by my royalties. If a young man really wants to make money, he should probably follow my wife's formula: Select a large, required course for which no good text is available, and then write something that students can read. Unfortunately, I did not grasp these essential requirements early enough but tended, as most professional men do, to write on topics that were of interest to me, without respect for practical considerations. So far as the books themselves are concerned, I have few regrets, although I admit freely that they contain some mistakes and occasionally express too much youthful intransigence. As for the repute they have brought, I could hardly be otherwise than content.

CHAPTER II

FIELD
WORK IN
GERMANY

My chance to do field work in a complex society came as an indirect result of the Second World War. During the war many universities organized courses intended to give our soldiers some familiarity with the language, geography, economic conditions, and the like of enemy countries that we might occupy. One of these "specialized training programs" for which the University of California assumed responsibility embraced Germany and southeastern Europe. Participating as an ethnologist, I naturally lectured on German and Balkan culture; what I had to say on the latter was based wholly upon reading, hence seemed hardly worth preserving, but with German culture I had had a lifelong acquaintance, hence felt emboldened to publish the gist of the relevant lectures in a hundred-page pamphlet entitled *The German People: A Social Portrait to 1914* (1945).

The essay interested Dr. Paul Fejos, Director of Research for the Wenner-Gren Foundation. He encouraged me to apply to the Foundation for funds enabling me to pursue the study in the field. Therefore, from September, 1950, till late in March, 1951, my wife, who donated her services to the project, and I traveled about western Germany, Switzerland, and Austria. The results of our inquiries I published in 1954 under the title *Toward Understanding Germany*.

There are two obvious differences between field work in so primitive a group as the Lemhi Shoshone and a civilized people like the
Germans. In the first place, one can survey the entire range of
Lemhi activities, whereas no one person is able to grasp all the
aspects of a European civilization, even if he manages to observe
as many phases of life as possible. Second, the inquirer on a small
reservation can have some acquaintance with every adult Indian, but he is obliged to limit his acquaintance in a large, modern,
civilized country to a very small fraction of the total adult population. Because of these restrictions, some limitation of the phases
to be studied was necessary from the start.

I decided therefore to restrict myself to a number of significant
social questions, such as particularism, the class system, student
life in the universities, treatment of Jews, attitudes toward democracy, and the much discussed family life of Germany, including the changes wrought in social structure and family life by recent events. To avoid too narrow a basis, I tried to secure a random
sampling of responses from the entire population. For a university
professor, the main danger lies in relying exclusively upon information obtained from or through academic colleagues. Fortunately,
there are several ways of expanding the investigator's horizons.

One fruitful source is the huge body of printed material written almost exclusively by Germans and bearing on the national culture. For example, on one of my special problems there are valuable monographs dealing especially with the stability of the family
bond under the stress of conditions between the two World Wars,
and others that deal with the second postwar period—notably
Hilde Thurnwald's study of Berlinese conditions immediately after
1945. Naturally, an ethnologist concerned with these questions
must make the fullest use of such publications. There are also many
unpublished theses that deal with the life of students before and
after the war, with the black market, with relations between natives and occupying troops, with delinquency, and with many
related topics, for which the original writer questioned, observed,
and studied a cross section of the entire population.

Again, there is an approach which, though also based on books,
corresponds strictly to one widely followed in the investigation of
"savage" peoples. We have long known that, fanciful as are the

tales told by primitives, they nevertheless embody much wholly trustworthy realistic detail from the life of the narrators. Indeed, attitudes that an investigator could never directly inquire about are often revealed spontaneously by the primitive storyteller. The printed novels and other realistic stories of civilized nations furnish corresponding data on a vast scale. The ethnologist may learn about the "upper crust" from writers like Baroness Marie von Ebner-Eschenbach, about Styrian peasants from Peter Rosegger, and so on. The technique is identical with that used by Classical scholars in reconstructing the Homeric Age from the Iliad and the Odyssey.

A much humbler form of literary effort may be equally instructive; namely, the editorials, news items, announcements, advertisements, and letters to the editor in the daily newspapers. My wife read every local paper in each of the more than forty cities and towns in which we stopped to pursue our inquiries, and clipped from them any items that reflected current problems and customs.

The clippings covered such diverse topics as: the Agricultural Week Festival in Bavaria, new laws governing the employment of domestics, problems of aging government clerks, fate of refugees in the French Zone, position of women, hardships and values of peasant life, reading interests of adolescents, growth of a League for Resistance to Communism, free vocational training for crippled veterans, types of scientific institutions in Munich, democratic ideals among German youth, draft evasion and the League for Avoidance of Military Service, the inadequate salaries of professors and of government clerks, differences between German and American secondary schools, competition among school children for the best essay on a living European statesman, number of refugees in the various parts of Germany, celebration of the wine harvests, surveys of sanitary conditions in factories, nutritional levels among a random sampling of Frankfurt adults, organizations of former German army officers, common types of hobbies, election activities in the Free City of Hamburg, the problems of the German family, gifts of American picture books for use by German children, free speech, nature of radio programs and suggestions for their improvement, letters from an orphaned Jewish girl, number and types of dialects found in Germany, problems of proper sex instruction for children, arguments for and against the former state of Baden becoming part of the newly formed Southwest State, reports on the numerous revolts against Hitler during his decade of power, results of surveys on the number of families still without homes and children still without schools, articles about the effects of extreme separatism on national unity, reports from East Zone refugees, protests against remilitarization. In short, in German newspapers, as in American, one can find out what the more verbal portion of the population is thinking about and striving for.

The papers also reflect customs and manners that are usually so taken for granted that natives do not mention them, no matter how freely they may talk to an investigator. Particularly revealing are the items in the personal columns and the letters to the editor. A few examples appear below.

To the Editor: Your article in yesterday's paper "Domestic Servants—a Concept from Yesterday" delighted me. It is like a fairy tale, that someone should have the courage and take the time to consider the problems of domestics. For twenty-five years I have worked as a cook, but only in the best of families. If I had ten daughters, I wouldn't allow a single one of them to become a domestic, because the freedom which we must sacrifice to our employers is never paid for in this life. Moreover, we soon come to realize that we are not regarded as people but merely as work animals. Forgive me for my extreme forms of expression, but the toll of years has made me bitter. [*Frankfurter Allgemeine*, February 13, 1952.]

In order to protest against the discharge of their teacher, the pupils in the seventh and eighth grades of the elementary school in the small industrial town of Stockstadt have been on strike for several days. As the mayor explains the matter, the strike will continue until the school commissioner of Bavaria instructs the local school board to re-hire the teacher. [*Süddeutsche Zeitung*, February 8, 1950.]

A hundred times I have read in the advertising sections of newspapers a request for a "daughter." Why does no one ever advertise for a son? Actually, what the advertiser is looking for is not a "daughter" but only a female domestic. In earlier times one called her a maid, and the term was no insult. But today the social conditions and relationships between employer and employee have become so distorted that no one dares any more to advertise for a "maid." [*Schweizer Frauenblatt*, December 29, 1950.] The writer of this contribution has probably missed one point. The Swiss regularly call a maid in a hotel "Tochter" because, for the period of her service, she becomes a member of the family that owns the hotel—and almost all Swiss hotels are owned by families; and often the same family has owned and managed a hotel for generations. So the use of "Tochter" may be a term of endearment!

Remilitarization? No! Draft evasion? Yes! That is the message from the pronouncements of the Enemies of Military Service among university students. They argue: "Armament never prevented war." The financial burden of remilitarization would plunge Germany into social and economic catastrophe. They would refuse military service because it is senseless and may lead to a senseless death. They are quoted as saying, "Ideologies are not fought with armaments." Let the politicians carry on their activities but "ohne uns" (without us). It takes more courage to be a pacifist than it does to march with the collective security of an army. Our past compels us to find a new way. [*Die Welt*, February 13, 1951.]

The phrasing of the requests for a marriage partner also reflect an approach to the matter that seems strange to a foreigner. For instance:

Little Eve sighs for an Adam with an educated heart and spirit, with cultured feelings, with a love for children, with a peace loving, tolerant nature, with a love of music and travel, but who also puts a high value upon industriousness. Dear You, dare to send me a note and a picture of yourself.

The obituary notices also have a flavor all their own. In addition to the announcement of death by the bereaved family, we often find a corresponding appreciation by the firm with which a man was connected. A single sample from the *Reinische Post* (Düsseldorf) must suffice:

On October 2, 1956, after a brief but serious illness, there passed on our chief mechanician

Herr Josef Meier

We sincerely mourn the demise of this upright man, who for forty years was associated with our plant. In him we lose one of our most competent and reliable engine fitters. The deceased has fulfilled his professional duties in exemplary fashion. He was not only very popular among us but also in the circles of our customers. We shall faithfully keep him in our memories.

Business Management and Personnel of
the Firm Poensgen Brothers.

Often the inferences to be drawn from articles are more important to an understanding of culture than the articles themselves. For instance, one learns something about the culture of Winterhur, a Swiss town of perhaps 65,000, when he reads that a second art gallery has just opened there. One learns something of the intellectual life of Hamburg when its newspapers advertise virtually throughout the year performances of classical plays and operas. One gets light upon the strong hold that the native speech has upon Swiss natives when he reads a letter written in almost unintelligible Bernese, in which the contributor complains bitterly that the use of the dialect is dying out. Precisely what a newspaper means when it announces an international lottery drawing by using two inkblots from the standardized Rorschach tests is not clear to me, but it seems to signify something to the inhabitants. Certainly the prestige of a university degree is reflected by the fact that an aspirant to matrimony does not fail to make it clear if he is an *Akademiker*. The advertisements about a mysterious *Znüniplättli* tell the reader—after he has resolved the dialect into the standard German *Zu neun Uhr Plättchen* (snack served at 9:00 A.M.)—that the native population gets up at such an early hour (actually around 5:00 A.M.) that reinforcements are needed by nine o'clock. And what can one think of the cultural level of a country when a publisher of a new edition of Schiller's works (price: about thirty dollars) thinks it economically profitable to use a full-page advertisement in every widely read local paper to announce the appearance of the edition? What American publisher would feel confident enough of sales to so announce a new edition of Irving or Hawthone?

Of course, the ethnologist who is studying a higher culture will not drop the commonest of techniques that has stood him in good stead in his usual professional practice in small communities— the interviewing of those best qualified to speak for others or the pursuance of whatever promising lines of investigation may open up as the result of casual contacts with natives. For once, in Germany, I had no need of an interpreter, since German is my native language, and since my wife speaks it well enough to collect data from informants who would be more likely to talk to a woman than to a man. My standing as a university professor gave me an entree into schools, universities, museums, clubs, libraries, and government offices. The initial contacts were with colleagues and students, through whom I became acquainted with various members of the educated classes. I was allowed access also to much un-

published material and was escorted to such diverse places as or-
phanages, camps for refugees, abandoned fortifications now used
as dwellings, ultramodern apartment houses in the suburbs, and
so on. My wife talked with chamber maids, garage mechanics,
clerks in stores, streetcar conductors, guides, small boys and girls,
policemen, and assorted strangers in tearooms. Because I lectured
in several universities and remained at least four weeks in each, I
became well acquainted with students, many of whom had never
before met a professor who wanted to talk with them and to listen
to their explanations of personal problems. By taking courses in
bookbinding and porcelain painting, we met a cross section of
the general population. By taking our afternoon tea in a large
number of different places, we struck up an acquaintance with
many people. In all cases I kept an eye open for particularly competent informants and pursued my inquiries whenever I discovered
someone with ideas to contribute, even if the original contact was
quite casual.

Nor did we neglect to note incidental happenings which, though
inadequate in themselves in the investigation of a large population,
nicely supplemented printed materials or more extended conversations with others. Thus the outburst against military training of
a tipsy fellow on a platform in suburban Hamburg lent support
to what we read in the daily papers. A middle-aged and extremely
respectable-looking seller of lottery tickets in Bern spoke with her
customers in five different languages, within a ten-minute interval
while we were waiting nearby for a bus. One day my wife observed
a stranger on a square in Zürich who asked a passerby where a certain street was; the information was given in a few words, after
which the two men involved in the brief colloquy took off their
hats and shook hands. And one can hardly fail to note that the
clerk in a small store accompanies each customer to the door, opens
the door, and says a polite farewell. No waiter ever brings a bill
until the customer asks for it, because he does not know how long
the diner may wish to linger at the table, reading a newspaper or
writing letters, and to hand him a bill would be to suggest that he
move on. The service in restaurants is slow and therefore a source
of much irritation to Americans, but not because the waiters are
inefficient; the European intends to spend two hours eating a

leisurely dinner, and he wants the service to be slow enough so that he may carry out his intentions in peace. These small and seemingly insignificant bits sometimes tell more about a culture than a formal interview does.

In 1950–1951 we used a technique of investigation that proved eminently rewarding. Hitchhiking has become a common practice among Germans, because of the disorganization of transportation after the war. We made it a rule to pick up women, children, boys, and old men, taking them to or near their destinations. On each occasion my wife did the driving while I quizzed our catch along whatever lines seemed most profitable. Many of our passengers were refugees. From them we obtained much information about the effect of the war on family life, about their postwar experiences as *Heimatsvertriebene,* about living conditions—number of cubic meters allowed per person, for instance—about their treatment by the military and by fellow Germans, about their work— past and present—their needs, and their attitudes. At various times we picked up students, working girls, farm laborers, housewives returning home from market, tottery old gentlemen, and assorted children. From everyone we garnered at least a little definite information about something, and often we could make deductions about social conditions that were not even mentioned. For instance, we picked up a ten-year-old Swiss girl who was walking through forest land to visit her aunt near St. Gallen. The child obviously came from a good family, but here she was walking a distance of some seven miles through thick woods and over hills all by herself. She clearly had no fear of being molested, and she showed no hesitation in getting into a car with strangers. An American mother would not permit such a trip through an uninhabited area, and most American children would not even consider making a seven-mile jaunt merely to carry a cake to auntie, nor would they accept a ride with strangers. From their earliest childhood, American girls especially, are trained not to behave in this manner. One can only assume that the molestation of children is practically unknown in Switzerland—as it is. In Austria a small boy who was on his way to a dentist in St. Gilgen, informed us that he had his teeth cleaned three times a year, that the dentist never hurt him, that he had no cavities, and that he enjoyed going to the dentist. If St. Gilgen were any smaller than it is it would not be there, and yet this country child was pursuing a modern course in oral hygiene. A young woman who was hitch-hiking from a summer's job in Oldenburg to her home in Bavaria, gave us information about jobs, about her reactions to life under the Nazis, and about the comparative friendliness of North Germans and Bavarians. An old peasant woman, a refugee from East Prussia, who spoke a horrendous dialect, wanted my wife's heavy coat. When I explained that my wife had no other, she answered, "But you're rich Americans. You could easily buy another." Later on she remarked plaintively that she wished and wished she might just once receive a food package from America. From a thirteen-year-old girl I got supporting testimony that the line of demarcation between the use of *Du* and *Sie* came at the time of confirmation. Since she was not yet confirmed, I addressed her as *Du*. She was working on a farm where she plucked hens, receiving 26 *Pfennige* (about six cents) per hen, as a reward for about a half-hour's work—of course, in addition to her room and board. She was not a bright girl, but even she had begun to think that there must be easier ways of making a living. From a middle-aged house-wife trudging home from market, we got our best exposition of monetary conditions during and after the war. And so on, ad infinitum. Such contacts, though brief, were rewarding. Our passengers often expressed, frankly, just what they thought and felt precisely because there was no likelihood that they would ever see us again.

It seems worthwhile to present in some detail two case studies, one of which developed from the transportation of a hitchhiker and the other from a casual contact. My account, except for the names, corresponds exactly to the facts of each case.

Driving northward from Göttingen we stopped just outside the city limits to pick up two women standing by the side of the road. They turned out to be mother and daughter. They were going to seek employment in a town not far from Göttingen, where they had heard that the sugar beet harvest needed more workers. As usual, we talked about various matters and learned that our pas-sengers originally came from Silesia, whence they had fled once from the invad-ing Russians, and, after returning to their home in Bunzlau, had been driven out again by the Poles. The father had served in the German navy during the war, after which the family, which included a teen-age boy as well as the married daughter who was with her mother at the time, had been reunited and had settled near Göttingen, largely because the daughter's husband was in a military hospital there. The woman's husband had been an official *Beamter* in the *Katasteramt* (Government Land Office) but was at the time an employee in the sugar factory. When we deposited our hitchhikers near their destination, they thanked us profusely and shook hands all around on leave-taking.

The quiet, dignified demeanor of these women and their excellent German, both of which contrasted sharply with the whining mendicacy and frightful dialect of some others whom we had previously taken up, impressed us most favorably. About six weeks later, toward the end of our sojourn at the Frobenius Institut in Frankfurt, my wife conceived a plan so quixotic that she kept it to herself, fearing that I might merely scoff at its impracticality. She had some clothing that was not worth carrying 6,000 miles home but still had a good deal of wear in it, and she wanted to send it to this particular woman, but ran up against the difficulty of knowing neither her name nor her address. By talking with the chambermaid at our hotel, however, she learned that any sizable German town had an *Einwohnermeldeamt,* which kept track of its inhabitants. She therefore wrote to this bureau in Göttingen, giving such meagre details about the family as we had extracted during a twenty-minute drive. In a surprisingly short time a letter came from Frau Hauff, as I shall call her. As we subsequently learned, the officials had scanned their lists not only in Göttingen but in all surrounding towns and had eventually run down the factory that employed a Silesian refugee who had served in the navy and had been an official in the Land Grant Office in Bunzlau before the War. Herr Hauff was asked to have his wife report to the bureau. Herr Hauff jocularly told his wife, upon getting home that evening, "Du bist steckbrieflich verfolgt." (The police have issued a description of you.) This remark threw his wife into a panic, after ten years of living in a police state. Frau Hauff went next day to the Bureau and was given our address, to which she sent a letter. In order to assure herself that the woman who wrote us really was our passenger, my wife wrote and asked some questions by way of identification: Which of us had been driving the car at the time? Where had the passengers sat in the car? Where had we said we came from? Exactly where had we dropped them? How long had they been in the car? What facts about the quarters for refugees had we elicited from them? and so on. None of these points had been mentioned in the letter previously sent. When Frau Hauff had given all the correct answers, my wife sent her a parcel of clothing and later a little money, for which the family was touchingly grateful. Towards the end of our relatively long stay in Europe we had again accumulated clothing that we did not wish to carry home with us, and since Frau Hauff was most anxious to see us again, she came to Munich to collect the clothes and remained for two days.

All this was only the beginning of an enduring intimacy. During her visit in Munich we were again impressed by her good manners, her pleasant personality, and her superior speech—the latter came from having been brought up on the von Bülow estate, where her father had been the old general's coachman. She is probably the only person of our acquaintance who can converse properly in German with important personages using the third person singular for the subject of a sentence and the third person plural for the verb, because she had to learn this artificial form in order to speak correctly with the general's distinguished guests. While she was in Munich, Frau Hauff told us that she had a sixteen-year-old son who was going through a trade school in order to qualify as a precision mechanic and that his dearest wish was to settle in the United States. My wife made this dream possible by supplying the initial funds and affidavits, and in the summer of 1952 young Otto, recently graduated from his trade school, joined us in California and lived in our house for three years. He obtained a job as a mechanic the day after his arrival, soon repaid his debts, was given raise after raise by a grateful employer, became a citizen, and is now serving a four year hitch in the Air Force.

Frau Hauff and my wife have maintained a regular correspondence. We were again in Germany in 1954, by which time Herr Hauff had regained his position in the Katasteramt in Göttingen. Later he was transferred to Bonn, where we visited the family in 1956, at the time of Otto's marriage to a German girl. We also took Frau Hauff with us for a three weeks' trip through the Black Forest and a northern section of Switzerland, and in 1957 she came to Berkeley for a visit of two months.

Now what was the scientific yield of these contacts? The special value for me lay in the fact that in the most natural way possible we gained an insight into the attitudes of a definitely non academic family. Further, within that family we were able to observe sharp differences between the two generations that had weathered the Second World War. These points require some further elucidation.

As regards education, Herr Hauff evidently enjoyed more formal education than either his wife or his son. He attended a *gymnasium* and both speaks and writes excellent German. Frau Hauff did not go beyond the public school, after which she attended a trade school and learned to be a seamstress. She is an excellent observer and adept at exploiting natural resources—one reason why the family lived through the postwar period. She is also most sensitive to the beauties of nature and has a good working knowledge of plants of all kinds. Notwithstanding her limited education she, like her husband, has a definite feeling for culture. I was surprised to hear her at once identify Grieg's *Peer Gynt Suite* on the radio, for instance. And she can often complete a quotation from the classics. Her written German is not as good as her speech, but she has great vivacity of style.

About the Hauff's daughter we have less information. Since she holds down a job as bookkeeper, she presumably went to a business college. She seems much less sophisticated than her parents; in a moment of depression, she once went to a fortuneteller and was reproved by her mother for indulging in such superstitions. The family is Lutheran, but with individual differences. Herr Hauff is deeply religious, probably from the influence of a still living nonegenarian mother. On Frau Hauff religion sits much more lightly. Otto has no urge whatsoever to attend church. Like his mother, he is a great nature lover, and he once told me, that walking through a beautiful wood gave him more emotional satisfaction than the best of sermons. He added, however, that he was no heathen, and he believes in a man's sticking to the faith in which he was born.

In this young man several attitudes bring out the contrast of generations. First, he has no great reverence for education. His own was limited and sketchy, since he was a child of eleven when the war began, and often during the family migrations he attended no school at all. Although he is very intelligent and seems to be successful in his chosen calling, he is quite unfitted for the life of an *Akademiker*. He totally lacks his parents' humanistic interests. He acquired in an amazingly short time an excellent English pronunciation and a vocabulary quite sufficient for his needs. But his spontaneous reading consisted wholly of boy's adventure stories, and his written English is full of misspellings and gross grammatical errors. His written German is not much better, and is full of translated Americanisms; such as "Ich will *mit* ihm eine Woche *stehen*." [This sentence should be: "Ich will eine Woche bei ihm bleiben." Otto has used "mit" (English "with") for "bei"; he has transliterated "stay" into "stehen" (meaning "stand"); and he has put his adverbial phrase of time into the English rather than the German word order.] He mixes English and German words in speech into a veritable mishmash, a procedure that his parents find highly offensive. The trials of the war and postwar periods seem to have left a deep imprint upon his personality. He is thoroughly upright and honest, and—being a tall, well-built young man with good manners—he creates a favorable impression. But there is a striking difference in attitude between himself and his parents. He shows a certain hardness and indifference to others and a tendency to withdraw from close contacts that contrast markedly to the outgoing character of both parents. His is self-centered and emotionally cold. He learned early that one must look out for oneself. At no time did he send any money home, although he was earning more than his father did. He also exhibited a strange suspiciousness. We advised him to join the YMCA and gain the use of a swimming pool. He went there once or twice but then dropped out because of alleged discrimination shown by college students against him. This conclusion is nonsense, since the students have their own swimming pool and their own YMCA and do not frequent the main rooms in the city. We also suggested his attending classes for foreigners so that he might learn English faster. He attended twice and then abstained because he thought the three German students in the group were slighted by the teacher. His mother, however, went to the English class three hours every day with great delight during her two months in Berkeley. The familial ties between the two children and the parents appear to be close—the son and daughter both addressing their father as *Vati* (dad) and their mother as *Mutti* (mom)—but sometimes two months went by without Otto writing a word home. In short, Otto shows the intensely self-centered attitude of a person who grew up during his more impressionable years in a disorganized environment in which it was every man for himself. The warmth and generosity of the parents find no reflection in him. The daughter, who was already married when the war began, shows a personality affected in another way. She is intensely dependent upon others, especially upon her mother. The excessive insecurity of the postwar years have left their mark upon her.

Another conspicuous difference between the parents and Otto appeared in their retention or rejection, respectively, of traditional class distinctions. Herr Hauff invariably kissed my wife's hand in greeting her, and both he and his wife have the time-honored reverence for the college professor, always addressing me by my academic title. In traveling with Frau Hauff we had the greatest difficulty in preventing her from carrying my luggage or snatching up any parcel that I had purchased. Otto has probably never kissed a hand in his life, and he always addressed me as plain "Mr. Lowie."

The close contacts we had with our friends led to their revealing to us unreservedly their political preferences now and in the past. Herr Hauff did not take to Nazism at all, but under pressure he became a party member in order to retain his government job. Frau Hauff had the typical German woman's indifference to politics, but she felt that no good could come of a regime that used force, so she never joined the party. At the close of the war, she was the only able-bodied woman left in her community who was still not a member. Her father also was against Nazism. She recalls hearing him tell his wife, "Von Hitler wirst Du am End keine Quarkscheibe bekommen." (In the long run you won't get a slice of curds out of Hitler.) Her brother, on the other hand, was a fanatical Nazi, which did not prevent him from being marched off to oblivion in a Russian labor camp. During the war Frau Hauff aided several Jews and Ukrainians to escape from Nazi wrath. The Hauffs give Adenauer credit for improving conditions but are not among his admirers. Both Hauffs comment on Adenauer's supercilious manner, contrasting it with President Heuss's affability. Heuss was reported, at the time of our last being in Germany, to have inquired kindly after the health of his chauffeur's wife, a rumor which inspired Herr Hauff to remark "That's something the Old One would never do." Neither of the Hauffs have any use for the Social Democrats who, they say, had their chance under the Weimar Republic and failed dismally. Neither has, or has had, any inclination toward communism. From relatives in the East Zone and from refugees they have a clear picture of harsh economic conditions and strong repressive measures. However, Frau Hauff gives the Communists credit for one good feature: the eastern government does aid the gifted children of poor parents, even though the object in doing so is to help the party rather than to help the children. Like most Germans, Herr and Frau Hauff are firmly opposed to remilitarization.

Chance meetings that proved profitable for our purpose were not limited to our transportation of hitchhikers. On one trip to Europe in 1950 we met as fellow passengers on the boat three well educated German ladies, the widow of a secondary school professor and her two daughters, both of whom taught in the elementary schools of Augsburg, though their training and cultural level would certainly have fitted them for work on a higher level. We grew fond of them and have since visited them three times at their home. The Theodors, as I shall call them, were valuable in illustrating the tension between Protestants and Catholics in the predominantly Catholic state of Bavaria. For instance, the older daughter was forced out of her position in the schools merely because she was a Protestant and was sent to teach in another town. The administration approved of her work, which was the teaching of arts and crafts, but stated that there were too many Protestant teachers in the Augsburg schools, so some of them must go. The school authorities found her new position for her and gave her the best recommendations, but she was not allowed to remain in Augsburg.

The Theodors exemplified very well what had long impressed me in certain types of German—the sense of minute gradations in social rank. Since Frau Theodor's husband had been only a gymnasium professor whereas I was a professor at a university, we were treated as beings of somewhat higher grade than themselves. Friendly relations with us were regarded as an honor. All members of the family adhered meticulously to our titles, though not without some individual variations. Frau Theodor once addressed a letter to us as *Herr Universitätsprofessor Doktor Lowie und Frau Gemahlin*, and the opening words were: *"Hoch verehrtes Ehepaar Professor Doktor Lowie."* The younger daughter regularly addresses her letters to my wife as *Herr Universitätsprofessor Doktor Lowie's Gattin*. The Theodors not only belonged to the upper middle class, but they tended to preserve ancient traditions even more than the average German of this status; in general, we found Bavarians to be more conservative than most Germans in their preservation of titles. Irrespective of governmental changes, there is an abiding loyalty to the Wittelsbach dynasty. In 1954 when Crown Prince Rupprecht celebrated his eighty-fifth birthday, the administrative council of the Bavarian Academy of Science made a pilgrimage to transmit the congratulations of the Academy "to the high collaborator (*Jubilar*) and the sole honorary member." At the meetings of the Academy the president still addresses the assembly as *Hochansehnliche Festversammlung*, and even corresponding members like myself rank as *Hochwohlgeboren* on the envelope of the official stationery.

The Theodors illustrate especially well the German attitudes about Christmas. To be sure, they do exchange some simple gifts, but the main emphasis is upon the coming together of the family and the emotional satisfactions therefrom derived. The excitement begins two weeks before Christmas with the preparation of sundry little cookies, many of which are hung on the tree. Then the tree is brought in and trimmed. Everyone works like a Turk for days in making ready for the family party, which takes place on Christmas Eve and lasts most of the night. The whole affair is an emotional steam bath, but is beloved of Germans.

Any such case studies as those above must of course be supplemented by the other sources of information previously mentioned. But the advantages of the procedure are obvious; the investigator gains a depth of understanding impossible in a mass study. Compared to the inferences drawn from fiction, the information is not only realistic, but real.

I was especially interested in the problem of parent-child relationships because of the then-recent publications of a psychoanalytic character that ascribed to the German father a dominating role in the family. Whenever I talked with a young person— and there were few days when I did not—I probed for attitudes toward the father. I uncovered some parent-adolescent conflicts of much the same character as we find in America, but the idea of paternal domination struck my young informants, without exception, as merely funny. Nor could I observe in our frequent visits in German homes any signs of the "patriarchal family" with which the Germans have been credited. In democratic Switzerland the father often is a patriarch, as far as I could determine, but in Germany this type exists only no more than about as often as it does here. Talks with parents reinforced this view. At one gathering a businessman regretted that his daughter had fallen in love with a Jewish refugee from Poland; but he added that all he asked of the pair was that they wait for six months before announcing their engagemenet and take time to assess their real feeling for each other and the difficulties that the marriage would almost surely involve. Another father, a chemist, was obviously sorry that his one son was interested only in the history of art, but he comforted himself with the reflection that, since his son was now married, there might soon be a grandson with scientific leanings. The main difference we noted between German and American children was that, while the former answered freely and easily any questions directed to them, they did not break into adult conversations, and they gave every evidence of considering it a privilege to be allowed to remain with an adult group and listen. They were less active and less boisterous, at least in the presence of adults, but they seemed to be "repressed" only to the point of being well-mannered.

Through our many social contacts we were able to visit German homes, to observe furnishings and equipment, and to hear opinions on a number of topics. Our continual dealings with people of all classes gave us an insight into interclass attitudes. An evening spent with a professor at Marburg gave me specific examples of how people managed to get enough food to stay alive just before

and just after the close of the war when the economic and transport systems of Germany were in collapse. From the Frau Professor
I gathered specific details about how one crossed "black" * the
borders into Switzerland or Austria during the time when all exits
from Germany were supposedly closed, and of how one entered
and left the East Zone if one wished to visit relatives there. This
professor's house had been rather difficult to find, and en route we
had picked up a sixteen-year-old lad as a guide. He turned out to
be the son of a bookstore proprietor. The next day I dropped into
his father's store, bought a book, and talked for a half-hour with
the father, who gave me a certain insight into the *Ohne mich*
(without me) attitude of German youth, then at its height. He
told me that his three sons were all against joining any movement
or organization, even one as undemanding as the Red Cross, because
they were "fed up" with catchwords and insignia, with compulsory
membership in youth organizations, with pomp and parades, and
were too disillusioned to have any beliefs left. They wanted only
to be left alone.

The well-known fondness of Germans for titles has by no means
disappeared, as in theory it should have done under the leveling
influences of democracy. We met personally Herr Sanitätsrat
Schmidt, Herr Oberlehrer Müller, Herr Justizrat Franz, Fräu-
lein Schriftsstellerin Klein, Herr Studienerat Ziegler, Herr Professor Extraodinarius Paulus, and more than one Magnifizenz (the
title used for the head of a university.) If a man had two Ph. D.
degrees, he used them both and became Herr Professor Doktor
Doktor Fishbein. There are also titles of an hereditary type, which,
while worthless in some ways, entitle the bearer to extra consideration. Thus, at an informal meeting held in a Bierstübli after a
lecture, the seat at the head of the table was taken, not by a professor, but by the local *Graf* (Count). He arrived somewhat late,
but the place was still empty and waiting for him. At all European hotels I long ago learned to register as Universitätsprofessor
Lowie, because I received preferential treatment. Any request I
might make to the portier was relayed by him to the proper factotum with the words: "Der Herr Doktor Universitätsprofessor

---

* The common phrase to go illegally into another country is, "Ich gehe schwartz"; the term
presumably comes from the "black"—or illegal—market.

wünscht . . ." and the service was immediate. This applies also in democratic Switzerland, where my wife got preferential treatment in stores by being a Frau Professor. In Vienna, one of the advanced graduate students was a countess; in manner she was as democratic as anyone else, but she always got a front seat. In offices one finds a similar arrangement: one of our friends will, upon retirement get one pension as an *Angestellte* (clerk), another as a *Beamter,* (official) and a third as an *Oberaufseher* (superintendent). Even in common speech the former phrases of class distinction linger on, as when a clerk in a store says, "Was wünschen die Herr-schaften?" (What would the gentry wish?)

From personal contacts with students I learned a great deal about student life, the conditions under which they lived, their means of obtaining financial support, their experiences and am-bitions, their chances of finding a job, their motives in getting a degree, their philosophy of life.

The low standard of living and the general insecurity in 1950 reacted on the social habits and mental orientation generally. Of the Hamburg students examined by one investigator, thirty per cent had no rooms of their own, and fifty-eight per cent were lodged in attics, cellars, outhouses, storage rooms, or on porches. Of those who did have rooms to themselves, only sixty-eight per cent were able to heat them. Some would get warm in the winter by working in hospitals or scientific institutes, some took refuge with parents or landlords, eight per cent had no recourse but to go to bed. Who, in such circumstances, can comfortably discuss topics of common interest with intellectual peers? Who, more-over, can afford the time? Forty-nine per cent had to do all their housework, which involved wasting hours in purchases, often wait-ing in queues. Such distractions, in addition to the hours spent in nonacademic jobs, seriously interfere with studies. After lectures some return to the family household, others dash to their jobs. Not infrequently, Germans of the old school lament the absence of the earlier idealism. Fellow students, it is said, now regard one another as competitors rather than as comrades; and they strive, above all, to complete prescribed courses instead of browsing widely in search of a generalized humanistic education. In my opinion these judg-ments are exaggerated. Obviously, economic necessity underlies the manifestations criticized. But to study at all despite existing difficulties and, in many fields, notwithstanding slim prospects for the future, betokens a high degree of idealism. The fact, attested by several sources, that some young people seek employment merely to stand on their own feet and to relieve their families points in the same direction.

The *Werkstudent*—that is, the student who is working his way through college—is a relatively new phenomenon in the German university, although the inflation after the First World War had already driven a few students into flouting the mores and taking on work that would earlier have been spurned as *nicht standesgemäss*. However, the situation is unquestionably very much worse now, for, bad as it was in 1918, Germany had not then been devastated nor had she experienced the invasion of more than ten million refugees. Of the advanced students I knew in Hamburg, where I remained for six weeks, only one was tolerably well off. According to Hans Wolfheim's investigation only twenty-six out of the one hundred students questioned by him did not need to work—or at least were not at the moment working—and forty-eight depended entirely upon what they could earn in their spare time. The position of night watchman in garages or on building lots is particularly popular, for it nets on the average 7 DM. (Deutsche Marks, value: about $.25) per night. Getting such a job three times a week is considered a stroke of good luck. On the other hand, a young man who has been up for fifteen hours is not likely to be alert during an eight or nine o'clock morning lecture. The most lucrative occupation shortly after the cessation of hostilities was the clearing of rubble, at which a man might make as much as sixty marks a day. In Frankfort I heard of students of both sexes spending the two hours from 5:00 to 7:00 A.M. selling newspapers or washing windows. A Hessian journal mentions a prospective physician who, while preparing for his examinations, sells scientific books and ladies' underwear. The women I met in Hamburg had undertaken a variety of jobs, including that of baby sitter; one of them had sold some goods in a public restaurant —a thing her professor characterized as simply *indiskutabel* (undiscussable) in former times. Wolfheim's informants had done laundry at five marks a week and delivered rolls in the morning, for instance at 6:00 A.M., a chore that brought them 15 DM a week. Other young women had the good fortune to get jobs as interpreters—companions to visiting foreigners at a daily fee of about 15 DM. Some students tutored, some did domestic chores, some took whatever jobs were available, whether in business offices, households, or factories. Naturally, both sexes depend largely on what they can earn during the vacation periods. In Vienna I met a mature woman student who served as agent to a beer dealer. A few specific histories of working students appear below:

R——: twenty-seven years old, a refugee from Stettin, who has lost all his savings, is a married medical student, obliged to help support his wife's parents, since his father-in-law is unable to work. Including fellowship fees, he has 230 marks a month, which he supplements as a common laborer on building lots, as a night watchman, by removing rubble, working on a farm, and in other jobs. All this has not yet gained him a steady income. He does not indulge in black-market trading and consumes his allotment of cigarettes himself. So far he has obtained only three or four textbooks, bought directly from the publishers. Except when on his rare jobs with a peasant, he depends on his ration card for food; once he received a Swedish relief parcel. The four persons of his household live in the country, occupying two small rooms, of which one can be heated. By digging peat he has obtained some fuel. The entire family are in poor health, worn out, and liable to sickness. R spends an hour going to his lectures, and his extra jobs sometimes keep him working all night. His case illustrates the obstacles facing those students who avoided illegal trading.

O——: twenty-five years old, also is a prospective physician. He lacks legitimate income, yet has to help support his parents and a young sister. He deals "black" in all articles, "from a locomotive to a collar button," as he himself puts it. His earnings vary enormously; sometimes he is in the red, in some months he nets thousands. He gets food for himself on the black market, but on moral grounds will not deal in it. He himself uses up his smoker's allowance. As for texts, he had kept some previously acquired, others he has bought "black." Though in poor physical condition and emaciated, he does not as yet exhibit edemas or other deficiency symptoms. He occupies a room of his own, which is heatable, buying fuel "black." Living outside Hamburg, he requires an hour and a half, and in the winter often up to four hours, to get to the university.

H——: a woman of thirty, is studying phylosophy. A fellowship of 200 DM plus exemption from fees has been granted her, and she makes 12 DM a week giving English lessons. During the summer she and a friend who cultivates a garden went into partnership, the friend furnishing flowers, which H sold in the streets. Thus during the season they made 324 DM, shared equally between them. H also traded some films and a watch for food, besides selling meat coupons and cigarettes. This enabled her to buy sugar. She dines with her parents, but lives by herself in a decent heatable room 11 square meters in area, paying 40 DM rent plus 10 DM for light and other utilities. Her stove is inadequate, but in need she can warm herself at her parents'; next winter she expects to steal coal. Her efforts to earn money, and the examinations to which stipendiaries are subject, consume a great deal of time.

In summary, I might say that for investigating the nature of a complex culture, I used six methods of investigation: the systematic interviewing of persons who were by common consensus best fitted to give evidence on any given point; the interrogation of a representative cross section of the population by developing casual contacts of all kinds; the excerpting of relevant data from newspapers and periodicals; the examination of what Germans have printed about themselves, either as books or as theses; the reading of realistic novels; and the direct observation of such techniques and phenomena as were to be seen or heard by the German speaking stranger. Many times I was able to obtain confirmation of certain points about the culture from several of these sources. The usual ethnographic technique of merely talking to everyone remained the basic method of inquiry; but when investigating a higher culture, oral methods can and should be supplemented with the written word.

CHAPTER 12

SIC
ET NON

According to general opinion, no man can fairly criticize his own work. On the other hand, he does enjoy one advantage over other judges, namely, a more intimate knowledge of the situations in which the work was done and of his motives in doing it. In that sense, then, his comments may have a certain significance in supplementing the objective appraisal of his peers, and so long as the remarks remain on a descriptive level, they ought not to become invidious. Naturally, I do not set up my own professional career as a model for my colleagues or students. As I view the experiences detailed in earlier chapters, I can see both failures and successes, weaknesses and points of strength, largely useless wastage and constructive additions to ethnology.

To take the debit side of the ledger first. At no time have I regarded myself as a particularly good observer. I am not capable of the spontaneous interest in detail that characterizes, say, Spier, Radin, Sapir, Kroeber, Nimuendajú, and others; still less am I possessed of the eidetic memory for sense impressions at which I used to marvel in the late Harlan I. Smith. Naturally, I am able to direct my attention toward phenomena that have been pointed out as significant; Clark Wissler was extremely helpful in pointing out such phenomena when I was on his staff. Correlated with this deficiency is what has been styled my "lack of interest in material culture." If the word "technology" were substituted, I should accept the stricture a hundred per cent. I simply cannot think in mechanical terms as Wissler and Spier do. On the other hand, when the mechanical factor is eliminated, I take as much interest in material culture as in any other phase. The problems involved in the domestication of animals, for example, have engaged my attention for many years.

I have the reputation of unusual steadfastness of purpose. In my opinion this is completely unmerited. What has evidently created this false impression is that I have generally tried to do particular tasks in a craftsmanlike fashion. In the long run, however, I have signally failed to accomplish any major project that might reasonably have been expected of me. My explanation for this failure is that I have always allowed myself to be distracted by matters that have little or no relation to my supposed lifework. As a graduate student, for instance, I read little ethnography, but a great deal of philosophy; and I was then and for many years thereafter much more concerned with problems of philosophy and of popular enlightenment than with those of anthropology. To be specific, I did each of my Crow jobs conscientiously and with the keenest enjoyment, but I emphatically have not become the sort of authority on the whole Plains area that Boas was for the Northwest Coast or Kroeber is for California. Still less did I feel the urge to inform myself on the problems of Mexican and Peruvian archaeology and ethnography. In short, I can hardly claim to be an Americanist in the sense of Kroeber or Boas.

Similarly, I clung to none of the subdivisions of culture with the expected and requisite tenacity. I started out with a thesis on mythology in 1908, but apart from the obvious collection of tales, when the opportunity offered, I did not revert to the subject until a few years ago. Again, the first logical sequence to my *Primitive Society* would have been a thoroughgoing interpretative synthesis of North American Indian sociology. This should have been followed by a variety of historical and functional studies: I should have attempted to reconstruct the development of social organization and usage in every major area outside North America; and I ought to have inaugurated an indefinite series of investigations bearing on the correlations of descriptively separate sociological phenomena—say, mode of residence and parent-in-law taboos, to take a classical instance. Or, I might have concentrated on kinship terminology and striven to supersede L. A. Morgan's *Systems of Consanguinity and Affinity*. Actually I did none of these things, but pecked at isolated bits of the field, as in my typology of kinship nomenclature. Notwithstanding my genuine interest in language I neither devoted much time to phonetics nor to linguistics—one of the oddest and (to myself) least forgivable sins of omission.

Moreover, I gather that I have an unearned reputation for erudition; when Boas introduced me to Bogoras in Sweden, for example, he described me as "the most learned of the younger American anthropologists." This notion seems to rest on an unwarranted interpolation: it so happens that in the course of my professional career I have thoroughly studied several very discrete sets of phenomena. Many colleagues have assumed that I was equally conversant with the connecting ranges of fact—a conjecture quite contrary to reality.

Finally, I have until recent years strangely neglected the social disciplines adjoining cultural anthropology. In this respect I contrast to my disadvantage with, say, Thurnwald, Malinowski, and Radcliffe-Brown. Boas, too, took far more cognizance of sociology, Kroeber of geography. I fear I qualify even less as a "social scientist" than as an Americanist.

I was very slow in adopting some of the points of view set forth as important in the preceding chapters. I long continued to regard the study of illiterate peoples as the ethnologist's real and only proper business. It seemed odd to me when, in the first edition of his *Anthropology*, Kroeber dealt at some length with problems of the more advanced cultures of the world. The unity of cultural history all over the globe had not yet become clear to me. When I saw the rich contributions of present folk ethnology in special museums devoted to them in Stockholm and Vienna, I was greatly impressed and was naïvely surprised that the specialists I conversed with were approaching the material in precisely the same way that we ethnographers of the savage cultures approached similar data.

In like manner I was tardy in grasping the significance of acculturation. It was the reconstruction of the ancient primitive life that interested me, though Boas had preached the need of concentrating on processes of change, and my friend and fellow student, Paul Radin, had given a fine sample of relevant investigation in showing in detail how the borrowed peyote cult had been fitted into the native religious scheme of the Winnebago Indians. Though of course dimly aware of the fact that I was myself an illustration of the adjustment of German-Austrian culture to the American scene, the full realization of the implications came to me comparatively late.

In my leisure reading I have shown an almost complete reluctance to read in any of the fields that adjoin anthropology. I do not, for instance, read sociology or economics or jurisprudence for pleasure. I have at all periods of my career preferred literature and philosophy, especially the philosophy of science. I have several shelves of books on this latter topic, and I read them often, yet I have only the merest handful in the fields into which one would suppose my interests might lead me.

Ernst Haeckel was the source of my youthful intransigence, and Ernst Mach was the dominant influence of my maturer years. No ethnologist—not even Boas—was ever my hero or my source of inspiration. To be sure, I have always liked to read history, although I am not such an omnivorous reader in the field as Kroeber or Radin. I intensely enjoy anything that reflects the general atmosphere of a civilization. Alfred Franklin's books on French culture history, Arthur Young's *Travels,* Ford's *Gatherings from Spain,* Troels-Lund's picture of sixteenth-century Scandinavia are among my special favorites. But my real love has always been German literature, in which I read avidly and widely—the classical writers, the Austrians—especially Rosegger, Nestroy, and Grillparzer—and modern authors, such as Stefan Zweig or Thomas Mann. I still keep a copy of Faust on my bedtable and dip into it when I cannot sleep. In my leisure reading I am still un-Americanized.*

* There is ample testimony of the truth of the above statements. Whenever my husband had to wait a few minutes for me—which happened often—he picked up, not a copy of *Time* or any of the hundreds of works in his professional library but some book from his grandfather's collection of Goethe, Schiller, Lessing, von Humboldt, Herder, or Wieland. These he read repeatedly. It is typical that on the last evening of his conscious life, as he waited for the doctor's injection to take effect, he asked for his Faust, turned to a favorite passage, which he had read aloud to me every Easter morning for twenty-five years, and went into his last sleep to the accompaniment of the long-loved words:

> Vom Eise befreit sind Strom und Bäche
> Durch des Frühlings holden, belebenden Blick,
> Im Thale grünet Hoffnungsglück;
> Der alte Winter in seiner Schwäche
> Zog sich in rauhe Berge zurück.   [L. C. L.]

There is also something to be said on the credit side. Perhaps my chief contribution has been my conviction that cultural anthropology is a science, which requires precisely the same logical and psychological processes as any of the supposedly more exact sciences. That our subject matter permits of artistic treatment I have never denied, but I have tried to keep apart objective findings and aesthetic interpretation. My attitude toward certain modern fashions in anthropology should be considered in this light. I do not necessarily deny all significance to them, but I do not care to join in these trends until I see some likelihood of objective procedure and verification of theories. This feeling holds especially for the attempted synthesis of psychoanalysis and anthropology.

I have been able to collect adequate and definitive material on a number of more or less isolated points, such as visionary experiences, age societies, or the structure of the Crow language. My work will not need to be done over, even though some younger man will probably need to finish and organize it.

My personal contacts with Indians have almost always been excellent. I have usually managed to overcome quickly any initial hostility a group of Indians may previously have generated toward white men and have had no more than temporary difficulties in establishing rapport.

Probably the greatest compliment of my life was given me in a little restaurant just off the Crow reservation, where I heard one Indian tell another (in Crow), "You see that white man over there? He looks like any other white man, but when he comes to the campfire, you'd never know him from an Indian." I feel that my ability to enter into the Indians' own attitudes and to convince them of my genuine interest in them has been my chief asset as a practicing ethnologist. Part of the story was mere Austrian *Gemütlichkeit,* but part of it was stern self-discipline. An interpreter or informant, after agreeing to turn up at nine o'clock, may appear any time from 6 A.M. to 10:30 P.M., or not at all. He may wander in on Wednesday instead of Sunday or Saturday instead of Tuesday. He may bring his grandmother, his children, or his neighbors. It took a great deal of self-control for a punctual, methodical person such as I to accept cheerfully the Indians' vague concepts of time.

I cannot see that I have invented any dramatic or new methods of investigation, but what I believe I have done is to select the right one for each investigation—or if I did not do so at first, I called a halt and started over again with some more apposite technique. It does not take long in the field to discover that not everything in the book will work; but if an investigator has a good grounding in methodology and is willing to try everything at least once, he can find the right approach and the right combination of methods for reaching each specific goal.

I feel that my roamings into a number of areas have had their positive side because, by these diversions of energy, I have been able to develop valuable work that might otherwise never have been done. Nimuendajú's work was saved for posterity largely because I neglected other lines of interest. And my "war work" precipitated me into an analysis of certain social problems in a modern, complex civilization, a type of research that I should not have chosen if left to myself; but I believe I have made some contributions that will be of value to students of similar subjects.

I am told that I have been a successful teacher, a development I had not anticipated. Indeed, after a disastrous experience trying to teach unruly fourth-grade children, I had determined to remain a "museum man," a line of work in which the chances of facing another class were remote. When I was thirty-four, Kroeber finally prevailed upon me to try teaching for a year, and four years later to leave the American History Museum and become a university professor. I was therefore rather slow in getting started, but once begun, I found a latent talent for the work.

To be sure, I have not had any urge toward "leadership" nor toward the establishment of a "school" of ethnology, and I have, thank God, no disciples. At one time I even went so far as to suppose that I had exerted little or no influence on my students. This assumption has been so vigorously denied by Theodore D. Mc-Cown, Cora DuBois, George Devereux, and many others that I gratefully accepted the correction. It is also pleasant to learn from men who never "sat under me," such as Alfred Métraux, Paul Kirchhoff, and Claude Lévi-Strauss, that they derived stimulation from my writings long before they had met me in the flesh. So perhaps I may rate myself as a success in my teaching.

It will appear from the foregoing that my appraisal of my own work differs rather sharply from that of my peers as regards my strong and weak points. In particular I am impressed with my grave ignorance of matters I ought to know well, with my easy distractability, and with my lack of fixed purpose as an anthropologist. But perhaps I have succeeded in my youthful ambition to "add my mite to the sum-total of human knowledge." And quite probably no man should hope for more.

VITA

1883   Born in Vienna, Austria, June 12.

1888   Entered the Cherninschule in Vienna; member of the Allgemeiner Deutscher Sprachverein.

1893   Accepted for a classical gymnasium in the spring. In the fall, brought to the United States by his parents; settled in New York; entered the fifth grade of Public School 83.

1897   Entered the City College of New York. ["In my youth," but presumably after coming to the United States, he was a founder of the Deutscher Literarischer Verein.]

1898   Received the Claflin Medal (Greek).

1901   Received A. B. degree from City College of New York; elected to Phi Beta Kappa; received the Serena Mason Carnes Prize (Spanish).

1901   Started working in the New York public schools as a substitute teacher. [Sometime between 1901 and 1904 attended summer courses at Columbia University in chemistry.]

1904   Became a full-fledged teacher in the New York public schools; eked out income by teaching evening classes in German. Entered Columbia University in the fall as a graduate student in anthropology under Professor Franz Boas.

1906   Made first field trip, visiting the Lemhi Shoshone of Idaho.

1907   Visited the Stoney Assiniboine; made a brief visit to the Northern Blackfoot in Gleichen, Alberta; made first trip to the Crow reservation in Montana. Elected to Sigma Xi. In November appointed assistant at the American Museum of Natural History under Clark Wissler.

1908   Received Ph. D. degree from Columbia (dissertation: "The Test-

Theme in North American Mythology"). Visited the Chipewyan in Northern Alberta.

1909   Appointed Assistant Curator, American Museum of Natural History.

1910   Elected a member of the American Association for the Advancement of Science. Elected Secretary of American Ethnological Society. Began regular summer visits to Crow (1910 through 1919) and Hidatsa (1910, 1911, 1913) reservations.

1912   Visited the Shoshone of Utah and Nevada. Appointed Associate Curator, American Museum of Natural History. Became Editor, *Current Anthropological Literature.*

1913   Elected Sectional Secretary of New York Academy of Sciences.

1915   Visited Hopi, Ute, and Paiute reservations.

1916   Elected President of American Folklore Society.

1917   Appointed visiting Associate Professor, University of California, Berkeley, for the 1917–1918 academic year.

1918   Called for military service on Armistice Day.

1920   Appointed Lecturer in Primitive Law, Columbia University for the 1920–1921 academic year. Elected President of the American Ethnological Society.

1921   Appointed Associate Professor in Anthropology, University of California, Berkeley. (Served as departmental chairman for the academic years, 1922–1923; 1923–1924; 1926–1927; 1934–1935; 1935–1936; 1936–1937; 1938–1939; 1939–1940; 1942–1943; 1944–1945; 1945–1946; 1946–1947; 1947–1948; 1948–1949.)

1924   Became Editor of the *American Anthropologist.* In the fall he attended the International Americanist Congress in Gothenburg, where he first met Father William Schmidt; traveled in England, France, Sweden, Norway, Germany, Austria. In Sweden he met Baron Erland Nordenskiöld and Paul Rivet, with whom he conceived the idea of a handbook on South American Indians.

1925   Appointed Professor of Anthropology, University of California, Berkeley. Elected Corresponding Member of the Société des Americanistes de Paris.

1926   Visited the Washo of California and Nevada. Baron Nordenskiöld called Lowie's attention to Curt Nimuendajú, but Lowie was not then interested in South America.

1927   Appointed Visiting Professor of Anthropology, Columbia University for the summer.

1930   Appointed Visiting Professor of Anthropology, Ohio State University for the summer. In the fall attended the International Americanist Congress in Hamburg; served as one of the meeting's vice presidents. Traveled in Germany, Austria, Denmark, and Spain. Inspected the Altamira caves.

1931   Elected to the National Academy of Sciences, Washington, D. C.

Made last visit to the Crow. Became Editor of the *American Anthropologist* and *Memoirs*. Elected Chairman, Division of Anthropology and Psychology, National Research Council, Washington, D. C. (As chairman, Lowie persuaded Baron Nordenskiöld to edit a handbook of South American Indians. After Nordenskiöld's death the Smithsonian Institution assumed "moral sponsorship" for the work.)

1933   Married Luella Cole. Elected Honorary Fellow of the Royal Anthropological Institute of Great Britain and Ireland.

ca. 1935   Began working with Nimuendajú; a relationship that continued untill Nimuendajú's death in 1945.

1937   Appointed Visiting Professor of Anthropology, Yale University for fall semester. Received the Townsend Harris Medal "for notable achievement" from the Associate Alumni of the City College of New York. Served as member of the jury awarding the Duc de Loubat Prizes.

1939   Appointed Representative of the American Anthropological Association to the Social Sciences Research Council.

1941   Elected Corresponding Member of the Institute do Ceará, Fortaleza, Brazil. Appointed representative of the American Anthropological Association to the Committee on Native Languages, American Council of Learned Societies. Received the degree of Doctor of Science (honoris causa), from the University of Chicago. Spent three months of the fall in Washington, D. C. working on the *Handbook of South American Indians*.

1942   Elected to the American Philosophical Society, Philadelphia.

1943   Began a series of training courses for the army in addition to his regular teaching program at the University of California.

1944   Elected to honorary life membership in the New York Academy of Sciences.

1945   Appointed Visiting Professor of Anthropology, Columbia University for the summer.

1948   Served as a Vice President and as a delegate from the University of California and the American Anthropological Association to the Third International Congress of Anthropological and Ethnological Sciences at Brussels. Visited several European countries, England, Belgium, Switzerland, France, and Austria. While in England was appointed Medalist and Lecturer, Thomas H. Huxley Memorial, Royal Anthropological Institute of Great Britain. Delivered three lectures at University College, three at Cambridge University and one at Oxford University. Returned to New York City in December to deliver Viking Fund lecture and receive the Viking Medal in Ethnology. Presided as one of three vice presidents of the Conference on Science, Philosophy and Religion.

1949   Appointed Faculty Research Lecturer, University of California. In the fall he presented a paper (on the "Heterogeneity of Marginal

American Cultures") at the International Congress of Americanists in New York.

1950   Appointed Professor Emeritus and Fellow of the University of California. Granted honorary membership in the Württembergische Verein für Handelsgeographie (Stuttgart) and the Deutsche Gesellschaft für Völkerkunde (Hamburg). Went to Europe in September to study German culture for six months under a grant from the Wenner-Gren Foundation. Traveled in Germany, Austria, and Switzerland. Lectured at the Universities of Hamburg, Frankfurt-am-Main (Frobenius Institut), Bonn, Zurich, Basel, and Vienna. Visited (without lecturing) the Universities of Marburg, Freiburg, Tübingen, Bern, Neufchâtel, Göttingen, Aix-en-Provence, Grenoble, Strassburg, Innsbruck, Leiden, Geneva, and Heidelberg.

1951   Elected a member of the Société Suisse des Americanistes (Geneva).

1952   Elected Corresponding Member, Bavarian Academy of Science. Presented paper at Wenner-Gren Symposium. Appointed Visiting Professor of Anthropology, Columbia University for the summer. Appointed Walker-Ames Professor of Anthropology, University of Washington (Seattle) for the fall term.

1953   Conducted a seminar on the "History and Theory of Ethnology" at the University of California, Berkeley.

1954   Traveled in Germany, France, Italy, and Switzerland. Elected to honorary membership in the Mark Twain Society.

1955   Appointed Visiting Professor of Anthropology, Harvard University for the summer. In the fall he attended a conference in Chicago sponsored jointly by the Universities of Chicago and Frankfurt-am-Main on the integration of the sub-disciplines of American anthropology. Visited Northwestern University and spoke to staff and graduate students on the field methods in the days of his early professional life.

1956   Appointed Visiting Professor of Anthropology, University of Hamburg for the summer semester, 1958. Traveled to Germany, Switzerland, and France (was aboard the *Stockholm* when it collided with the *Andrea Doria*). Represented the University of California as well as the American Anthropological Association at an August meeting of the International Americanists Congress in Copenhagen; presented a paper on the culture-area concept in America.

1957   Became ill in February and died September 21, of cancer.

BIBLIOGRAPHY OF ROBERT H. LOWIE

ABBREVIATIONS

A   *Anthropos*
AA   *American Anthropologist*
AJS   *American Journal of Sociology*
AMer   *American Mercury*
AMJ   *American Museum Journal*
AMNH–AP   American Museum of Natural History, *Anthropological Papers*
BAE–B   Bureau of American Ethnology *Bulletin*
CAL   *Current Anthropological Literature*
D   *Dial*
ESS   *Encyclopedia of the Social Sciences*
Fr   *Freeman*
ICA   *International Congress of Americanists*
JAFL   *Journal of American Folklore*
NIYB   *New International Yearbook*
NR   *New Republic*
S   *Science*
Soc   *Sociologus*
SWJA   *Southwestern Journal of Anthropology*
T   *Tomorrow*
UC–PAAE   University of California, Publications in American Archaeology and Ethnology

BIBLIOGRAPHY

1898

"Edgar Allen Poe," in *New Yorker Review*, February 13.

1901

"Haeckels Verhältnis zu Amerika,"*Sonntagsblatt der New Yorker Staatszeitung*, August. (Reprinted without permission in Heinrich Schmidt, ed., *Was wir Ernst Haeckel verdanken*, Leipzig, 1914, 2:404–407.)

1905

"Neue Gedanken über die Abstammung des Menschens," *Sonntagsblatt der New Yorker Staatszeitung*, June 18.

"Ludwig Feuerbach: A Pioneer of Modern Thought," *Liberal Review*, February, pp. 20–31.

"Spencer and Tolstoi," *Liberal Review*, December.

1907

With Livingston Farrand, "Marriage," BAE–B, 30. 1:808–810.

1908

"Catchwords for Mythological Motives," *JAFL*, 21:24–27.

"The Test-Theme in North American Mythology," *JAFL*, 21:97–148.

"Anthropological Publications of the American Museum of Natural History for 1907–1908," S, 28:522–524.

1909

"The Northern Shoshone," AMNH–*AP*, 2:165–302.

"The Assiniboine," AMNH–*AP*, 4:1–270.

Edited with H. H. St. Clair, II, "Shoshone and Comanche Tales," *JAFL*, 22:3–20.

"Additional Catchwords," *JAFL*, 22:332–333.

"Hero-Trickster Discussion," *JAFL*, 22:431–433.

"An Ethnological Trip to Lake Athabasca," *AMJ*, 9:10–15.

"The Fijian Collection," *AMJ*, 9:117–122.

Review of John R. Swanton, *Social Condition, Beliefs, and Linguistic Relationships of the Tlingit Indians*, *JAFL*, 22:2–3.

Review of George Laurence Gomme, *Folklore as an Historical Science*, *JAFL*, 22:3–5.

1910

"Notes concerning New Collections," AMNH–*AP*, 4:271–337.

With Clark Wissler, "Anthropology," *NIYB* for 1909, pp. 27–32.

Review of C. Hart Merriam, *The Dawn of the World: Myths and Tales told by the Mewan Indians of California*, *AA*, 12:464–466.

1911

"The Methods of American Ethnologists," S, 34:604–605.

"A New Conception of Totemism," *AA*, 13:189–207.

"Industry and Art of the Negro Race," *AMJ*, 11:12–19.

"The New South Sea Exhibit," *AMJ*, 11:53–56.

"The Crow Indians of Montana," *AMJ*, 11:179–181.

"A Forgotten Pragmatist: Ludwig Feuerbach," *Journal of Philosophy*, 8:138–139.

With Clark Wissler, "Anthropology," *NIYB* for 1910, pp. 34–40.

Review of W. S. and K. Routledge, *With a Prehistoric People: The Akikuyu of British East Africa*, *AA*, 13:130–135.

Review of C. C. Uhlenbeck, *Geslachts-en Personsnamen der Peigans*, *AA*, 13:324–326.

Review of Lord Avebury, *The Origin of Civilization and the Primitive Condition of Man*, *AA*, 13:623.

1912

"On the Principle of Convergence in Ethnology," *JAFL*, 25:24–42.

"Some Problems in the Ethnology of the Crow and Village Indians," *AA*, 14:60–71.

"American and English Methods in Ethnology," *AA*, 14:398–399.

"Social Life of the Crow Indians," AMNH–*AP*, 9:179–248.

"Chipewyan Tales," AMNH–*AP*, 10:171–200.

"Cosmogony and Cosmology; Mexican and South American," in *Hastings, Encyclopaedia of Religion and Ethics*, 4:168–174.

"Crow Indian Clowns," *AMJ*, 12:74.

"Convergent Evolution in Ethnology," *AMJ*, 12:139–140.

"Dr. Radosavljevich's 'Critique' of Professor Boas," S, 35:537–540.

"Menschheitskunde und Rassendünkel," *Sonntagsblatt der New Yorker Volkszeitung*, May 26.

With Clark Wissler, "Anthropology," *NIYB* for 1911, pp. 46–50.

Review of Hans Cornelius, *Einleitung in die Philosophie*, *Journal of Philosophy, Psychology and Scientific Methods*, 9:238–246.

Review of John Roscoe, *The Baganda*, *CAL*, 1:34–37.

Review of R. Neuhauss, *Deutsch Neu-Guinea*, *CAL*, 1:116–119.

Review of Hans Vogel, *Eine Forschungreise im Bismarck-Archipel*, CAL, 1:116–119.

Review of Karl Weule, *Leitfaden der Völkerkunde*, CAL, 1:177–178.

Review of Fritz Krause, *In den Wildnissen Brasiliens*, CAL, 1:199.

Review of Clark Wissler, *Ceremonial Bundles of the Blackfoot Indians*, CAL, 1:286–288.

1913
"Dance Associations of the Eastern Dakota," AMNH–AP, 11:103–142.

"Societies of the Crow, Hidatsa and Mandan Indians," AMNH–AP, 11:145–358.

"Charms and Amulets, American," in *Hastings, Encyclopaedia of Religion and Ethics*, 3:401–409.

"The Inferior Races," *The New Review*, 1:934–942

"Military Societies of the Crow Indians," AMNH–AP, 11:145–217.

With Clark Wissler, "Anthropology," NIYB for 1912, pp. 30–35.

Review of Alice C. Fletcher and Francis La Flesche, *The Omaha Tribe*, S, 37:910–915.

Review of Fritz Graebner, *Krückenruder*, CAL, 2:1–4.

Review of Otto Reche, *Der Kaiserin-Augusta Fluss*, CAL, 2:19–20.

Review of Leo Frobenius, *Und Afrika Sprach*, CAL, 2:87–91.

Review of H. von Buttel-Reepen, *Man and his Forerunners*, CAL, 2:138.

Review of Edward Clodd, *The Childhood of the World*, CAL, 2:227.

1914
"The Crow Sun Dance," JAFL, 27:94–96.

"Crow Rapid-Speech Puzzles," JAFL, 27:330–331.

"Social Organization," AJS, 20:68–97.

"Ceremonialism in North America," AA, 16:602–631.

"International Rivalry in Science," NR, December 19, pp. 15–16.

"Ernst Haeckel," *The New Review*, 2:354–356.

"Some Recent Expressions on Racial Inferiority," *The New Review*, 2:542–546.

"A Pro-German View," *The New Review*, 2:642–644.

"Reviews of Anthropological Literature," *Psychological Bulletin*, 11:391–394.

"German Scientists," in *Evening Sun*, January 27.

With Clark Wissler, "Anthropology," NIYB for 1913, pp. 34–39.

1915
"The Sun Dance of the Crow Indians," AMNH–AP, 16:1–50.

"Dances and Societies of the Plains Shoshone," AMNH–AP, 11:803–835.

"Societies of the Arikara Indians," AMNH–AP, 11:645–678.

"The Crow Indian Sun Dance," AMJ, 15:23–25.

"Exogamy and the Classificatory Systems of Relationship," AA, 17:223–239.

"Psychology and Sociology," AJS, 21:217–229.

"Oral Tradition and History," AA, 17:597–599.

"Exogamy and the Classificatory System of Relationship," *Proceedings of the National Academy of Sciences*, 1:346–349.

"American Indian Dances," *AMJ*, 15:95–102.

"The Crow Indians," *The Southern Workman*, November:605–612.

"Ute Indians the Real Troublemakers," in The New York *Sun*, February 28, p. 8.

"Morgan's 'Ancient Society'," *The New Review*, 3:101–104 (reprinted in *Solidaritat*, 11:10–12).

With Clark Wissler, "Anthropology," *NIYB* for 1914, pp. 35–39.

Review of W. H. R. Rivers, *Kinship and Social Organization, AA,* 17:329–340.

Review of Felix Speiser, *Südsee, Urwald, Kannibalen, AA,* 17:177–180.

Review of Berthold Laufer, *Some Fundamental Ideas of Chinese Culture, AA,* 17:350–352.

Review of Baldwin Spencer, *Native Tribes of the Northern Territory of Australia, AA,* 17:354–355.

Review of W. J. Sollas, *Ancient Hunters and their Modern Representatives, AA,* 17:575–576.

Review of W. H. R. Rivers, *The History of Melanesian Society, AA,* 17:588–591.

1916

"Historical and Sociological Interpretations of Kinship Terminologies" in *Holmes Anniversary Volume,* pp. 293–300.

"Plains Indian Age-Societies: Historical and Comparative Summaries," AMNH–*AP,* 11:877–992.

"Societies of the Kiowa," AMNH–*AP,* 11:837–851.

"A Note on Blackfoot Relationship Terms," *AA,* 18:148.

"Ernst Mach," *NR,* April 9, pp. 335–337.

"Theoretical Ethnology," *Psychological Bulletin,* 13:397–400.

With Leta S. Hollingworth, "Science and Feminism," *Scientific Monthly,* pp. 277–284.

"A New Shakespeare," *The International,* August, pp. 246–247.

With Clark Wissler, "Anthropology," *NIYB* for 1915, pp. 31–35.

Review of James Marchant, *Alfred Russel Wallace, NR,* November 18, pp. 14–16.

Review of Leo Sternberg, *The Turano-Ganowanian System and the Nations of North-East Asia, AA,* 18:287–289.

Review of J. Marquart, J. D. E. Schmeltz, and J. P. B. de Josselin de Jong, *Ethnographisch Album van het Stromgebied van den Congo, AA,* 18:436–437.

Review of Hartley Burr Alexander, *The Mythology of All Races, Vol. X: North America, AA,* 18:563.

1917

Culture and Ethnology. New York: Douglas C. McMurtrie. 189 pp.

"Notes on the Social Organization and Customs of the Mandan, Hidatsa, and Crow Indians," AMNH–*AP,* 21:1–99.

"Oral Tradition and History," *JAFL,* 30:161–167.

"The Kinship Systems of the Crow and Hidatsa," 19 *ICA* [December, 1915], pp. 340–343.

"Edward B. Tylor," *AA*, 19:262–268.

"Ojibwa," in *Hastings Encyclopaedia of Religion and Ethics*, 9:454–458.

"Peyote Rite," in *Hastings Encyclopaedia of Religion and Ethics*, 9:815.

"Age Societies of the Plains Indians," *AMJ*, 17:495–496.

"Noted in Hopiland," *AMJ*, 17:569–573.

"The Universalist Fallacy," *NR*, November 17, pp. 4–6.

With Clark Wissler, "Anthropology," *NIYB* for 1916, pp. 31–36.

Review of R. B. Dixon, *The Mythology of All Races, Vol. IX: Oceania, AA*, 19:86–88.

Review of W. H. R. Rivers, *Kin, Kinship, Marriage; Mother-right, AA*, 19:269–272.

Review of *Harvard African Studies: Vol. I, AA*, 19:546–547.

Review of Conklin, *Heredity and Environment*, *NR*, May 12, pp. 59–60.

Review of Ernst Haeckel, *Eternity, the Masses*, April, p. 28.

Review of J. Joly, *The Birth Time of the World*, *NR*, September 15, pp. 196–197.

1918

"Myths and Traditions of the Crow Indians," *AMNH–AP*, 25:1–308.

"Age Societies of the Plains Indians," *Scientific American*, 85:201.

"More Light: a Rejoinder," *AA*, 20:229–230.

"Survivals and the Historical Method," *AJS*, 529–535.

"The True Authority of Science," *D*, May 9, pp. 432–434.

"Anthropology put to Work," *D*, August 15, pp. 98–100.

With Clark Wissler, "Anthropology," *NIYB* for 1917, pp. 31–37.

Review of A. M. Czaplicka, *Aboriginal Siberia, AA*, 20:325–326.

Review of Marie L. McLaughlin, *Myths and Legends of the Sioux, AA*, 20:451–453.

Review of W. Max Muller and Sir James G. Scott, *The Mythology of All Races, Vol. XII*, *NR*, August 24, pp. 113–114.

Review of Sedgwick and Tyler, *A Short History of Science*, *D*, September 5, pp. 157–158.

Review of Jean-Henri Fabre, *The Wonders of Instinct*, *D*, August 15.

1919

"The Tobacco Society of the Crow Indians," *AMNH–AP*, 21:101–200.

"The Sun Dance of the Shoshone, Ute, and Hidatsa," *AMNH–AP*, 16:387–431.

The Matrilineal Complex, *UC–PAAE*, 16:29–45.

"Family and Sib," *AA*, 21:28–40.

"Biometrics," *The International Journal of Orthodontia and Oral Surgery*, 5:219–227.

"The Economic Interpretation of History: a Footnote," *D*, January 11, pp. 35–36.

"Primitive Ideas on Numbers and Systems of Measurement," *Natural History*, 19:110–112.

"Ernst Haeckel and his Work," *Christian Science Monitor*. October 29, p. 3.

"Biology and Anthropology," [Unsigned review of various books.] *NR*, November 26, p. 3.

With Clark Wissler, "Anthropology," *NIYB* for 1918, pp. 37–41.

Review of Edward Sapir, *Time Perspective in Aboriginal American Culture*, *AA*, 21:75–77.

Review of *Harvard African Studies*, Vol. II, *AA*, 21:208–210.

Review of Fritz Sarasin, *Neu-Caledonien und die Loyalty-Inseln*, *AA*, 21:311–315.

Review of John A. Macculloch and Jan Máchal, *The Mythology of All Races*, Vol. III, *NR*, February 1, pp. 29–30.

Review of John M. Macfarlane, *The Causes and Course of Organic Revolution*, *D*, January 11, pp. 48–49.

Review of H. F. Osborn, *Men of the Old Stone Age*, *D*, February 8, p. 150.

Review of P. A. Means, *Racial Factors in Democracy*, *D*, July 12, p. 32.

1920

Primitive Society. New York: Boni & Liveright. viii + 463 pp. [French translation by E. Métraux, title: *Traité de sociologie humaine*, Paris: Payot, 1935. 460 pp. New preface; some corrections; appendix in translation of "The Family as a Social Unit," see 1933. Japanese translation. I. Kawanura; Dailchi, 1939, 494 pp. Chinese translation. Date unknown.]

"Mysticism and Science," *Fr*, March 31, p. 63–64.

"Applied Psychology," *Fr*, April 7, p. 91–92.

"Herbert Spencer, " *Fr*, May 19.

"The Father of Eugenics," *Fr*, July 28, pp. 471–474.

"Wilhelm Wundt," *Fr*, September 22, p. 42.

"An Ethnologist's Memories," *Fr*, August 11, p. 517–518; October 6, p. 85–86.

"The Divine Right of Lineage," *Fr*, November 3, pp. 179–181.

"The People of Unknown Lands," *The Bookman*, pp. 156–160.

With Clark Wissler, "Anthropology," *NIYB* for 1919, pp. 42–48.

Review of W. Koppers, *Die ethnologische Wirtschaftsforschung*, *AA*, 22:72–73.

Review of R. Thurnwald, *Vorläufiger Bericht über Forschungen im Innern von Deutsch-Neu-Guinea*, *AA*, 22:80–81.

Review of Herbert E. Cory, *The Intellectuals and the Wage Workers*, *AA*, 22:186.

Review of Leona Cope, *Calendars of the Indians North of Mexico*, *AA*, 22:188.

Review of A. Jacobi, *Eine völkerkundliche Sammlung von den europäischen Samojeden*, *AA*, 22:189–190.

Review of W. D. Wallis, *Messiahs; Christian and Pagan*, *AA*, 22:383.

Review of Edward A. Ross, *The Principles of Sociology*, *The Nation*, 111:418–419.

Review of E. Gaupp, *August Weismann*, Fr, May 26, pp. 256–258.
Review of Paul Radin, *The Autobiography of a Winnebago Indian*, Fr, June 16, p. 334.
Review of R. R. Marett, *Psychology and Folk-Lore*, Fr, July 21.
Review of F. Soddy, *Science and Life*, Fr, September 1, pp. 20–21.
Review of R. Vallery-Radot, *The Life of Pasteur;* and E. Duclaux, *Pasteur: The History of a Mind*, Fr, November 24, pp. 259–260.
Review of F. Schleiter, *Religion and Culture*, NR, February 18.
Review of Wilfred N. Beaver, *Unexplored New Guinea*, NR, June 2, p. 26.
Review: J. A. Thomson, *The Secrets of Animal Life*, NR, July 28, p. 260.

1921
"A Note on Aesthetics," *AA*, 23:170–174.
"The Eugenicists' Programme," *Fr*, October 19, pp. 129–130.
"An Hidatsa Love Story," *Fr*, September 14, p. 8.
With Clark Wissler, "Anthropology," *NIYB* for 1920, pp. 41–46.

Review of W. Schallmayer, *Vererbung und Auslese*, AA, 23:77–78.
Review of Bernard Hart, *The Psychology of Insanity*, AA, 23:215.
Review of A. L. Kroeber and Waterman, *Source Book in Anthropology*, AA, 23:226–227.
Review of D. Jenness and Ballantyne, *The Northern D'Entrecasteaux*, AA, 23:216–217.
Review of Clark Wissler, *North American Indians of the Plains*, Fr, May 4.
Review of J. G. Frazer, *Folklore in the Old Testament*, Fr, March 30, pp. 67–68.
Review of G. B. Grinnell, *When Buffalo Ran*, Fr, April 20.
Review of E. S. Hartland, *Primitive Society*, and W. Koppers, *Die Anfange des menschlichen Gemeinschaftslebens*, Fr, August 31, pp. 595–596.
Review of G. Stanley Hall, *Recreations of a Psychologist*, Fr, March 2.
Review of Hartley Burr Alexander, *The Mythology of All Races: South America*, Fr, February 9.
Review of James Sully, *My Life and Friends; a Psychologist's Memories*, Fr, February 9.
Review of W. Wundt, *Erlebtes und Erkanntes*, Fr, May 25, pp. 260–261.
Review of Carveth Read, *The Origin of Man and of his Superstitions*, NR, September 14.
Review of John M. Tyler, *The New Stone Age*, NR, October 19, pp. 223–224.

1922
"The Material Culture of the Crow Indians," AMNH–AP, 21:201–270.
"Crow Indian Art," AMNH–AP, 21:271–322.
"The Religion of the Crow Indians," AMNH–AP, 25:309–444.
"The Avunculate in Patrilineal Tribes," *AA*, 24:94–95.
"Science," in Harold Stearns, ed., *Civilization in the United States*. (New York: Harcourt, Brace & Co.) pp. 151–161.
"Takes-the-pipe, A Crow Warrior," in Elsie Clews Parsons, ed., *American Indian Life*. (New York: B. W. Huebsch) pp. 17–33.

"A Crow Woman's Tale," in Elsie Clews Parsons, ed., *American Indian Life.* (New York: B. W. Huebsch) pp. 35–40.

"A Trial of Shamans," in Elsie Clews Parsons, ed., *American Indian Life.* (New York: B. W. Huebsch) pp. 41–43.

"Windigo, a Chipewyan Story," in Elsie Clews Parsons, ed., *American Indian Life.* (New York: B. W. Huebsch) pp. 325–336.

"The Origin of the State," *Fr,* July 19, pp. 440–442; July 26, pp. 465–467.

"The Plains Indians," *Fr,* May 10, pp. 211–212.

"Rejoinder to Objector to Review of Madison Grant," *Fr,* March 29, p. 66.

With Clark Wissler, "Anthropology," *NIYB* for 1921, pp. 43–47.

Review of Alfred Korzybski, *Manhood of Humanity, NR,* February 8, pp. 313.

Review of H. H. Newman, *Readings in Evolution, Genetics, and Eugenics, NR,* March 1, pp. 25–26.

Review of Park and Burgess, *Introduction to the Science of Sociology, AA,* 24:215.

Review of René Maran, *Batouala, Fr,* November 29, pp. 284–285.

Review of Albert Churchward, *The Origin and Evolution of the Human Race, Fr,* May 3, pp. 595–596.

Review of Madison Grant, *The Passing of the Great Race, Fr,* January 25, pp. 476–478.

Review of A. A. Goldenweiser, *Early Civilization, Fr,* November 15, pp. 235–236.

Review of Emily P. Cape, *Lester F. Ward, Fr,* August 30, pp. 595–596.

Review of Clark Wissler, *The American Indian, Fr,* August 16, pp. 547–548.

1923

The Cultural Connections of Californian and Plateau Shoshonean Tribes, UC-PAAE, 20:145–156.

"The Buffalo Drive and an Old World Hunting Practice," *Natural History,* 23:280–282.

"A Note on Kiowa Kinship Terms and Usages," *AA,* 25:279–281.

"Psychology, Anthropology, and Race," *AA,* 25:291–303.

With Clark Wissler, "Anthropology," *NIYB* for 1922, pp. 43–48.

Review of O. W. Von Engeln, *Inheriting the Earth, Fr,* February 21, pp. 572–573.

Review of G. A. Bartsell, ed., *The Evolution of Man, Fr,* May 30, pp. 284–285.

"Races and Psychological Tests," [unsigned editorial] *Fr,* June 20, pp. 342–343.

Review of J. G. Frazer, *The Golden Bough, abridged, Fr,* June 20, pp. 353—355.

Review of Jeremiah Curtin, *Seneca Indian Myths, Fr,* June 27.

Review of W. F. Ogburn, *Social Change, Fr,* July 11, p. 431.

Review of C. Wissler, *Man and Culture, Fr,* October 3, pp. 93–94.

Review of Ernst Haeckel, *Letters to his Parents; The Story of the Development of a Youth, Fr,* October 24, pp. 164–165.

Review of Hermann Klaatsch, *The Evolution and Progress of Man*, *NR*, August 1, pp. 268–269.

Review of Roland B. Dixon, *The Racial History of Mankind*, *The Nation*, June 13, p. 698.

Review of Paul Radin, *The Winnebago Tribe*, *The Occident*, November, p. 43.

Review of E. Sapir, *Language*, *AA*, 25:90–93.

Review of *Harvard African Studies*, III, *AA*, 25:103–105.

Review of Sidney Hartland, *The Evolution of Kinship; An African Study*, *AA*, 25:272–273.

Review of R. Thurnwald, *Psychologie des primitiven Menschen*, *AA*, 25:417–418.

Review of F. G. Speck, *Beothuk and Micmac*, *AA*, 25:418–419.

Review of A. R. Brown, *The Andaman Islanders*, *AA*, 25:572–575.

1924

Primitive Religion. New York: Boni & Liveright. xix + 346 pp.

"Shoshonean Tales," *JAFL*, 37:1–242.

"Notes on Shoshonean Ethnography," *AMNH–AP*, 20:185–314.

"The Origin and Spread of Cultures," *AMer*, April, pp. 463–465.

"Minor Ceremonies of the Crow Indians," *AMNH–AP*, 21:323–365.

With Clark Wissler, "Anthropology," *NIYB* for 1923, pp. 42–47.

Review of W. J. Perry, *The Children of the Sun*, *AA*, 26:86–90.

Review of Hermann Dengler, *American Indians; Tribes of the Prairies and the East*, *AA*, 26:269.

Review of W. Koppers, *Unter Feuerland-Indianern*, *AA*, 26:404–415.

Review of Rafael Karsten, *The Toba Indians of the Bolivian Chaco*, *AA*, 26:538–540.

Review of J. A. Thomson, *What is Man?* *NR*, December 10, p. 18.

1925

"The Historical Connection between Certain Old World and New World Beliefs," *21 ICA* [1924], pp. 546–549.

"Five as a Mystic Number," *AA*, 27:578.

"A Note on History and Race," *AMer*, March, pp. 342–343.

"Is America so Bad after all?" *Century Magazine*, 109:723–729.

"A Woman's Ceremony among the Hopi," *Natural History*, 25:178–183.

"African Ethnology," in *New International Encyclopaedia*, 2nd ed., 1:212–214.

Review of W. H. R. Rivers, *Medicine, Magic and Religion*, *AA*, 27:457–458.

Review of P. Radin, *Monotheism among Primitive Peoples*, *AA*, 27:560–561.

Review of Max Ebert, *Reallexikon der Vorgeschichte*, *I–II*, *AA*, 27:561–562.

1926

"Zur Verbreitung der Flutsagen," *A*, 21:615–616.

"The Banana in America," *Nature*, 117:517–518.

Review of Danzel, *Kultur und Religion des primitiven Menschen, id., Magie und Geheimwissenschaft*, AA, 28:281–283.

Review of W. Schmidt and W. Koppers, *Völker und Kulturen*, AA, 28:283–285.

Review of A. M. Tozzer, *Social Origins and Social Continuities*, AA, 28:285, 286.

Review of Verneau, *Les Récentes découvertes préhistoriques en Indochine*, AA, 28:289, 424.

Review of Schebesta, *Unter den Zwergen von Malakka*, AA, 28:298–299.

Review of Birkner, *Der diluviale Mensch in Europa*, AA, 28:420.

Review of Olivier Leroy, *Essai d'introduction critique à l'étude de l'économie primitive*, AA, 28:549.

Review of C. Wissler, *The Relation of Nature to Man in Aboriginal America*, NR, November 10.

1927

The Origin of the State. New York: Harcourt, Brace & Co., 117 pp.

"Note of the History of Anthropology," S, July 29, p. 111.

"Theoretische Ethnologie in Amerika," *Jahrbuch für Soziologie*, 3:111–124.

"Prestige among Indians," AMer, December, pp. 446–448.

Review of Buschan, *Illustrierte Völkerkunde, II, Zweiter Teil*, AA, 29:112–113.

Review of Ebert, *Reallexikon . . .* , III–VII, AA, 29:332–335.

Review of Eickstedt, *Archiv für Rassenbilder*, AA, 29:339.

Review of W. Schmidt, *Der Ursprung der Gottesidee, I*, AA, 29:689–690.

Review of R. R. Marett, *The Diffusion of Culture*, AA, 29:690–691.

Review of P. Amaury Talbot, *The Peoples of Southern Nigeria*, AA, 29:715–717.

Review of H. J. Massingham, *Downland Man*, NR, July 20, p. 234.

1928

"A Note on Relationship Terminologies," AA, 30:263–267.

With E. W. Gifford, Notes on the Akwa'ala Indians, UC–PAAE, 23:339–352.

"Individual Differences and Primitive Culture" in *Schmidt Anniversary Volume*, 495–500.

"Incorporeal Property in Primitive Society," *Yale Law Journal*, 37:551–563.

"Edward Sanford Burgess, 1855–1928," AA, 30:481–482.

"Word Formation in the American Indian Languages," AMer, July, pp. 332–334.

"Bathing through the Ages," AMer, September, pp. 62–64.

"Aboriginal Education in America," AMer, October, pp. 192–196.

Review of K. G. Lindblom, *The Use of Stilts*, AA, 30:317–319.

Review of Herbert Kuhn, *Beziehungen und Beeinflussungen der Kunstgruppen im Palaolithikum*, AA, 30:327–328.

Review of Schebesta, *Bei den Urwaldzwergen von Malaya*, AA, 30:483–486.

Review of W. Jochelson, *The Yukaghir and the Yukaghirized Tungus*, AA, 30:487–490.

Review of N. Vavilov, *Studies on the Origin of Cultivated Plants*, AA, 30:716–719.

1929

Are We Civilized? New York: Harcourt, Brace & Co. xiii + 306 pp.

"Notes on Hopi Clans," AMNH–*AP*, 30:303–360.

"Hopi Kinship," AMNH–*AP*, 30:361–388.

"Relationship Terms" in *Encyclopaedia Britannica*, 14th ed., 19:84–89.

Review of W. Jochelson, *The Yukaghir and the Yukaghirized Tungus*, *AA*, 31:163–165.

Review of Marcel Cohen, *Instructions pour les voyageurs*, *AA*, 31:499.

Review of Ebert, *Reallexikon . . . , X, XI*, *AA*, 31:499–500; 780–785.

Review of Sandford and Arkell, *First Report of the Prehistoric Survey Expedition*, *AA*, 31:501.

Review of H. S. Harrison, *Pots and Pans*, *AA*, 31:504–506.

Review of Margaret Mead, *Coming of Age in Samoa*, *AA*, 31:532–534.

1930

"Adoption, Primitive," *ESS*, 1:459–460.

"Age Societies," *ESS*, 1:482–483.

"Avoidance," *ESS*, 2:369–370.

"Ceremony, Primitive," *ESS*, 3:313–314.

"The Kinship Terminology of the Bannock Indians," *AA*, 32:294–299.

A Crow Text, with Grammatical Notes, UC–PAAE, 29:155–175.

"American Indian Cultures," *AMer*, July, pp. 362–366.

"Freemasons among North Dakota Indians," *AMer*, February, pp. 192–196.

"Literature and Ethnography," *AMer*, April, pp. 454–458.

"The Omaha and Crow Kinship Terminologies," in *Verhandlungen des XXIV. Internationalen-Amerikanisten Kongresses, Hamburg*, pp. 103–107.

Review of J. H. Driberg, *The Savage as He Really Is*, *AA*, 32:557.

Review of M. Heydrich, *Ethnologischer Anzeiger*, *AA*, 32:660.

Review of G. Elliot Smith, *In the Beginning;* and W. J. Perry, *Gods and Men*, *AA*, 32:165–168.

Review of Gerrit S. Miller, *Some Elements of Sexual Behavior in Primates . . . ,* *AA*, 32:168–169.

Review of W. Schmidt, *Ein Versuch zur Rettung des Evolutionismus*, *AA*, 32:169–170.

Review of Ebert, *Reallexikon . . . , XII, XIII*, *AA*, 32:170–171; 300–301.

Review of W. Jochelson, *Peoples of Asiatic Russia*, *AA*, 32:178.

Review of Joseph Maier, *Adoption among the Gunantuna*, *AA*, 32:178.

Review of Hjalmar Stolpe, *Collected Essays in Ornamental Art*, *AA*, 32:301–302.

Review of T. M. Durlach, *The Relationship Systems of the Tlingit, Haida, and Tsimshian*, *AA*, 32:308–309.

Review of A. B. Lewis, *Melanesian Shell Money*, *AA*, 32:312–313.

Review of Arthur W. Hill, *The Original Home and Mode of Dispersal of the Coconut*, *AA*, 32:320–321.

Review of Halfdan Bryn, *Der nordische Mensch*, *AA*, 32:547.

1931

"Hugo Obermaier's Reconstruction of Sequences among Prehistoric Cultures in the Old World," in Stuart Rice, ed., *Methods in Social Science*, pp. 266–274.

"Indian Theologians," *AMer*, pp. 472–479.

"Inventiveness of the American Indian," *AMer*, pp. 90–93.

Review of C. Wissler, *An Introduction to Social Anthropology*, AA, 33:111–112.

Review of K. T. Preuss, *Tod und Unsterblichkeit im Glauben der Naturvölker*, AA, 33:626–627.

Review of Robert Briffault, *The Mothers*, AA, 33:630–631.

Review of H. C. Shetrone, *The Mound Builders*, NR, January 28, pp. 305–306.

1932

"Proverbial Expressions among the Crow Indians," *AA*, 34:739–740.

"Kinship," *ESS*, 8:568–572.

"Marriage and Family Life among the Plains Indians," *Scientific Monthly*, 34: 462–464.

Report of the Chairman, Appendix Q, Annual Meeting of the Division of Anthropology and Psychology, National Research Council (mimeographed).

Review of Frank B. Linderman, *American*, AA, 34:532–533.

Review of Truman Michelson, *The Narrative of a Southern Cheyenne Woman*, AA, 34:534.

Review of Frank B. Linderman, *Old Man Coyote (Crow)*, AA, 34:717–718.

1933

"A Crow Indian Medicine," AA, 35:207.

"Crow Prayers," AA, 35:433–442.

"Erland Nordenskiöld with Bibliography of his writings," AA, 35:158–164.

"The Family as a Social Unit," in *Papers of the Michigan Academy of Science, Arts and Letters* [1932], 18:53–69. (Published also as appendix to French translation of *Primitive Society*.)

"Marriage," *ESS*, 10:146–154.

"Nordenskiöld," *ESS*, 11:396–397.

"Queries," *AA*, 35:288–296.

"Land Tenure, Primitive Societies," *ESS*, 9:76–77.

"Selk'nam Kinship Terms," *AA*, 35:546–548.

"Primitive Skeptics," *AMer*, July, pp. 320–323.

Review of Paul Kirchhoff, *Die Verwandtschaftsorganisation der Urwaldstämme Südamerikas*, AA, 35:182–183.

Review of A. Métraux, *Les Hommes-dieux chez les Chiriguano* . . . AA, 35: 183–184.

Review of R. Thurnwald, *Die Menschliche Gesellschaft, II, III*, AA, 35:343–345.

Review of F. Pospišil, *Ethnologiské materialie* . . . , AA, 35:359.

Review of Carleton S. Coon, *Flesh of the Wild Ox*, AA, 35:372–373.

Review of M. Leenhardt, *Notes d'ethnologie Néo-Calédonienne*, AA, 35:362.

Review of A. B. Lewis, *Ethnology of Melanesia, AA,* 35:527.
Review of R. W. Fortune, *Omaha Secret Societies, AA,* 35:529–533.
1934
An Introduction to Cultural Anthropology. New York: Farrar & Rinehart.
xxii + 350 pp. (French translation by E. Métraux, *Manuel d'anthropologie culturelle.* Paris: Payot, 1936. 390 pp.)
"Religious Ideas and Practices of the Eurasiatic and North American Areas,"
in *Essays presented to C. G. Seligman,* pp. 183–188.
"The Omaha and Crow Kinship Terminologies," *24 ICA,* 1930:102–108.
"Some Moot Problems in Social Organization," *AA,* 36:321–330.
"[Heinrich] Schurtz (1863–1903)," *ESS,* 13:587.
"Social Organization," *ESS,* 14:141–148.

Review of A. Goldenweiser, *History, Psychology and Culture, AA,* 36:114–115.
Review of F. B. Linderman, *Red Mother, AA,* 36:124–125.
Review of Hortense Powdermaker, *Life in Lesu, AA,* 36:129–130.
Review of Schubesta, *Bambuti, die Zwerge vom Kongo, AA,* 36:469.
1935
"Eine kaukasisch-lapplandische Parallele," *A,* 30:224–225.
The Crow Indians. New York: Farrar & Rinehart, xxii + 350 pp.
"[Franz Theodor] Waitz (1821–1864)," *ESS,* 15:321.
1936
"Cultural Anthropology: a Science," *AJS,* 42:301–320.
"Alfred L. Kroeber: professional appreciation," in *Essays in Anthropology Presented to Alfred Louis Kroeber* (Berkeley: University of California Press),
pp. xix–xxiii.
"Lewis H. Morgan in Historical Perspective," in *Essays in Anthropology Presented to Alfred Louis Kroeber* (Berkeley: University of California Press),
pp. 169–181.

Review of Baumann, *Lunda; bei Bauern und Jägern in Inner-Angola, AA,*
38:118–120.
Review of H. Thurnwald, *Die schwarze Frau im Wandel Afrikas,* 38:120–121.
Review of A. Métraux, *Introduction à la connaissance de l'Ile de Paques, AA,*
38:126–127.
1937
The History of Ethnological Theory. New York: Farrar & Rinehart, xiii + 296 pp. (Spanish translation by Paul Kirchhoff, *Historia de la Etnología.* Mexico City: Fondo de Cultura Económica, 1946. 358 pp.)
With Curt Nimuendajú, "The Dual Organizations of the Ramkókamekra (Canella) of Northern Brazil," *AA,* 39:565–582.
"Dr. Wissler on 'The Crow Indians'," *AA,* 39:366.
Introduction to W. Lloyd Warner, *A Black Civilization* (New York: Harper & Brothers), pp. xv–xviii.

Review of Baumann, *Schöpfung und Urzeit des Menschen im Mythus der afrikanischen Völker*, AA, 39:346–347.

Review of G. Herzog, *Jabo Proverbs from Liberia*, JAFL, 50:198.

1938

"Subsistence," in F. Boas, ed., *General Anthropology* (New York: Heath & Co.), pp. 282–326.

"A Note on South American Parallels to Maya and Aztec Traits," *American Antiquity*, 4:157–159.

"The Emergence Hole and the Foot-Drum," AA, 40:174.

Translation of: C. Nimuendajú, *The Social Structure of the Ramkókamekra*, AA, 40:51–74, 760.

Review of W. Schmidt, *Handbuch der Methode der kulturhistorischen Ethnologie*, AA, 40:142–144.

Review of W. I. Thomas, *Primitive Behavior*, AA, 40:144.

Review of G. D. Wagner and W. A. Allen, *Blankets and Moccasins*, AA, 40:309.

Review of Martin Gusinde, *Die Feuerland-Indianer. II. Die Yamana*, AA, 40:495–503.

Review of H. Thurnwald, *Menschen der Südsee*, JACL, 51:352–353.

1939

Ethnographic Notes on the Washo, UC–PAAE, 36:301–352.

Translation: Curt Nimuendajú, "The Apinayé," The Catholic University of America, Anthropological Series, No. 8. 189 pp.

With Curt Nimuendajú, "The Associations of the Serénte," AA, 41:408–415.

With Z. Harris and C. F. Voegelin, "Hidatsa Texts," in Indiana Historical Society, Prehistory Research Series, 1:173–239.

1940

An Introduction to Cultural Anthropology, new and enlarged edition. New York: Farrar & Rinehart, 584 pp.

"Native Languages as Ethnographic Tools," AA, 42:81–89.

"American Culture History," AA, 42:409–428.

Review of Franz Boas, *Race, Culture, and Language*, S, 91:598–599.

1941

"Intellectual and Cultural Achievement of the Human Races," in Jennings et al., *Scientific Aspects of the Race Problem* (New York: Longmans, Green & Co.), pp. 189–249.

"A Note on the Northern Gê Tribes of Brazil," AA, 43:188–196.

Review of Leslie A. White, ed., *The Bandelier-Morgan Letters*, American Antiquity, 7:196–197.

1942

The Crow Language; Grammatical Sketch and Analyzed Text, UC–PAAE, 39:1–142.

"The Transition of Civilizations in Primitive Society," AJS, 47:527–543.

Studies in Plains Indian Folklore, UC–PAAE, 40:1–28.
Translation: Curt Nimuendajú, "The Serénte," Publications of the F. W. Hodge
  Anniversary Publication Fund, Vol. IV. ix + 106 pp.
"Soviet Russia and Religion." *T*, November, pp. 43–44.
"A Marginal Note to Professor Radcliffe-Brown's Paper on Social Structure,"
  AA, 44:519–521.
"The Professor Talks Back," *The Antioch Review, Summer*, pp. 317–321.

Review of S. A. Sieber and Fr. H. Mueller, *The Social Life of Primitive Man*,
  AA, 44:313–314.
Review of K. N. Llewellyn and E. A. Hoebel, *The Cheyenne Way*, *AA*, 44:478–
  479.
Review of Clellan S. Ford, *Smoke from their Fires*, *T*, February, pp. 59–60.
Review of Leo W. Simmons, *Sun Chief*, *T*, August, pp. 62–63.

1943
"Property Rights and Coercive Powers of Plains Indian Military Societies,"
  Journal of Legal and Political Sociology, 1:59–71.
"A Note on the Social Life of the Northern Kayapó," *AA*, 45:633–635.
"Franz Boas, Anthropologist," *The Scientific Monthly*, 56:183–184.
"Franz Boas; his Predecessors and his Contemporaries," *S*, 97:202–203.

Review of A. H. Quiggin, *Haddon, the Head Hunter*, *AA*, 45:478–479.

1944
"Franz Boas (1858–1942)," *JAFL*, 57:59–64.
"Bibliography of Franz Boas in Folklore," *JAFL*, 57:65–69.
Translation: Curt Nimuendajú, "Serénte Tales," *JAFL*, 57:181–187.
"American Contributions to Anthropology," *S*, 100:321–327.
"Jean Bassett Johnson," *AA*, 46:528–529.
"South American Messiahs," *T*, December.

1945
The German People; a Social Portrait to 1914. New York: Farrar & Rinehart.
  143 pp.
"A Note on Lapp Culture History," *SWJA*, 1:447–454.
"A Case of Bilingualism," *Word*, 1:248–259 [actually published August, 1946].

Review of *One Hundred Years of American Psychiatry*, *The American Journal
  of Psychiatry*, 102:129–141.

1946
Translation of: Curt Nimuendajú, The Eastern Timbira, UC–PAAE, 41:1–357.
"Evolution of Cultural Anthropology: a Reply to Leslie White," *AA*, 48:223–
  233.
Translation of: Curt Nimuendajú, "Social Organization and Beliefs of the
  Botocudo of Eastern Brazil," *SWJA*, 2:93–115.
"Professor White and Anti-Evolutionist Schools," *SWJA*, 2:240–241.
"Eastern Brazil; an Introduction," *BAE–B*, 143. 1:381–397.

"The Bororo," BAE–B, 143. 1:419–434.
"The Northwestern and Central Gê," BAE–B, 143. 1:477–517.
"The Southern Cayapó," BAE–B, 143. 1:519–520.
"The Tapuya; the Cariri; the Pancarurú; the Tarairiu; the Jeico; and the Guck," BAE–B, 143. 1:553–569.

Review of B. Malinowski, *A Scientific Theory of Culture and Other Essays, AA*, 48:118–119.

1947

"Biographical Memoir of Franz Boas (1858–1942)" in *National Academy of Sciences, Ninth Memoir*, 24:303–322.
"Letters from Ernst Mach to Robert H. Lowie," *Isis*, 37:65–68.
"Some Problems in Plains Indian Folklore," *JAFL*, 60:401–403.
Primitive Society, 2d. ed. New York: Liveright Publishing Company, xii + 463 pp.

1948

Social Organization. New York: Rinehart & Company. ix + 465 pp.
"Some Facts About Boas," *SWJA*, 4:69–70.
Primitive Religion, rev. ed. New York: Liveright Publishing Corporation. (New preface, v–vii; new chapters, pp. 321–337).
"Some Aspects of Political Organization among the American Indians," in *Huxley Memorial Lecture* (London: Royal Anthropological Institute), pp. 1–14.
"Robert H. Lowie," *Boletín Bibliográfico de Anthropología Americana*, 10:324–337. (Bibliography through 1946)

Review of Kaj Birket-Smith, *Geschichte der Kultur, JAFL*, October–December, p. 401.

1949

"Supplementary Facts about Clark Wissler," *AA*, 51:527.

Review of Bertram Schaffner, *Fatherland: A Study of Authoritarianism in the German Family, Man*, 48:131.
Review of Geoffrey Gorer, *The American People, Man*, 49:34.

1950

"Observations on the Literary Style of the Crow Indians," *Beitrage zur Gesellungs- und Volkerwissenschaft* [Thurnwald Festschrift], pp. 271–283.
"Parochialism and Historical Instruction," in *8th Symposium: Learning and World Peace* (Conference on Science, Philosophy and Religion), Chap. IX, pp. 89–98.
"Social and Political Organization of the Tropical Forest and Marginal Tribes," BAE–B, 143. 5:313–350.
"Property among the Tropical Forest and Marginal Tribes," BAE–B, 143. 5:351–367.

Review of Hilde Thurnwald, *Gegenwarts-Probleme Berliner Familien, AA*, 52:105–106.

Review of W. Schmidt, *Der Ursprung der Gottesidee,* Vol. IX, *AA,* 52:519–521.

1951
"Some Problems of Geographical Distribution," in *Südseestudien* (Basel: Museum für Völkerkunde), pp. 11–26.
"Beitrage zur Völkerkunde Nordamerikas," *Mitteilungen aus dem Museum für Völkerkunde in Hamburg,* 23:7–68.

1952
"The Heterogeneity of Marginal Cultures," in *Selected Papers of the XXIX International Congress of Americanists, New York,* 3:1–7.
"The Wenner-Gren Foundation International Symposium on Anthropology," *Soc,* n.s., 2, 2:145–148.
C. Nimuendajú, The Tukuna, Edited by R.H.L., UC–PAAE, 45:1–207.
"The Song 'Frohe Botschaft'," *JAFL,* 65–187.

Review of R. Thurnwald, *Des Menschengeistes Erwachen, Wachsen, und Irren, Psyche,* 4:50–52.
Review of A. E. Jensen, *Mythos und Kult bei Naturvölkern, JAFL,* 65:102–104.
Review of A. E. Jensen, ed., *Mythe, Mensch und Umwelt; Beiträge zur Religion, Mythologie und Kulturgeschichte, AA,* 54:400–401.

1953
"Ethnography, Cultural and Social Anthropology," *AA,* 55:527–534.
"The Relations between the Kiowa and the Crow Indians," *Société Suisse des Américanistes, Bulletin* 7:1–5.
"On Historical and Ethnographic Techniques," *AA,* 55–280.
"The Comanche, a Sample of Acculturation," *Soc,* 3:122–127.
"Alleged Kiowa-Crow Affinities," *SWJA,* 9:357–368.
"Contemporary Currents in American Ethnology," [translated by I. Obayashi] in *Ethnological Research,* 17, 2:61–76.

Review of Franz Caspar, *Tupari, AA,* 55:441–442.
Review of Sol Tax et al., *An Appraisal of Anthropology Today, Soc,* 3:137–141.
1954
Indians of the Plains. New York: McGraw-Hill. xiii + 222 pp.
"A Crow Tale" in *Anthropological Quarterly,* n.s., 2:1–22.
Toward Understanding Germany. Chicago: University of Chicago Press. ix + 396 pp.
"Field Research in South America," *Man,* 54:100.
"Richard Thurnwald (1869–1954)," *AA,* 56:863–867.
"Richard Thurnwald," *Soc,* n.s., 4:2–5.

Review of Kunz Dittmer, *Formen und Entwicklung der Kultur, AA,* 56:1114.
Review of Raffaelo Pettazzoni, *Miti e Leggende III: America Settentrionale, Western Folklore,* 13:218–220.
Review of M. J. Herskovits, *Franz Boas: The Science of Man in the Making, Scientific Monthly,* 78:47.

1955

"Reflections on the Plains Indians," *Anthropological Quarterly*, April, pp. 63–86.

"Contemporary Trends in American Cultural Anthropology," *Soc*, n.s., 5:113–121.

"The Military Societies of the Plains Cree," in *Separata dos Annais do XXXI Congreso Internacional de Americanistes*, 1–9. (1955 [i.e., 1956] author's reprints in Spanish).

Review of Margaret Hasluck, *The Unwritten Law of Albania*, AA, 57:1076.

1956

"*Boas Once More*," AA, 58:159–164.

"Choosing Reviewers," *Man*, 55:188. December, 1955 (Issued in March, 1956).

"Supernormal Experiences of American Indians," *T*, 4, 3:9–16.

"Reminiscences of Anthropological Currents in America Half a Century Ago," AA, 58:995–1016.

"Notes on the Kiowa Indians," *Tribus*, n.f., pp. 4–5.

Review of Edward P. Dozier, *The Hopi-Tewa of Arizona*, Soc, 6:189–191.

Review of George C. Homans and David M. Schneider, *Marriage, Authority and Final Causes; A Study of Unilateral Cross-Cousin Marriage*, AA, 58:1144.

1957

Edited: The Nature of Compromise, Paris: UNESCO (in press).

"Primitive Compromise" in *The Nature of Compromise*; Chap. I (in press).

With Luella Cole, *A Practical Handbook for Planning a Trip to Europe*. New York: Vantage Press. 206 pp.

"Primitive Messianism and an Ethnological Problem," *Diogenes*, 19:62–72.

"Generalizations, Field Work, and Materialism," *AA*, 59:884–885.

Posthumous Publications in Press

"Oral Literature of the Crow Indians," *JAFL*.

"Empathy," in Memorial Volume to Paul Radin.

"My Crow Interpreter," in *Native Interpreters*, edited by J. Casagrande.

"Die Religion der Naturvölker," *Zeitschrift für Ethnologie*.

"Religiöse Erscheinungungen im Allstagsleben der Crow Indianer," *Zeitschrift für Ethnologie*.

"Crow Curses," *JAFL*.

"Evolution and Diffusion in the Field of Language," in *Lowie's Selected Papers in Anthropology*, edited by Cora Du Bois. University of California Press.

"Economic Factors and Culture," *ibid*.

"Berthold Laufer as Ethnologist," *ibid*.

"Development of Anthropology as a Science," in *Essays in the History of Science*, edited by H. M. Evans. University of Washington Press.

Crow Texts. Collected, Translated, and Edited, by Robert H. Lowie. University of California Press.

Crow-English and English-Crow Vocabularies.

"Facts and Ideas in American Anthropology," *AA*.